ESCAPE
FROM THE
ORDINARY

ESCAPE FROM THE ORDINARY

JULIE BRADLEY

Close Reach Publishing LLC
First Printing, December 2018
©2018 Close Reach Publishing

Colophon is the trademark of Close Reach Publishing.
All rights reserved. Published in the United States by Close Reach Publishing.
closereachpublishing.com

Cover Design: Cyndie Shaffstall
Cover Photograph: J.M. Rieupeyrout, Amel
Photographs: Glen or Julie Bradley and J.M. Rieupeyrout, Amel

Identifiers: LCCN 2018913162 | ISBN 978—1—7329184—0—5

The Library of Congress has cataloged as follows:
Bradley, Julie M.
Escape from the Ordinary / Julie Bradley

SUBJECTS:
Fiji (South Pacific)—Description and Travel. 2. Bradley, Julie—Travel—South Pacific. 3. Bradley, Julie—Biography and Memoir—South Pacific—French Polynesia. 4. Bradley, Julie—Adventure and Adventurers—Biography. 5. Sailing—Pacific Ocean. 6. Sailing—Caribbean. 7. Escape (Psychology) 8. Life-changing events. 9. Moving, Household. 10. International and World Politics—Caribbean and Latin American. 11. International and World Politics—Russian and Former Soviet Union

Printed in the United States of America
DOC 10 9 8 7 6 5 4 3 2 1

CLOSE REACH
PUBLISHING

*For Glen,
who taught me how to
dream big.*

Author's Note

When people hear that we sailed around the world (I let that tidbit drop a lot), they all have the same questions: *Did you have any bad storms? Did you encounter any pirates? How did you afford it?* But the most common is: *How did you and your husband live in such close quarters?*

This account of our early retirement adventures answers all those questions about the perils of escaping from it all. My hope is that it will inspire all who read it to consider taking time off from wherever they are in life to pursue a great personal quest. If some of the adventures I describe sound too edgy, and staying home sounds more your cup of tea, you can share the experience in this book. Fair warning however: after lurching out for life changing adventure, it is very difficult to live an everyday life and the confines that come with stability.

Another question often asked is *"How much of this is true?"* The answer: basically all of it. I kept a journal during our entire seven-and-a-half-year circumnavigation and published articles in newspapers and magazines. As I reviewed those writings for this book, I was reminded of events, people and sometimes even entire islands I had forgotten. Those diaries provided frightening insight into our lack of preparedness the first year out. Lessons learned from bad experiences are the most lasting and this book, from the Bay of Biscay, France to Fiji, is full of our stupid mistakes as well as incredible adventures. In the sequel, *Crossing Pirate Waters*, the death-defying experiences are more a consequence of being in places like the Indian Ocean and Gulf of Aden, where bad stuff like piracy and tsunamis tend to happen.

Sometimes, in the interest of moving the story, or respecting privacy I skip the names of many boats and people we sailed with and befriended along the way. Also, it would be too hard to track them all down to ask their permission. I've tried to convey dialogue faithfully, but when you see quotations it means that *something approximately like this was said.* I have tried to extract only the juicy bits of over seven years of daily adventures and travel. Exploring so many places and countries required making hard choices about what and whom to include.

You can enjoy more pictures of our voyage and travels as well as updates on what Glen and I have been doing since we sold our boat, at *www.juliebradleyauthor.com.*

Prologue

S omewhere off the coast of France, I woke up drenched in frigid seawater from a monster wave breaking over the bow of the boat. Recovering from the cold shock I looked around and saw that while I slept, Glen had furled the foresail into the size of a hand towel. The weather was worsening.

The sky was ominously dark, and BB pellets of freezing rain peppered my foul-weather gear before swirling their way down the cockpit scupper drain. Our electronic autopilot was pulling heavy duty; at times it whirred and slipped, thumping the boat into the next wave instead of riding up and over. Glen sat clipped in at the helm, ready to steer manually if needed. We were sailing as close to the wind as the laws of physics allowed, and it required supreme concentration to keep us so near to the edge. If the powerful waves completely overwhelmed our rudder the boat could round up into the wind and stop dead in the water. In the jaws of a Force 10 storm, dead in the water could be taken literally. I was scared. We were scared.

Unhooking my safety tether from a bolt, I slid toward Glen. He had been at the helm 30 minutes beyond our self-imposed watch schedules. I thought he had lost track of time, then remembered it was Christmas morning. His overtime was a sort of last-minute holiday present to me.

Fighting against the wind, I pulled myself up to the helm and held Glen—rather, I held onto him. The storm pelted us both and I laid my head on his shoulder.

"Happy Christmas!" I said into his ear.

Glen turned and brushed his beard against my face. Did I imagine it or were his eyes moist? In full understanding we clung there together. I kissed him lightly and tried some humor. "This is an extreme way to get out of Christmas shopping. If we end up in a life raft eating each other's limbs, I will never forgive you for the worst Christmas ever." Glen gave me a weary smile, but we both knew that if our sailboat foundered, we would never find the life raft. Even if by some unlikely chance it should happen to float right in front of us, we would be devoured by the massive, pounding waves before we could inflate the tiny survival craft.

The dream we worked so hard for was becoming a nightmare. Self-doubt froze me more than the frigid water battering the boat. Could we really make it all the way around the world? How many more mistakes like this could we handle?

Chapter 1

I woke in the cold, dark room with a headache. Slowly, with effort, my vision adapted, and I eyed my surroundings. The peeling faded wallpaper and musty odor flashed memories of my grandparents' house, before the reality of subzero Russia pushed the nostalgia away. The window was open a slit to allow in what bitterly cold fresh air I could tolerate, making it damp enough to see my breath. I burrowed into the layers of blankets covering the nun-sized bed—mine for the months of my final Army deployment—and looked toward the glowing red eyes of the digital clock. 0-4-3-0—too early to get up and too late for more sleep. Cocooned and dreading the day, I thought about what I was leaving behind and what waited ahead. My restless sleep was expected after the three-day trip from my home in Washington, D.C., to the Ural Mountains, and I knew my pounding head was to be expected after the night of toasting vodka with my Russian counterparts. As though the Russians needed an excuse… last night's clinking of glasses marked the arrival of our American nuclear weapons inspection team. Waking up in this room would feel normal within a few days, but I hoped tossing back Russian vodka never would.

Before leaving for Russia, I promised my husband, Glen, I would make an effort to enjoy this last gasp of my 20+ year Army career, but I still expected the time to pass slowly. A nine-week calendar hung on the wall in our operations room and one of the inspection team members used a Sharpie hanging from a string to mark the passing of days. As the team leader it would not be appropriate for me to keep a countdown calendar anticipating my rotation home. But I was glad it was there; as the weeks passed the large, X'd out dates would give me comfort.

It was Friday night back home in D.C. and I would not bother calling Glen on the dedicated phone line provided by the American government for our safety and sanity. With nothing to keep Glen at home in our soulless, claustrophobic Alexandria condominium, he would be at anchor on our pre-retirement, training sailboat in a snug cove on the Chesapeake Bay working through a list of projects that would make the boat more attractive when we put her on the market. I sucked deeply at the frigid air, forced myself to stop dwelling on what I was missing and shifted to the reality of my present situation.

Outside, the rising sun overtook the security light's dim beam signaling it was time to get up. I unwound from the hefty layers of bedding, shut the heavy, double-paned window, and walked into the bathroom in nothing but my socks. The clothes I wore yesterday were well traveled and I had been too woozy to find my PJs in the duffle bag last night. It was all the same to me though—three years of constant video and audio surveillance by the Russian government had toughened me to the audience I knew was ever-present. There was no hope of privacy here and I no longer possessed any remnants of self-consciousness. My modesty had been forced out the window three years ago after a visiting American counter-surveillance team pointed out the locations of the hidden Russian cameras and listening devices.

During that first rotation I had clenched my fists and narrowed my eyes at a Russian counterpart who, with a knowing wink, commented on me being a "real redhead." I flushed at the thought of that day, but I had toughened since then, and their feeble attempts to rile me with references to private conversations with my husband no longer fazed me. The Russians had by this time pieced together almost everything about my life, including our plans for sailing around the world when I retired. My life was a favorite subject for the curious Russians during our twice-daily perimeter and portal monitoring rounds when it was low risk enough to converse with them. This was a time when there was some semblance of socializing—unlike the quiet demanded during inspections of real or suspected nuclear weaponry. Those were intense, high-risk, high-consequence events when no one let their minds stray from the task at hand, not even to comforting thoughts of the future.

Showered, I retrieved my extreme-cold-weather gear from my duffle and robotically dressed for work. During the short, outdoor walk to the small dining room and base operations offices, the biting cold stole my breath away and my watering eyes stung as my tears became frozen. After some hot oatmeal, I read reports from the last inspection team and took comfort in finding nothing radical had transpired. It was now up to our team to account for the numbers of treaty-prescribed nuclear warheads. I desperately hoped my last tour in Russia would pass with no surprises, disasters, or political gamesmanship. I rapped my still cold knuckles on the wooden tabletop for luck.

Like a snowplow, I pushed through six inches of snow to reach the monitoring office for the day's first inspection. Two of our folks were thumping the thermometer in an attempt to persuade the mercury to drop further—the silver thread of both despair and hope.

Thwack! Thwack!

I glanced toward the hidden surveillance camera and imagined Russian colleagues at their monitors, watching and laughing their asses off at our unbridled and unwarranted optimism that it would be cold enough to cancel the inspection. They were likely tossing back vodka to stave off their own hangovers, relying on the hair of the dog that bit them technique. Shortly, both Americans and Russians alike would be sweating out the smell of alcohol as our bodies powered through the snow pack on our cross-country skis on the day's monitoring mission.

Turning away from the tableau of American inspectors still huddled around the not-to-be-coaxed thermometer, I scraped blue-white crystals from the window. An ocean of sparkling diamonds seemed to have poured from the sun to blanket the earth and I found myself surprisingly eager for the exertion. Though cold enough to freeze my nostril hairs, it wasn't cold enough to cancel the inspection.

"We're on," I told the team. Their disappointment in the thermometer showed. If it had been twenty degrees below zero—a certifiably badass cold—the Nuclear Inspection Treaty ruled that it was a health hazard to conduct our inspections and we could have stayed in the warmth of our offices. Though we came close many times, the *too cold* rule had only been applied once in my three years of work in Russia. Preparing for the slap of Mother Nature's icy hand, I gave a pep talk and tried to keep it light-hearted. With my retirement from the Army only a few months away, I felt as though I should take advantage of these last opportunities to be all I could be—even in a place where neither side wore military uniforms. As an Army Major, I was in charge of our little band of military defense contractors—cold or hot.

Leading the team of well-paid American defense contractors was not all that challenging. Some had been working at this location for a decade and knew their job as well or better than I. Knowing I was surrounded by experts in a job where mistakes could not be undone took the weight off my shoulders. Out here, leadership was more about being congenial, professional and detail-oriented while using my ability to speak Russian to communicate with our counterparts.

Back in the real Army, leadership was graded on a daily basis, and had never come easy for me. With plenty of role models in high leadership positions, I noticed that it helped to look the part. I discovered early that an athletic, 5'9" redhead can define leadership by encouraging and supporting subordinates who could be helpful—or not—to the officers in charge of their mission area. I had also been fortunate enough to serve with excellent noncommissioned officers during my career. The NCOs made me smarter and more successful with every passing assignment. Bracing myself for that day's frigid excursion, the thought of letting down those NCOs and soldiers—doing less than my best—put me in overdrive and kept me there. I had always been committed to the Army and in truth, it had always come first over the past twenty years. As a result, I had never used all my allotted leave days, and, because of work requirements, had canceled planned vacation trips with Glen on more than one occasion.

After 20 years of endless challenges, I had begun to feel whittled down physically and mentally. Even though this particular assignment did not require tactical Army skills, it was peculiar and arduous in its own way. Working with nuclear weapons is never an easy assignment, but it was far more demanding during long Russian winters that could clamp around one like a vise.

"Downright balmy at two below," I told my team. "Let's gear up!" I was glad to hear the usual mild banter despite their disappointment. Layering on outerwear in the coatroom, we looked like astronauts suiting up for a spacewalk. The enviable idea of no gravity made me wistful. Heavy outerwear and gear left me feeling burdened, both physically and emotionally. The remnants of my headache and heavy boots tugged at me as I strapped on my cross-country skis. If the Russians were going to pull something unusual, it would likely be during the first days of our rotation, before we hit our stride, and this added to the load I felt.

"Ready everyone?" I asked, not wanting to keep the door open too long. We trudged forward into another frosty day during my last tour in Russia.

Stepping outside, I adjusted the woolen covering around my nose and squinted my eyes against the sun reflecting off the snow, obviously intent upon blinding us all. However, even if just imagined, the glowing sun provided some help in allowing me to feel my hands and feet. I stretched my legs forward, one after the other, and sought the rhythm of the ski glide across the snow. With the physical exertion, my body warmed, and I could feel the heat of my core snaking its way to my fingers and toes like snow melt.

At the designated time, our Russian counterparts skied out from the missile installation. Puffy coats made their bodies look large in contrast to their gaunt, serious faces, and their outerwear and boots looked flimsy in comparison to our Special Forces issue subarctic gear. I greeted the men in Russian.

These were not military personnel—they were rocket scientists. Not the kind you affectionately call your super smart friend who kicks your ass in every round of Trivial Pursuit, but *real* rocket scientists. We were at a missile factory where the Russians built and refurbished rocket motors and intercontinental ballistic missiles. The missiles were capable of carrying nuclear warheads more than 6,000 miles and hitting a target within 200 meters of accuracy.

After the Soviet Union collapsed there was no shortage of missiles to inspect, both old and new, as part of the arms treaty between the former Soviet regime and the United States. I felt lucky to be assigned to these old school nuclear missile systems. My appointment could have been to the chemical and biological weapons arsenals that the United States was trying to buy and dispose of from newly independent Republics and former Warsaw Pact countries. Illogically, I felt safer working with the nuclear weapons and took cold comfort that the dosimeter on my collar would let me know if the worst happened before my internal organs melted from radiation exposure.

I glanced over at my Russian colleagues easily keeping pace with us on their own skis. It wasn't my imagination—they looked thinner each time I rotated in. Food was scarce after the chaos of the breakup of the Soviet Union. The factory employees had taken to planting gardens and hunting mushrooms in the summer on the very grounds of the missile facility we were inspecting. Back in the Soviet days, places such as this had commanded respect and its workers received priority in food, clothing, and housing. Now, the opposite was true. Priorities had shifted toward industries that made hard currency. As I traveled through Russia, I met more and more Western businessmen buying up vast resources of minerals, timber, and petroleum.

On the plane to Moscow, I had spent hours conversing with my former boss, a recently retired Army colonel who was opening an office for IBM in Moscow. He pressed a business card into my hand and urged me to "come make the big bucks." I took his business card, but the only thing that sounded worse than long deployments in Russia with only an occasional three weeks stateside, was to live in Russia full time. Glen, for sure, was not going to join me in something like that. Might as well draw up the divorce papers if I brought that idea home. It was hard enough as it was, and every time I rotated back home I made every effort to bridge the emotional distance of long separation. *In just a few months I will retire and my marriage will grow stronger*, I thought to myself. My eyes watered at the thought—or perhaps because the wind had picked up— and stung as I blinked fast to clear my vision. We were still only halfway to the weapons-inspection site.

Soon, very soon, things would be far different, and I took consolation in that. During this rotation, Glen would sell our house, furniture, and cars in what was our planned life-simplification phase. When I returned, we would both retire from our jobs, live on an ocean-capable sailboat, and explore the world, island by island. Picturing the two of us on the deck of a sailboat anchored in front of a tropical island made me feel warmer and much happier.

Brrrr!

The icy north wind whipped through my woolen head covering, penetrating the open area around my sunglasses. There and then I vowed to voyage only to warm climates; crossing oceans, visiting exotic places, and meeting people who did not care about rank or what I had done for a living. It would be a life of catching fish to eat, reading stacks of books, and having adventures in balmy, exotic places.

I'm so ready!

No more long separations from Glen, no more obsessing about promotions and performance evaluations, no more braving sub-zero temperatures. Sure, sailing around the world would be tough at times; there would be storms and hazards to be avoided, sails would tear, boat stuff would break. I was aware of the realities. The ocean is hard on both people and equipment but we would learn as we went. I wasn't afraid. I had an ace in the hole—Glen—a skilled sailor and electronics engineer who enjoyed fixing what was broken, even when he had to MacGyver something together with whatever was at hand.

Sailing had become the glue that bonded us. The few weekends I was home, Glen and I were out on our training boat—even in bad weather—to better hone our skills. Glen had been at it longer than I and was a regular at Friday night sail races with a local sailing club on the Chesapeake Bay. We were not sure exactly which skills would be the most important for world voyaging but we had read countless articles and books on heavy weather sailing, navigation, world sailing routes, cooking in a small galley... We had even taken emergency medical courses. (Lord help Glen if he really needed me to remove his appendix!) Despite our book learning, neither of us would be the most experienced sailor to ever cross an ocean, but we felt ready enough. After a lifetime of Army do-or-die thinking, I figured whatever I lacked in skills could be learned along the way. We would be a team, sailing our home to far off places and exploring them together. Our dream was about to become our life.

In only a few months, the Army and Russia would all be a memory.

When the inspection concluded, I brushed snow and ice from our boots and waved our team into the heated cloakroom. I climbed out of my extreme-cold-weather gear, headed in to write my report, and then read more of Heavy Weather Sailing, a book I had brought with me. Not that I expected to ever have to use those storm survival tactics. We, of course, were going to be careful and avoid bad weather whenever possible.

Was Glen thinking of me?

That weekend he was replacing the bank of worn-out batteries on the boat and taking photos for the sale listing. I already yearned to be back home with him. Army deployments are famously tough on relationships; Mission First is the Army way. Many of my female Army colleagues had resigned to have children or save their marriage. For me, having children was unimaginable, so great were the demands of the military. As far as saving marriages, Glen was my third husband; proof that I had put more into my career than personal life. From the very beginning, my Army career had been a hard road, but it was also full of new experiences and the unexpected. The Army had offered me numerous advancement opportunities, some I had declined to keep this marriage intact. But my military career had never been something I was willing to give up.

At the age of 19, I enlisted in the Women's Army Corps (WAC) at the lowliest rank of private. During my WAC basic training, the separate women's branch was disbanded, the WAC title dropped, and training for women soldiers was integrated with the men's. Seemingly overnight I had to perform both physically and professionally at a much higher level. It felt good to work in what was nearly a level playing field. The Army was still a man's world, but we were allowed to do more. At basic training there was no lack of encouragement to "be all you can be" by drill sergeants. I figured they cared enough to yell, and from them I learned the self-discipline that allowed me to achieve things I never thought possible. After basic, I attended two years of Russian language and cryptologic code training, then worked as a translator at a field station in Germany. While there I attained the rank of sergeant, and eventually a supervisor recommended me for Officer Candidate School. Those three months at the Infantry Center for Officer Candidate School were the hardest of my life, but I graduated as a second lieutenant. I was proud to be an officer, the first ever in my family. With strong language skills, I was posted as a Russian foreign area officer in the Military Intelligence Corps. Over the years my wide range of assignments included debriefing Soviet and Warsaw Pact defectors, and bizarre Cold War era training for psychological interrogation techniques and cutting edge, on-demand, never predictable, and doubtfully possible out-of-body travel to learn *secrets*.

In the more traditional assignments, I had been a company commander, and assigned to male-only designated jobs in an Infantry Division and then with a Special Forces unit in a combat environment. I had entered the Army as a private and at 40 years old was retiring as a major in Military Intelligence. Though my Army *handlers* told me I had a good chance for promotion to lieutenant colonel, I had already submitted a request for retirement and within months would exit the Army with as much grace as I could muster.

My early life had been marked by deep financial insecurity, and it was almost too good to believe that I would receive the lifetime pension that comes after 20 years' service in the military. My commitment to the Army had been driven as much by loyalty for all it had given me as by fear of poverty. Glen too had put in enough time to retire and we would be able to live a comfortable life together on our pensions. My entire adult life I had scrimped and saved so that I would be able to retire completely and then live the life of my dreams.

When Glen and I married, we recognized that the trouble with early retirement for Type A people like ourselves was that we would go batty due to a lack of purpose. We came up with a sure-fire solution to that dilemma: retire early but keep living an adventurous life by sailing around the world. This dream had nurtured our marriage when things were tough. The long separations had been hard, so it concerned us both that we might sell everything we owned, buy a boat with our nest egg, and then regret it. We were also concerned about whether our marriage could survive such close quarters after multiple deployments and separation. Discussion of those possibilities went far into one long, tearful, heart-open night. In the end, we mutually decided we could and would make it work. We wanted to build a stronger, deeper, more-committed version of our marriage by following through on our shared dream. Glen, who had already retired early once from the government, notified his defense-contracting company of our plan to wrap up work and go sailing.

Soon we would be completely free of ties to life on land.

ESCAPE FROM THE ORDINARY

Chapter 2

Glen sold our 23-year-old boat while I was working in Russia, and it was time for a new one that could take us around the world. Most sailboats built in the United States are designed for coastal and inland waters—not the rigors of crossing oceans. There were custom built sailboats built in the United States that could do the job, but they had a price tag well beyond the value of our nest egg. However, Glen and I had read about a Frenchman named Henri Amel, who built sailboats designed to be handled comfortably by two people wanting to tackle ocean voyages.

The US dollar was remarkably strong in Europe at the time, and taking advantage of the favorable exchange rate, we almost doubled our investment value by buying a boat built in France. Once we sold all our possessions and converted our dollars to French currency, we were able to afford a modern Amel ketch design called a Super Maramu. Our savings and the proceeds from our 23-year-old sailboat gained us a brand-new ocean-going sailboat, which surpassed our wildest dreams. As star struck as we were, it was a big commitment. Even with the powerful dollar, the new boat consumed our savings. But when we did the math, discovered we could live modestly day to day off our pensions. This gave us the courage to make the purchase. As our new sailboat was being built in France, we watched the exchange rate fluctuations, and at a prime moment, wired our dollars to take the plunge. The transaction finalized just days before my retirement from Army life.

* * * * *

My last deployment to Russia was the best I could ask for: uneventful. Back in Washington, D.C., I had been placed on light duty for out-processing during my final month before retirement. This gave me the free time I needed to focus on the countless chores of disposing with a lifetime accumulation of goods.

As I looked around the empty condo decorated with stacks of packing boxes it looked like a miniaturized city of brown, paper skyscrapers. I was officially a civilian who owned little more than the duffle bags of clothing we would take with us and a sailboat located 4,000 miles away. The boxes held my battle-dress Army uniforms and combat boots that Glen was going to drop off at the thrift store on a nearby Army base. Soon, they would display different nametags and ranks—Godspeed to the next soldiers to wear them.

While boxing these last possessions, I thought about how I had routinely been boxing myself into difficult Army assignments on the far side of the world. However, this was different. Like the Army, this voyage would take me to faraway places, but with out-of-the-ordinary challenges. Life on a sailboat would be different—I was not sure what to expect. With a long history of blooming where I was planted, I figured I would adjust. What gave me pause was that there would not be anyone to call when something went wrong. No Army medevac, no calling in reinforcements if attacked by bad guys. "Just you and me, baby," I told Glen.

Some of my Army colleagues had gone into high paying jobs in defense contracting when they left the military, and many had remarked that, at 40, I was too young to settle into retirement. "I don't think sailing around the world is a quiet retirement," I responded. Glen and I felt that we were embarking on something that would be more demanding than anything either of us had ever done before.

Carrying a box of uniforms to the car, the enormity of what was happening—what Glen and I were causing to happen—began to hit me. I stowed the box and watched Glen drive off to the thrift store with my Army belongings. The car disappearing down the road somehow symbolized the end of all I had known. I felt shaky and sunk to the curb. "I've only been a civilian for one day and already I'm losing my grip." Would I feel even more disconnected on the water or would I find myself out there?

Slumped on the pavement, I worried. It wasn't as though family ties were holding me back; my parents, sister, brother, and I had little contact. From that vantage point it sounded like a jukebox country western song kind of background. Our family was thrown apart when my father suffered a brain tumor and the family business went into bankruptcy. My relationship with my mother was especially strained. Before I joined the Army, she had left for a better life to follow her own career as a pilot. It was strange that I resented her actions so much because like her, I had also put my own career above my family relationships. After 23 years I realized my mother had been a convenient target for my anger. But at that time, I was a devastated seventeen-year-old left to deal with debt collectors. It was unimaginable that my father would be able to help pay for my education beyond high school. Though diminished from his brain tumor, he still wanted more for his children than he could offer and the idea of enlisting in the Army came from him.

Dad grew up in an Italian immigrant family and, after serving in World War II, paid for his university education using the GI Bill. He knew first-hand the Army could be my path to advancement, and correctly predicted I would thrive there. Perhaps he guessed my strict Catholic education with uniforms, rules, and structure had prepared me well for a life of regulations. He had been right.

I had believed I would draw closer to my family once I retired from the Army but sailing around the world would not make it easier to smooth out relationships bent at odd angles and made more disjointed by the passing of time. My sister, Jeanne, a year older, was the family member I knew best. Quiet, but internally strong, she made her mark on the world the hard way. When our family scattered, Jeanne, always strong in math and science, enrolled in an engineering program and financed her way through five years of university, accumulating massive student debt lessened slightly by a part-time job conducting autopsies at a VA hospital. After becoming an electrical engineer, she worked her way up to a high-level position at Boeing in Seattle, cranking out patents and improvements to aviation systems as a testament to her education and perseverance.

My brother John, five years my junior, also managed to thrive. He shared Jeanne's interest in engineering and established his own career, a path he carved out at the side of his brilliant wife Marta, a cellular biologist. John is in a class of people who make leadership look easy. That, combined with his engineering skills, assured his continued and steady climb toward the top at Boeing.

After my mother left, she took a position instructing flight crew on commercial planes, and eventually remarried. They—my sister, brother, and mother—all worked at Boeing in Seattle, loved their jobs, and grew closer as a family. I, however, was separated from them by more than just distance. Glen was the only family to attend my Army retirement ceremony. At the time, I was rankled by this, but I came to realize sharing is a two-way street. To be fair, I had not involved them in my life any more than they had included me.

I got up from the curb, still shaky, and returned to the condo. When Glen came back, he noted that this would be our last night in the condo—we would turn in our keys the next day. I busied myself with cleaning and scrubbing for the final walk-through when I felt a buzzing build inside my head. The pressure of the sound grew and drove me to my knees. With an abrupt searing pain in my chest, I went from standing, to kneeling, to flat on the floor. I was forced into a ball, like clay at the hands of an angry giant. A hypodermic of adrenalin must have pierced my heart because it was trying to escape my chest; beating fast and hard as though I was being chased by a predator. As the world around me blurred, I struggled for breath, gasping for air through an open mouth. Sweat sprang forth from every pore, ran down my neck and soaked my clothing. I wanted to scream for help, but my efforts produced silent croaks. At 40 years old, I thought I was dying.

Glen was in another room and had not heard my pitiful squeaks for help. As I lay on the floor, I searched for breath enough to speak, but it was some time before my heart rate and breathing returned to normal and the worst of the crisis had passed. I dragged myself into a chair, and called again for Glen, this time louder. I was convinced I had suffered a heart attack. "Take me to the hospital!" I begged.

Glen, an engineer, has always had a strong aversion to overreacting. When people freak out, he tends to polarize and becomes calmer. He is from the school of thought that the only reason to take someone to the hospital is an injury involving massive amounts of blood or a state of unconsciousness. According to Glen, I did not belong to a category calling for medical attention. He rejected my heart attack assessment and pointed out that other than looking a little pale, I seemed fine to him. Since by that time my heart had returned to beating normally, he held firm. Glen was right. Within the hour I was feeling better—normal even.

The next day we handed our condo keys to a realtor, got a ride to the airport, and took off for France. Amel does not deliver their sailboats or ship them to customers on a freighter. Unique among boat builders, Amel insists all their sailboats leave the factory on their own bottom. We were to pick up our boat and embark on our new life thousands of miles from home.

The Amel shipyard is located in La Rochelle, France, on the Bay of Biscay, in the North Atlantic. We planned to take delivery of our new boat and immediately head south in pursuit of warmer—and hopefully better—weather. December is a dangerous time to sail the North Atlantic, known for its fitful storms. We would have to be careful. The big life changes of retiring, selling everything we owned, buying a sailboat overseas with different currency, and dealing with a language we didn't speak were challenging enough, but winter in the North Atlantic... my only explanation is we felt cocky that all the great luck with the currency exchange would hold. "How hard can it really be?"

Whatever my body had been trying to tell me, whatever had happened the day before on the floor of our condo, I was back to my resilient self and now everything seemed to be working fine. But that episode still bothered me. I had heard stories of soldiers dying shortly after their retirement, and I had a lingering fear I was about to be counted among their numbers. Fairly young and a very fit woman, surely I wasn't a candidate for a heart attack. I tried to convince myself because I needed to be healthy and able-bodied; sailing around the world was going to require all the strength and stamina I possessed.

Before departing, I phoned my sister and we had a long conversation about what I called my heart attack. "It sounds like a panic attack," Jeanne told me. "A woman I work with here at Boeing has panic attacks—strangely enough she is a former Air Force officer. The panic seems to come while she is doing something ordinary. She told me it doesn't happen during a stressful situation, but at an unpredictable, later time. What you are describing sounds a lot like what happens to her, and I'm not surprised. Julie, don't you think it stressful to take all your savings to buy a boat on a different continent and then start your first voyage with a major ocean crossing? Can't you buy a boat in Florida and start from there when it gets warmer? If you don't like living on a boat, you will have to sell it at a loss and start from zero with no furniture, no car, no... well, nothing. Why leave from the North Atlantic in the dead of winter? I think Glen is right; it wasn't a heart attack. But it does sound like you have lots of reasons to have a panic attack."

It was too late to turn back, but I knew there was truth in Jeanne's warnings.

This was at best a bold endeavor. Leaving behind a lifetime of structure and predictability, we were heading, literally, into a sea of uncertainty; escaping from what we believed would be an overly tame retirement and what we knew as the real world. Were we equipped for the challenges before us?

I was the weak link in the plan. I always deferred to Glen when it came to hands-on sailing decisions, partially because Glen had more sailing experience, but also because he excelled at everything he did. He was the guy always chosen for the team because he made things happen. I was convinced that as long as Glen was involved, everything would be alright. In truth, though, all our combined coastal experience would count for little; we had zero experience crossing oceans. That realization was first driven home when, due to our lack of experience, we were unable to find a company to insure our new boat and us. When Lloyds of London wouldn't insure us at any price, we had to think twice. Our boat builder finally directed us to a French company willing to write the insurance policy, but we were forced to pay double the standard premium for possessing nothing in the way of ocean-going experience

When Glen and I boarded the plane in D.C., carrying four bulging Army duffel bags with what was left of our worldly belongings, it was snowing hard. It was just as cold when we landed in Paris.

Driving through the frozen countryside from Paris to LaRochelle, France set off an alarm in our heads with the force of a cracked liberty bell—the weather was not cooperating. We checked into a quaint, poorly heated inn of the Loire Valley, shivering and wondering when things would finally be warm. Our sightseeing plans were ditched and instead, we drove directly to LaRochelle. The walled, medieval city, situated in the northern part of the Bay of Biscay, is the center of boat building in France and lovely.

We managed to negotiate the French language road signs and drove straight to the Amel boatyard to meet our new sailboat. It was still on land in the cradle where it had been built. Standing before it, we were in awe. It was more than we'd hoped for or thought we could ever afford. The beautiful boat met all our criteria: legendary strength, easily sailed by two people, and capable of crossing oceans. It was the first new sailboat we had ever owned and even the cold, wet weather could not keep us from being filled with joy. Our dream of sailing around the world could come true with this boat.

We watched as a tractor harnessed our boat out of its cradle and slid her into the water as smoothly as setting a rubber duck into a tub. It floated! The Amel employees looked surprised we ever considered any other possibility. Someone from the company climbed aboard and started the engine, piloting it to the LaRochelle marina. Glen and I wasted no time boarding with our four duffel bags and settled into our new floating home.

It was to be a night of firsts: the first meal I cooked aboard, the first shower, the first night in our new home. My euphoria was soon overtaken by reality: the cost and burden of equipping our boat for a globe-circling voyage. It had taken us years to equip the old boat we had just sold, but we had to get this boat prepared within weeks. The marina berth cost more than $100 dollars a day and it was adding up. We needed to depart quickly or risk draining our already low supply of funds. But this was no time to skimp on safety or take half steps; when we departed LaRochelle, it would be the real thing. The sea trial of our new boat would be an offshore passage from LaRochelle in the North Atlantic to the Canary Islands, totaling some 2,000 miles, give or take depending on the wind direction. If the wind was from the north we would zoom, if from the west or south it could be long, hard going.

With boat manuals in French, it took us a week to learn all the new boat systems. The hands-on deck practice with the unique furling and sail systems was canceled several times due to high winds and frequent rain. An Amel engineer spent two days going through every inch of the engine compartment with Glen, taught us how to operate our reverse-osmosis, desalination water maker, and the other new-fangled equipment not present on our former 23-year-old sailboat. At night we walked from the marina to the walled, medieval, waterfront city of LaRochelle but during the day we worked relentlessly to get the boat and ourselves ready.

Our credit card was also doing hard duty as every day we purchased things we would need to equip the boat: life raft, radar reflectors, radios, sheets, spices, blankets, food, the list went on... I wished I could have just moved everything off the old boat and onto the new one, but a condition of the sale was that all equipment remained aboard. Though still thrilled about our new boat, the entire experience was far more challenging than we could have imagined.

On the plus side, the many tasks kept us from becoming obsessed with the weather. Even if we immediately had a fully-stocked boat, there was no way we could take off in such horrible conditions. The freezing

23

temperatures and endless storms in the north of France were breaking records that year. We regretted taking delivery of the boat in the dead of winter. If we had been able to afford to keep our boat in that marina—and had anywhere else to live—we would have holed up and waited for spring. The expenses were mounting and since we already announced to our friends and family we were leaving, we felt the pressure to persevere. With the financial pressures and in truth, stubbornness, we did not step back and sufficiently look at other options.

Another major issue had also been overlooked.

Before we could take possession of our boat, it had to be registered. When the Amel manager asked us what name to put on the registration, we were totally unprepared. It's embarrassing to confess, but though we spent weeks deciding which life raft to purchase, and days deciding which dinghy to buy, we only had a few hours to come up with a name for our boat. As unbelievable as it seems even now, we showed up to take delivery of our new boat without a name for her.

We had been so absorbed with selling our possessions and getting our savings together, we had not thought too much about a name. Other sailboats we had owned were bought used and already named by the previous owner. We understood we would need to name the boat but thought we could think about it and let the right name settle on us. Big mistake. With only one day of notice before Amel registered the boat, we made a hasty and unfortunate decision.

The name came to us while buying supplies and offshore gear at a marine store in LaRochelle. I noticed a poster on the wall with pictures of frolicking whales and dolphins titled C'est Assez – Cetace. I asked the English-speaking store salesman what it meant, and he explained the two words were pronounced the same with different meanings. In French, C'est Assez means *It's Enough*; Cetace means cetaceans—whales and dolphins. As used on the poster, it meant: it's enough killing of whales and dolphins. Glen and I looked at each other and said, "C'est Assez – a perfect name for our boat because this is all we have, so it has to be enough."

I can only say now, the name we chose seemed a good idea at the time.

We learned soon enough that it was a horrible name for a boat. C'est Assez is a French expression that non-French speaking people did not understand and could neither spell nor pronounce. Every time we identified ourselves on the radio to another boat or the authorities of a country, they asked us to spell the name phonetically. If you ever have the opportunity to name or rename a boat, consider something extremely simple everyone understands. Avoid being too clever.

Eventually, I took to calling our boat by her English name: *It's Enough*.

Glen and I were competent coastal and bay sailors but knew we could get walloped in the kind of weather that hung over us in LaRochelle. It was the wrong time of the year to sail the North Atlantic, but that year was particularly problematic because of endless La Niña weather fronts rolling through the high seas. Fighting to walk against the powerful winds, pelting rain and snow during our trips into town, we resolved to wait for a weather window. We figured we needed only a couple days of better conditions and could scoot south fast enough to reach the milder weather of the mid-Atlantic before the next storm arrived. We monitored the weather closely at a meteorological station inside the LaRochelle harbor, which posted the weather forecast every day.

The only drawback: the forecast was, of course, written in French.

* * * * *

"So, you don't know French? If I travel to America will everyone speak French to me?"

[Long pause.] "Americans think everyone should speak English. Is that fair?" whined the French meteorologist in perfect English.

I was stunned speechless in both English and limited French. This very same French meteorologist had walked away from us with a shrug of *No English* during our first visit two weeks earlier. Suddenly he spoke perfect, if rude, English. We had visited the French Maritime Weather Office in La Rochelle harbor every day, looking for a weather window to head south to the Canary Islands. The printed forecast was in French, with poorly printed graphics of the fronts and pressure systems. Our scant French language skills and limited weather chart experience required us to seek help, which came in the form of Jean Luc, an Amel boatyard employee who had learned considerable English watching Seinfeld. On that day, three days before Christmas, Jean Luc, and all Amel employees, had departed for their Christmas holiday. The boatyard was closed for the next three weeks and Jean Luc was out of town visiting family.

On that particular morning the weather looked hopeful. We opened the hatch of our boat and blinked like moles. It had been that long since we had seen the sun. I sat in the cockpit with my face toward the warmth, basking in the blue skies and voicing hope that the break would last long enough for us to depart the Bay of Biscay and head south to a warmer and gentler climate. Our belief was that even a narrow window of calmer weather would allow us to get past the endless storms marching across the North Atlantic hitting the Bay of Biscay mid-center. The sun shone like a sign from the weather gods that we could leave for the Canary Islands. We grabbed our French dictionaries and ran, not walked, to the

Meteo office hoping for that precious good weather window in which to depart.

I was tortured by the taking apart of each sentence to make a word-for-word translation of the weather forecast, a technique that produces unimpressive results. At its best, French is a language where the subject of a sentence can reside in curious places. Stephan, the cranky harbor meteorologist who updated the weather maps several times a day, usually ignored us. He had been no help whatsoever and, claiming to speak no English would walk away during our daily visits. That visit to the weather office started out normally as he sneered at my linguistic trips and falls. Then, as though something snapped in his mind—as if he had endured enough—Stephan cocked his head in disbelief at my halting French and pages of garbled translation and, in perfect English, asked, "So… you don't speak French?"

We stared at him in disbelief. I searched Glen's face and silently willed him to not get angry as we needed this man's help. It was a shock to hear Stephan's excellent English. Two weeks earlier when I asked the man to *s'il vous plais* (please) help us with the weather forecast, he shrugged us off with *ne parle pas anglais* (I don't speak English) and walked away. Suddenly for some reason—perhaps the thought of having to listen to our broken French every day for the foreseeable future— he offered assistance laced with contempt.

Stephan proceeded, "I can tell you everything you need to know about this weather, but of course it does not depend so much on what this weather forecast says. It all depends on three things: the boat, the crew, and the captain. First off, you have an Amel, an excellent French-built boat made to sail in any conditions. No problem with the boat. Second, you have the crew. (Here he looked at me and raised his eyebrows.) I know nothing about the crew. Maybe they can take it, maybe not. Third – and most importantly – the captain. A French captain would say this weather is *sportif.* Yes, a French captain would go. So, have a Happy Christmas at sea." With that, he walked away.

Could I blame Stephan or was the burden ours alone for departing that afternoon? Probably both. Either way, during our world voyage we had plenty of opportunity to get to know a lot of French sailors, some well enough to tell that story and ask why some Frenchmen come across as arrogant. During a long, candid, wine-assisted talk on an ivory-colored, sandy beach in French Polynesia, a young, lanky French solo sailor offered us his explanation.

"My home country, France, was for a long time the strongest country in the world. At one time, France owned much of America and helped win her freedom from England. We aren't the best of the world anymore, but Americans think we should learn English for them? *Mon Dieu*, Americans, who eat fake cheese and drink box wine, want to teach us? Even if we do learn English, we make sure we have the thickest French accent so no one can ever think that French person made a real effort. You are Americans sailing a French boat known to all French sailors. I think it would be a wise choice for you to learn French."

Did we take his advice? Let's say we learned to sit tight in port when the weather is *sportif.*

Chapter 3

We departed LaRochelle hastily. The plan was to take advantage of the short window of calmer weather, tack west to get out of the Bay of Biscay—a gulf of water half the length of France itself—and once clear of the coast of Spain, head south on a fast point of sail toward the Canary Islands. With optimism suppressing a bit of anxiety, we motored *It's Enough* out of the marina and set our sails for the first time.

After two days of endless tacking in the Bay of Biscay, we were still not even close to being able to head south. Our inability to make progress against the headwinds had trapped us in the next storm. The building waves grew more ominous as we struggled against ferocious winds blowing directly into us from the west. Boats cannot sail directly into the true direction of the wind, so we fought hard, knowing that if the bow of our boat turned too far into it, the forward motion would be stopped and the snarling waves could pitch pole our sailboat end over end. The boat could not survive that kind of destructive violence, let alone its exhausted sailors.

The sad irony of the past eleven years of planning, saving, doing my utmost in all things to get to this place was that my life—both our lives—might end at the very start of living our dream. A person can recover from most mistakes in life, but the building winds and waves were eroding my *can-do* Army confidence. My fear came to focus when a monster rogue wave broke upon us with such staggering force it seemed we would be washed overboard despite the stainless-steel clips tethering our safety harness to the boat. As calf-deep seawater drained from the cockpit I broke our stunned silence, "Glen, are we going to make it through this?" Quickly regretting my question, Glen, my rock, answered, "I don't know."

I prayed to every force I could reach with my mind; God, the universe, my ancestors… "Please let us make it through this storm. I promise to respect and appreciate every single thing, creature and person in the world." Prayers and miracles aside, evidence was building that Glen and I had a lot to learn about our new dream life such as sailing across oceans, weather forecasting, and even more about patience.

Shivering against freezing rain in the immense North Atlantic, I realized misnaming our boat was not the worst of our bad decisions. With my arms tightly wound around Glen at the helm in 60 knots of wind on Christmas morning, I would have given anything to be safe and secure back at the docks in LaRochelle, and yes, complaining about the rude weather forecaster.

I grasped for the only consolation and hope of getting through the storm. Our boat was a truly capable, ocean-going vessel; among the best blue-water crafts in the world. Maybe it could compensate for our foolish decision to leave safe harbor for the jaws of a storm. Our very lives depended on the boat staying in one piece.

The loss of a mast, rudder… there were many scenarios that could end this so-called dream of ours in a boat haplessly named *It's Enough*. We would see if it really was enough.

She was living up to her strong reputation as she clawed up 20 to 30-foot waves so high it was a wonder our small engine could make any advances at all. Yes, our engine was running. As counterintuitive as it may sound, in winds surpassing 60 knots, we were forced to run our small, auxiliary engine through the looming waves. That extra boost from the propeller was needed when the boat was at the bottom of each wave trough. It helped lift the boat up and out of the wind shadow with enough momentum to crest the next wave, before careening and falling down the other side. It was a process that repeated itself over and over again, like a horror scene on a video loop. Falling off the high wave crests left my stomach twisted into a knot. Each fall down a wave felt as though it would surely be the one to break the boat into a collection of nothing more than floating debris. If only she could stay intact for the next 1,700 miles. Our only hope was that *It's Enough* really was, enough.

* * * * *

We did not know that the storm we were sailing through was making history. Our miscalculation had landed us in the middle of what we would later learn was violent enough to sink boats both at sea and at anchor in LaRochelle harbor, a history-making Christmas storm. Pelted by rain and wave spray, I wished to be anywhere but in the middle of it. We were truly on our own and did not know if the weather was worse in front or behind us. Should we turn around or keep going forward?

During the night, our long-range HF radio antenna broke and after Glen's nail-biting foray on deck to retrieve it, was now strapped securely to the deck. All we had left for communications was our short distance VHF radio, 12 miles at best, to call for help. If the worst came to pass, help from the French Coast Guard—before the waves of the North Atlantic consumed us—seemed far from likely.

Without a long-distance radio to download weather faxes, we had no idea how long the storm would last or how far it extended south. Could we ride it out—would this be over tomorrow—or would we be on the edge of survival the entire way to the Canary Islands? As though the universe was listening, I heard a high-pitched sound above the roar of the wind. Our only working radio, the close-range VHF, squawked. The caller had to be close.

Glen grabbed the helm as I unhooked the safety line of my life vest from a large bolt screwed into the cockpit seat. I made my way down below deck to the navigation station using cold, wet hands for balance and to pull myself forward. The radio call was coming in over the hailing and distress channel. I dreaded answering the call. If it was a boat in trouble, there was no way we could lend assistance. We were well beyond distressed ourselves.

"Jingle bells, jingle bells, jingle all the way…" a cheerful voice sang over the airwaves. Dumbstruck, I turned up the volume so Glen could hear from the cockpit.

"This is sailing vessel *It's Enough!*" I called to the unknown caroler.

"Well, ahoy there! I'm the duty officer on watch of a cargo ship."

I glanced at our radar display—he was calling from a freighter that was a mere speck in the distance. "Saw you on radar," he said, "but never imagined you were a sailboat. This ship is 400 feet long and we're having a rough go of it. What is a sailboat doing out here in this storm? Did you say that your boat was named Enough or is that just how you're feeling right now?"

"Both!" I yelled over the din. "We named the boat *It's Enough*, but maybe we should have named it Too Much! Hey, Santa, do you have a weather fax to fill our Christmas stocking? We're trying to get to the Canary Islands."

"Standby for a stocking stuffer," he said.

The voice on the radio read the latest forecast and told us we needed to hold on for only 36 more hours and the winds would subside further south.

"Get south as fast as you can," he warned. "There's another front moving in across the North Atlantic almost as big and bad as this one."

Advice to live by. I left the radio, then Glen and I inched out a little more sail and risked more speed. If we could survive 36 more hours, we would be free of the storm.

There's this thought and feeling, somewhere between excitement, desperation, and fear, when you say to yourself, "I can get out of this. I can do this. Soon I will be safe." Even though 36 hours would be a long time to sail in hurricane-force winds, for some reason that bleak weather forecast gave us hope. I had to believe our boat could pull us through and take us to the Canary Islands and beyond so we could enjoy our new life. I had to believe…

Revived by the thought of just two more days and one more night until freedom, I grabbed a jar of peanut butter from the galley and made my way back up to join Glen, still at the helm. I spooned out some peanut butter and passed the jar to Glen. We savored it while staring out at the gray, powerful and intimidating waves.

"Every Christmas from here forward, we will have peanut butter to commemorate this event," I announced. He raised his eyebrows and said, "I'll settle for turkey and pumpkin pie."

Despite my new-found optimism, the storm seemed a bit stronger than when I had woken from my nap – the wave tops were higher and roiled into foam at the crest. Sea foam blowing off the top of gnarly, massive waves meant we had graduated to a Force 10 storm. In my mind at that moment, that label was a sanitized nautical version of *you're screwed*.

As lightly as Glen and I bantered during all of this, the realization that we were inside a Force 10 storm was an emotional blow. We had to be a little crazy to dream of sailing around the world, but a Force 10 storm in the cold North Atlantic was life threatening, let alone that we were novice ocean voyagers on a sea trial in a brand-new boat. We had let our impatience, an arrogant meteorologist—and yes, bad judgment—get us into this predicament.

"Please, let us make it through this," I prayed to anyone listening out there in the middle of a hurricane-force storm.

* * * * *

EMAIL: IT'S ENOUGH

TO: Jeanne

FROM: Julie

Jeanne, I am using our small satellite radio system to send this, so don't respond – we'll never receive it. Please call Aunt Cat and ask her to pray for lighter winds and our safe arrival in the Canary Islands. I don't want to worry you but we could use some divine intervention (or even a miracle!). Aunt Cat has powerful influence in the prayer department.

Don't know the exact wind speed or wave height – we lost our anemometer during my watch last night. I was at the helm while Glen slept below (we stay exhausted). The wind instrument ripped loose from the top of the main mast but was still connected by a cable. The noise was piercing as the metal equipment banged against the aluminum mast, whipped about by unimaginable winds. Glen ran up to the cockpit in his skivvies and life vest to see what happened. Finally, the wind instrument tore itself to pieces and flew off like sea foam. Boat parts as missile projectiles are a bad sign.

Please ask Aunt Cat to pray for 20 MPH winds out of the west to get to the Canary Islands, then southeast trade winds to cross the Atlantic to the Caribbean Islands. Will let you know when we arrive in Canary Islands. Please forgive every time I have been a bad sister to you and Johnny.

Love, Julie

* * * * *

I wish I could say the last 36 hours of that storm went quickly, but the truth is we clawed and fought our way up every wave and crashed down an equal number with the force of hitting something solid. Despite every setback, we made it to the Canary Islands, as exhausted as I had ever been in my entire life. Glen and I were dehydrated, thinner, and sorely in need of showers. We arrived in one piece—nothing major such as a broken mast marred our boat—but a good number of important smaller things had suffered damage.

We called the Amel emergency contact phone number and they instructed us to sit tight in the Canary Islands; they were sending a workman to repair the fixtures and small parts broken during the passage. Our boat builder sounded shocked that we had departed LaRochelle marina and relieved that we had survived sailing through what the French were calling the Christmas Storm. After the devastation to our spirit and confidence, we were at a loss for words. Regardless of whether it was because of our boat's warranty, or they were thankful we had not foundered, we were grateful for their help. We knew we had purchased the best boat possible.

ESCAPE FROM THE ORDINARY

Chapter 4

We stayed at a marina in the Canary Islands for more than a week, busy with boat repairs, catching up on sleep, and stocking fresh food. Soon, our boat was like new again and we felt prepared for what we hoped would be an uneventful three-week crossing of the Atlantic.

Looking to depart the Canary Islands and sail west to cross the Atlantic Ocean, we then had the opposite problem: no wind. With all radios now working, Glen printed off a weather fax showing 5- to 10-knot winds at our latitude. Light winds... It seemed a gamble to rely on our diesel engine with only enough fuel on board to motor 1,000 miles. Should we wait for stronger winds or could we find them further south? The storm had humbled us, and we were no longer too proud to ask a more experienced sailor on the dock for advice. The British owner of the boat next to us was preparing for his fifth Atlantic crossing and seemed friendly enough.

"Should we wait here or sail south to find steady trade winds?" I asked. His reply was simplicity itself, "The southeast trades establish themselves a couple hundred miles south of here. Head south 'til the butter melts," he told us, "then turn right."

That's exactly what we did. Our course took a gentle curve southwest from the Canary Islands and after a few days the trade winds blew steadily. Clear skies and comfortable, downwind sailing merged quietly from one day to the next. Glen and I unfurled the massive sails the French call *papillon* (butterfly) sails. The boat's wing-on-wing *papillon* arrangement was more than just a pretty sight—it kicked up our speed a couple of knots as the sails caught the breeze and propelled us to our next destination. Each sunrise I would run the generator and reverse-osmosis water maker for an hour to keep the batteries and water tank topped. When the generator started, I called "Wakie, wakie, sleepyhead!" to Glen sleeping below.

I waited until Glen was up, so he would notice if I fell overboard while streaming two fishing lines off the stern. I was intent upon jazzing up our meals, and though the middle of the ocean is not the greatest place to catch fish, we appreciated the surprise tuna when it happened.

The horror of the storm recessed further into our memories as we enjoyed sunshine, gentle seas and watched the occasional pod of dolphins playing in our bow wake. On occasion, the wind was so low we only shambled toward our destination. Those were times we should have powered up our 65-horsepower auxiliary Volvo engine. The spanking new engine, however, was having serious problems—possibly due to running it at a low RPM full time for the five days we spent in the storm powering up the wave crests. We turned that problem into a feature and learned all we could about adjusting and trimming the sails to get the most out of the little puffs of breeze skimming across the ocean. I, personally, was grateful for the low winds and not inclined to do much wishing for anything stronger after our Force 10 storm experience.

We headed west (turned right when the butter melted) a couple days south of the Canary Islands and pointed our thoughts and boat toward the Caribbean. Most days, 15- to 25-knot trade winds on a broad reach (rear port/left quadrant) allowed us to sail comfortably upright and relieved us of the need to clutch at handholds below deck.

Whenever a tuna found its way onto our fishing line, Glen would clean it on deck. I was cheery and grateful for the bounty and sang along with Jimmy Buffett songs as I sautéed the fish in butter and soy sauce. While there is no such thing as a good night's sleep with alternating watch on an ocean voyage, we enjoyed naps with the off-duty person stretched out on the cockpit cushions or dozing in a nearby bunk. Afternoons before sunset, we would sit in the cockpit for sundowners, eat dinner together, and unfurl a large, paper navigation chart to pencil in our position and progress of the last 24 hours. As comfortable and happy as humanly possible on a major ocean crossing, we enjoyed ourselves and covered 125 to 200 miles a day.

Before nightfall, Glen and I would reef the 180-degree downwind sails so there would be no need for me to wake the sleeping, off-watch Glen for help in reducing the sail if the wind piped up. At nightfall, we switched to onboard red lights to preserve our night vision. We valued comfort over speed, and happily adjusted course to avoid the occasional rainsquall easily spotted ahead.

Life was good.

* * * * *

EMAIL: IT'S ENOUGH

TO: Jeanne

FROM: Julie

Heading South 'til the Butter Melts

We stayed in the Canary Islands a week for rest and repairs. Now that we've lived through it, here's the rest of the story. Through impatience and bad weather information, we spent five days clawing our way through a Force 10 hurricane strength storm.

It was bad. A container ship to our west broke in two at a welded middle bulkhead, and somehow both ends floated. Many of the shipping containers on board that ship fell into the ocean, heading our way. We followed the story on the radio, not knowing if the series of catastrophes would affect us. The Portuguese Navy towed one half to the Canary Islands where we saw it sitting forlornly in the harbor. The other half was towed to the Azores Islands. French military aircraft fired on the dozens of floating 50-foot containers, so they would sink and not be what they announced, in a strong French accent, a "Hazard to Navigation."

We heard the Mayday and rescue on the radio, then saw the fireworks in the distance. Then we heard that dozens of shipping containers were heading toward us… We would have been goners if a wave dropped a shipping container on or into us. Somehow, we avoided disaster. It should now be plain sailing across the Atlantic. Missing you! Please forward this to Dad, Johnny, and Mom.

Love, Julie

Chapter 5

G len is a master at fixing things, but even he was unable to identify what had gone wrong with our 65hp auxiliary, turbo-diesel engine. Sailboat engines are secondary to the sails but needed for maneuvering in tight spaces such as marinas and harbors or taking over from the sails during periods of calm. Though a motor is not intended to be the main source of power on a sailboat, it is essential when needed. We could start our distressed Volvo but not get it to run much above idle. It was sluggish at even the highest engine throttle positions, which was troubling as it slowed our Atlantic crossing. Instead of motoring at six to seven knots during days of calm, we were forced to keep our sails up, despite the banging and flapping, making a mere two to three knots speed. We had plenty of food and ran the generator to desalinate water, so a few days of calm and a longer passage time did not matter. However, our broken engine was a concern. Not knowing the details of our coverage for the Volvo diesel, we emailed Amel using our satellite phone and asked for guidance on where it could be repaired under warranty. Amel instructed us to head straight for the French island of Guadeloupe where they maintain a service boatyard, and they would arrange for the engine to be repaired when we made landfall.

Glen understood engines and was justifiably concerned that having run a new engine at low RPMs during its break-in period for five days in the Bay of Biscay had possibly ruined it. We rummaged through our stack of boat paperwork and read through our Volvo engine manual to see if it specified breaking-in rules. That was one of the few manuals written in both French and English (and Swedish!). The manual only stated that the engine should be run at full throttle for five minutes after every few hours of continuous operation. Despite our unusual break-in technique, the engine was still under warranty. With that, we adjusted our course to arrive at Guadeloupe, midway up the islands in the Caribbean chain.

Even when becalmed, our Atlantic crossing was magical. The days grew steadily warmer allowing us to wear bathing suits and shorts during the day, only changing to long pants and sweatshirts when the cool evening breeze settled in. The sounds of rushing water beneath the hull made it easy to sleep and, on many nights, dolphins performed a leaping race and burst from the ocean surface in the phosphorescent wake of our bow or stern. At sunset, the ocean edge was ablaze with oranges and pinks layered across the horizon, and night settled with quiet dignity. As darkness descended, countless stars illuminated the black night. A star chart taught the names of constellations or my eyes caught trace of a falling meteor or slow-moving satellite. The red and green navigation lights of the occasional airplane were the only proof that humans besides us existed. Enthralled with the beauty and in need of me time, I laid claim to permanent night watch. Ah, the luxury of having the cockpit to myself, and to gaze at the sky, and all that it held.

South of the commercial shipping lanes, there was little boat traffic to concern us. I saw only one other vessel in the 21 days we spent crossing the Atlantic—a sailboat passed close but did not respond when I hailed her on the radio. She must have been much longer and faster as she slipped out of sight within hours.

* * * * *

"Guadeloupe is somewhere ahead there. Look out for it," said Glen as he disappeared below to sleep. I had just taken the helm for my night watch and that comment was a huge lapse in our normal navigational precision. It made me realize the past few weeks of an incident-free and enjoyable Atlantic crossing had lowered our guard. Inspecting the GPS, I saw the reason for Glen's casualness. We were more than 60 miles from the closest point of landfall, it was 11 p.m., and we were sailing at 7 knots. Glen and the sun would be up in time to help negotiate any tricky reefs or obstacles near land. With no pressure, nice weather, and plenty of ocean, I settled in the dark next to Otto (our name for the autopilot, our most valuable crew member), watched for traffic, and listened to a book on tape until the sun showed the horizon ahead.

"LAND HO!" I cried, holding up my binoculars in triumph. No sighting of land is complete without a wee bit of drama and an air of expectancy. Glen roused, came on deck, and we studied the harbor details on our electronic GPS chart plotter, which also showed our boat as it moved position on the map. Things had been wonderfully monotonous on the Atlantic crossing but now it was time to pick our way through the surrounding reef. Using computer-based charts, I identified the harbor opening, gave a bearing, and Glen steered us carefully through the surrounding reef. We pulled up to the dock in Pointe-a-Pitre, the capital of Guadeloupe, and basked in the realization we had just crossed the Atlantic Ocean. It had been so pleasant that I hated for the passage to end. Then the thought of having the entire Caribbean to explore—combined with my yearning for fresh fruits and vegetables—dismissed the nostalgia.

Our fresh food had run out at day 15 and for the past six days we had eaten beans, rice, canned goods—and fish. Glen and I were mastering the simple hand line and bungee cord technique of fishing, and every few days were lucky enough to catch a tuna or dorado. Fresh fish jazzed up our diet on the passage, but I surely wouldn't order fish for our landfall celebration dinner at a local restaurant. I was craving fresh vegetables and fruit, and since Guadeloupe is a French possession, I expected that culinary-wise, good things could be found on shore.

I was an avid runner in the Army and antsy to get off the boat. I missed my five miles a day and had driven Glen to the point of madness over the past 21 days, stair-stepping up and down the four-rung companionway ladder leading from our below-deck living area up to the cockpit. However, French immigration and customs quickly put the brakes on my plan to go on a short run to check things out. When I reported in on the radio an official told us to wait in the marina and someone would be out in a few hours to check us in. To stay hours longer on the boat after 21 days at sea would be pure torture. So, despite the protests of Glen, I stepped off the boat and onto the marina dock for a quick look-see.

Putting my feet on solid ground, I felt like Neil Armstrong taking those first steps on the moon's surface. I leapt for joy and announced that as first officer, I had an official duty to perform: find an ATM machine and get some French money so we could go out to dinner and celebrate. I set out with my French dictionary in hand and a debit card in my pocket to search for a freedom-bearing money machine.

I looked forward to that first step on solid ground, until I stepped off the boat and lost my balance on the dock. I was land sick, which I learned is to be expected after 21 days at sea. I tried to stabilize myself— or the world around me—then slowly made my way toward the ATM sign in the distance. Light headed, I sat on a bench trying to acclimate to the unforgiving ground. I saw an older Frenchman down the street, complete with jaunty beret and man purse under his arm, standing by the ATM. I decided to stay on the bench until he finished to give him some privacy. He retrieved his cash and as he walked away from the ATM kiosk, a car screeched to a halt next to him. A large and dark man with a bat jumped out, hit the Frenchman over the head, snatched the money and purse, jumped back in the car, then sped away. A group of Frenchmen ran up to help the unconscious man who was lying on the ground with blood streaming from his head. I was so frightened by the experience, I ran back to the boat as fast as my wobbly legs would propel me.

"That didn't take long," Glen said. "Why are you out of breath?"

I leapt on the boat and told him of the attack while struggling to slow my breath and racing heart. I was now oh-so-happy to occupy myself with boat washing and laundry-organizing chores until the French immigration showed up. A combination of land sickness and a small dose of luck saved my butt that day. I learned two lessons in my first ten minutes on land: islands are not all mellow beaches with friendly natives, and sometimes stuff sucks. After a parochial-school upbringing and two decades in the military, I should have known enough to follow the rules and do the right thing. Instead, I ignored the directives and got off the boat before we could legally do so. I was by myself and intended to withdraw a wad of cash from the ATM. If I had walked any faster, I would have been the unconscious person lying on the ground with a wounded, bleeding head.

I took those lessons to heart. One of the worst experiences of my life was the five-day storm at the start of our voyage. We were nearly lost at sea because we broke the rules about respecting the power of the North Atlantic during winter. No matter how long it took, we should have waited for a clear-weather window. Our lifetime dream could have been all over before it started, if not for our sturdy boat and incredible luck.

The violent mugging in Guadeloupe reinforced our do-the-right-thing motto—even when following the rules was a pain.

From that day forward, we checked in with officials in every country. Even in the countless remote islands where some sailors opted-out because of the unlikelihood of discovery. We also flew the courtesy flags for every country we visited while we were in their territorial waters, even though the flags were expensive and often difficult to find.

Like the good nuns taught me years earlier, "Follow the rules and everything will turn out just fine."

* * * * *

It isn't easy living and working in the close quarters of a sailboat for even short periods of time. Marriages have split, friends have become enemies, and relatives can end up hating each other. None of that disharmony happened between Glen and me despite all that had gone sideways in the short span of time since we retired. Our life was full of kidding around, laughing, slow meals, and meaningful conversations. Our relationship had developed to a level of intimacy and honesty that I had never known with anyone else in my life. Sure, it would have been great to have had do-overs about so many things, such as sailing the North Atlantic in winter and the ill-conceived boat name. We had not developed a great track record so far. Yet, despite all we had been through, Glen and I had grown closer. Glen is not a demonstrative person, but ever since that violent storm, he showed more appreciation for me. He held my hand as we explored shores, and from time to time came up from behind, and put his arms around me. Unimaginable, but the storm had been good for our relationship, forging it with iron as we fought for survival. It was not despite but because of the hardships that we had drawn closer.

Not that I recommend a Force 10 storm as marriage therapy...

JULIE BRADLEY

* * * * *

EMAIL: IT'S ENOUGH

TO: Dad, Jeanne, Johnny, and Mom

FROM: Julie Bradley

We are docked on the large, industrial island of Guadeloupe where we stocked up with excellent French wine, cheese, and other so-called staples subsidized and imported by the French government. I only recently learned that Triple-cream Brie cheese is a staple.

We have been in Guadeloupe for three weeks and leave tomorrow for Miami. Volvo was unable to repair our new engine here and they think 1,500 miles is not too far to ask us to sail for warranty work. We need our engine to maneuver among the reefs so we are skipping a lot of the Caribbean and heading straight for Miami. We will return and visit every island next winter. Due to the change of plans, we'll sail to the Bahamas this spring for a couple of months, then up to New England as summer approaches. Can you make it for a visit? Maine in the summer should be extraordinary.

Love, Julie

* * * * *

"Oh my God, those kids are going to get killed!" I exclaimed to Glen.

We were on the dock of the town marina in Guadeloupe among French sailors who lived aboard with their families. Many of the French boats were used as family housing and were likely stuck to the ocean floor with barnacles. A number of small children lived on the derelict boats, playing on the dock the way other kids play in their backyards.

I don't have children of my own but I figure once a child is born, he or she should live a good, safe life. On the other hand, as a stranger in a foreign land, I knew to keep quiet about others' parenting techniques. The French parents on our dock subscribed to the *what doesn't kill them will make them stronger* school of child rearing. I say this because for hours at a time, the oldest child, a girl who looked to be about ten and whose daily outfit was only underpants, put all the smaller children in a grocery cart that one of the parents brought back from a store, and pushed the younger kids at full speed up and down the rickety dock, thrilling them by teetering the front wheels off and barely stopping before the cart fell into the water. They may have all been fine swimmers, but the very youngest would never have survived trapped in the folding child seat of that shopping cart. When I tried to reason with the children, they taunted me in French and tried to run me down with the cart as one of their mothers sat on the deck of her boat placidly reading a fashion magazine. There was only one other American sailboat on our dock, the rest were French. The other American couple had been there a few weeks for sail repairs, and the woman told me she too had been worried about the kids at first, but... She did not finish her sentence and the way her eyes narrowed, I could guess her thoughts.

It's very possible those French kids may one day work as physicists on the atomic particle collider, or they could still be down in Guadeloupe living on the same dock. That was the first time I had been around children raised on boats, but I would later discover there are many of them out there. Mostly, they are very interesting, homeschooled and sailing the world with their parents. Called *kid boats* by the rest of us, the vessels with children aboard tend to voyage together. All is quiet onboard kid boats during the morning school sessions, and in the afternoons the kids head to the beach or water and play until dinner. Those young voyagers grow up as interesting citizens of the world. I cannot imagine how they could ever adapt to the structure of normal, land-based work and life.

I had arrived in Guadeloupe with stars in my eyes, envisioning a Margaritaville song kind of life on tropical islands. Though still a novice, I soon realized that in most places, living goes on just like in more traditional towns. Island life includes the full range of social problems, bureaucracy, and crime.

With our first island behind us, it was time to pick up the pace and make a nonstop push for Miami. Our Volvo auxiliary engine had stumped the French engine mechanics in Guadeloupe, and an email from the Swedish company told us we would have to go to Miami to truly solve our engine problem. What's 1,500 miles at 6 knots? A very long way to travel for warranty work! It was barely light when we cast off from the docks and picked our way through the reef to the open ocean. After a collective deep breath to relax, Glen turned the boat over to ever-ready Otto as we raised sail and doused our gasping engine.

On the dark quiet water, I realized that this was what we dreamed of. Just the two of us, a sailboat, and the muted hum of her hull gliding through the water beneath the planets and stars.

* * * * *

Glen and I spent a month in Miami as expert mechanics attempted to resolve our engine problem. The Volvo folks could not figure out what was wrong, despite replacing most major parts such as the turbo charger. After considerable wrangling, they agreed to replace the entire engine, but because of their contractual blah blah blah fine print agreement with America Volvo, we had to take delivery of the new engine in a European country. Crossing the Atlantic again for warranty work was crazy, so Amel stepped in and insisted Volvo stand by their product and ship a new engine to their boatyard in Guadeloupe, a French territory, where it would be switched out at our earliest convenience. That was a relief, and we decided to endure our limping engine a while longer to explore more of the east coast of America. Despite the crippled engine, our next stop would be the Bahamas.

Chapter 6

L ook Glen, the water is so blue, clear and shallow, we can see the shadow of our boat on the sandy ocean floor! How cool is that?"

The scene rivaled any tropical island screensaver. With windswept trees leaning far over the white-sand beaches, as though they were stretching to preen in the mirrored water's surface. Starfish and conch on the bottom were barely distorted by the water and appeared close enough to pluck from the fine sand wafting back and forth around them in the movement of the waves.

The term "paradise" is overused, but that was the word that most often came to mind in the Bahamas. I like being warm; I like white, sandy beaches; I like water so sparkling I can see fish from the deck of the sailboat. In the Bahamas, anchor anywhere with a sandy bottom and you're guaranteed all those things.

Looking at a map you might think, "Big deal, the Bahamas are so close to the Florida Keys—how different can they be?" The differences are countless. The Keys, which we had explored from Miami, seemed off-limits to boaters. Any place we wanted to anchor was posted, "No Anchoring." In the Keys, boats are forced to berth in marinas, some that charge four dollars per foot (boat length!) per day. On a typical 40 to 50 foot liveaboard sailboat, that can get darned expensive. Add in a lot more people and boats to either enjoy, or contend with, depending on your mood, and the Keys didn't hold nearly the allure of the Bahamas.

Only a day sail from Florida, I thought the Bahamas would be packed with boats, but the tricky Gulf Stream crossing and cruising fees kept Floridians from invading in larger numbers. The Gulf Stream might look like a mere 30 to 40 miles wide area of strong currents, but it can be a bugger to cross. We did not want or need any more war stories, and a pleasant crossing was our goal. Having learned patience and humility (to an extent), we waited in Miami for the perfect conditions before setting out to cross the Gulf Stream.

There is one hard and fast rule about crossing the Gulf Stream in northerly winds: don't. Not even if it's blowing just a little north of east or west. In the center, the Gulf Stream currents reach speeds of 5 knots and so much water is forced through the area between the Bahamas and Florida that you actually travel uphill for the first half of the crossing. The strong north-flowing Gulf Stream current coupled with a wind blowing from the north—against the current—has a tremendous wave-building power. Steep seas can be created which are way out of proportion to the actual wind speed. On the other hand, in winds blowing with the current, from the bottom of the compass rose, the crossing can be downright pleasant. That's what we waited for.

On an early morning of mild, southerly winds, we departed Miami and dropped anchor in the Bahamas at dinnertime. We spent the night in solitude in what looked like still, open water, bordered by a stand of mangrove trees next to where we were moored. The water below was only 15 feet deep, which was shallow for us. The draft of our boat (the part of the vessel beneath the water), was six and a half feet, so we would be close, or on the bottom at low tide. That day marked the beginning of three months of getting used to the possibility of bumping the sandy bottom during low tide. My personal pucker tolerance didn't allow us to do that often—only where we could snorkel and inspect the bottom, checking for coral reefs or anything we could hit if we swung full circle on our anchor during the night. It may sound overly cautious, but on one of those inspection dives, Glen found a large refrigerator someone had dumped, which we would have hit when our anchor veered us in that direction. I could imagine Lloyds of London scoffing at an insurance claim for impacting with a refrigerator at sea.

On most of the sun-warmed days, Glen perfected his free-diving and spearfishing skills, and I snorkeled the reefs or walked the beach. We met sailors in the Bahamas who years earlier had planned a circumnavigation but could never find enough reason to leave behind those white sand islands and crystal blue waters. There were some 700 islands to explore and the Bahamian people were welcoming and friendly. I considered that I too would find it difficult to leave such a wondrous place.

* * * * *

EMAIL: IT'S ENOUGH

TO: Dad, Jeanne, Johnny, and Mom

FROM: Julie Bradley

The Bahamas are fantastic; non-crowded, friendly, and welcoming. Sailboats are in the minority here. We anchor in bays next to huge powerboats that come for the sport-fishing. Unlike those powerboats, we fish to eat. I like the powerboaters well enough, but they don't consider sailors real fishermen: 1) We troll off the back of the boat with a hand line, clothespin, bungee cord, and a hot pink, plastic squid; and 2) All we ever seem to catch is dorado (alias, mahi-mahi) or tuna. Normally we are not able to talk the talk with our brethren powerboaters at the dock. Today all that changed.

ESCAPE FROM THE ORDINARY

We left Bimini Island, a former home of Hemingway and base for dozens of sportfishing charter companies. Our destination was Cat Island, only five miles south. We decided to throw out the line on the hour-long sail. The boat was on autopilot and Glen was reading in the cockpit while I looked out for boat traffic. Glancing backward, I saw a big fish strike and yelled, "FISH ON THE LINE!!!" as the hook set. Then things happened fast. Battle stations! CODE RED!

We had hooked a huge wahoo. If you don't know what that is, it's no surprise because you don't often see them on a menu. Wahoo have the fighting ability and looks of a barracuda with the sweet and firm taste of an albacore tuna. Bringing it onboard is never a sure thing because its teeth are vicious and with a lucky snap, can cut through wire fishing leaders. We were motoring when we hooked the fish, so I cut power and let the boat drift in order to help Glen muscle and gaff the 30-plus pound fighting *wahoo* onboard.

All this activity didn't go unnoticed. Out of thin air, sport fishermen saw us grappling with a prized wahoo. We were so absorbed bringing the fish aboard, we didn't notice several sportfishing boats had moved within 300 yards of us.

One fisherman hailed us on the radio, "Hey, sailboat, what kind of rig did you use to catch that wahoo?" I laughingly described our set up and gave full credit to the hot pink plastic squid we towed on a handline attached to our stern cleat. Which made us members of the sportfishing elite for about five minutes!

Love, Julie

* * * * *

White sand beaches, turquoise waters, and red sky sunsets... I guess it's easy to get jaded anywhere, and I confess that was happening to me, until fate offered up a place totally unique within all the Bahamas. Having picked Cat Island at random from dozens of other islands on our path, we found it to be in a category of its own. Cat Island offered all the many delights of the Bahamas we enjoyed, as well as a chance to safely enter the dark underworld of potions, hexes, and voodoo.

When America won independence from England, many Loyalists—mostly wealthy plantation owners—were given land in the Bahamas under the British flag. Some set up plantations on Cat Island and brought slaves to tend the cotton and sugar crops, with many still operating. There were 15 or so family names on the island that reflected the planters from those days. The farming tradition persisted, and Cat Island was one of the few places in the Bahamas where inhabitants still worked their gardens, growing bananas, yams, papayas, and peas, just like their British ancestors did after fleeing post-revolution America.

Walking in search of fresh produce to buy, we saw a tree adorned with strange hanging objects. Like a windblown Christmas tree, it sported the kind of ornaments one could find washed up on a beach like bleached whale and shark bones, fishing net floats, and glass bottles. It wasn't until we met Samuel, a British descendant who sold garden vegetables, that we learned what made the objects so special.

"You're not afraid, are you? You're not superstitious?" Samuel asked. (I lived on a sailboat—of course I was superstitious, but wanting to get the full scoop, said nothing.) Samuel continued, "Those slaves brought over from America started the Obeah. It's voodoo."

Samuel's voice took on a conspiratorial tone as he told his story of salt Obeahs. It was five minutes into the tale before I realized by *salt*, he meant *assault*. Samuel described the power of an assault Obeah and the ceremony necessary to empower it in the local *patois*. He said, "There are other spells: love Obeahs, death Obeahs, wealth Obeahs, protection Obeahs…"

My ears perked up and I interrupted with, "How much for a protection Obeah?"

"Julie's just kidding," Glen said, not wanting to get involved in the hex business on a remote island in a foreign country.

Samuel explained that important Obeah ceremonies were only held at midnight—hours after we would be fast asleep on our boat—so participating in the underworld would not be on our schedule. Samuel had now hit his stride and we were getting the full story. The tree-hanging paraphernalia represented a more passive form of Obeah. Believers prayed to the good and bad spirits they hoped to convince to occupy their everyday articles such as bottles, fishing floats, hats, and so on. When an item is hung on the tree, there is a special ceremony for the spirits to occupy the item, and once done, believers count on the spirits' influence and ask them for assistance. The darker side of Obeah involved placing curses on one's enemy; there were stories of islanders dying from Obeah hexes. There were also tales of people being saved through help from friendly, tamed Obeah spirits. According to Samuel, Obeah still thrived on the island. "Even up there," Samuel concluded and pointed up a hill to a monastery called the Hermitage.

Curiosity goaded Glen and me to climb to the top of Mount Alvernia, a whopping 206 feet, the highest elevation in the Bahamas. On the historical marker, we discovered it was also a Christian pilgrimage site where Father Jerome, a monk, built The Hermitage (no relationship to the renowned museum of art in St. Petersburg, Russia). Father Jerome was a recluse who lived in a cave while he constructed the retreat as a penance, stone by stone. We had seen the structure from the deck of our boat in the anchorage—after all it was the highest spot in the Bahamas—

but never guessed it was a monastery. It appeared more like a decayed medieval castle from the Dark Ages with parapets, domed roof, and bell tower. From the water, it looked quite large but I was surprised how small it was as we stood before it.

Samuel told us Father Jerome was an architect before he felt the calling to be a monk. The monastery building had its oddities; constructed low and sparse, Father Jerome must have been very small. There was a feeling of foreboding, as though the reclusive monk had built it in such a manner as to discourage visitors. On the road leading up to the mount, Father Jerome had also built a sort of Stations of the Cross, which was more like a prayer obstacle course. You would certainly avoid its rocky path if wearing sandals, after a rain, or in the dark. A heavily ornamented tree close to the Stations of the Cross reminded us that Obeah voodoo played its hand even here, waving in the breeze on the monastery grounds.

* * * * *

SAILMAIL: IT'S ENOUGH

TO: JEANNE

FROM: JULIE

Hey, Jeanne! Daddy's advice about getting our HAM radio licenses really paid off. The Morse code was a pain. I promptly forgot most of those dits and dots but the ability to send and receive email over the radio instead of the expensive satellite system has improved life on the boat.

I thought we were accustomed to the shallow waters of the Bahamas but were reminded that we are still rookies in this voyaging life. Our good friends Phil and Nancy Bower flew in from DC to visit us. Phil, a former operations officer on the USS Nimitz aircraft carrier, really *gets* what we are doing. We were excited to show them the wonders of the area and forgot to check the tides. We anchored, then all sped off in the dinghy to snorkel some pretty reefs. We came back to It's Enough, and she was canted on her side in the water with the port holes inches from the lapping water. We were hard aground. She had swung on her anchor close to shore at high tide and it was now low tide. The water depth was less than that of our keel, and the boat had tipped on its side. It would be the middle of the night before the water raised enough to set her right. She was so canted we could not even climb aboard to batten the windows. This was serious trouble. We were at a disadvantage without a working engine, and I stood with the Bowers in shallow water while Glen sought help from other boats. After a couple hours of pulling and tugging we finally got the boat into deeper water thanks to an armada of dinghies and our bow thruster. I don't think that aircraft carriers go aground very often, so that was a bonus experience for Phil!

Love, Julie

* * * * *

"IT'S GONE"! I yelled to Glen.

I stood on the stern of the boat in shock. Our nearly new, $3,000 dinghy and its $2,000 outboard motor were nowhere in sight. We purchased it only six months earlier in LaRochelle and had not even been able to use it until the Bahamas. Normally we stowed the dinghy on the mizzen deck (beneath the shorter second mast) when we made a passage, but that day it had been my idea to tow the dinghy in case we needed to scout a path through the coral heads. When we departed that morning, I tied it to a cleat on the back of our sailboat, close to the stern, so it would not swing and get crosswise to our wake. I had not looked back even once the whole day.

We left the Abacos Islands at daylight, and since then I had been focused forward. Due to the tricky, shallow passage, my job was to help pick our way through a gauntlet of coral reef from the bow of the boat. We were heading to Eleuthera Island; motoring through shallow ocean and patches of coral that could rip a hole in the bottom of *It's Enough* if we were unlucky to hit one. Tools for that hot and sweaty work in direct sun were my hat, polarized sunglasses, and stabilized binoculars. We left early in the morning, so I was still wearing my pajamas—a short night-gown with fuzzy sheep on the fabric and a long sleeve cotton shirt over it for sun protection. My original plan had been to change clothes once we were underway but there had been so much coral I did not feel comfortable going below long enough to change. After spending most of the day in the glaring sun, I needed a shower and a good dinner—but first we had to find the dinghy!

The only way to describe the profound importance of a dinghy is to say what you are unable to do without one. You no longer have a way to get to shore to explore, buy food, go for a walk, wash your laundry, or get repair parts, for starters. No more dropping anchor for free in pictur-esque bays. Without a dinghy we would be forced to find a marina for a monstrous daily charge of $2 – 4 a foot! *It's Enough* would rack up more than $100 for every day it sat docked at any of those marinas, which are few and far between in the Bahamas. Without a dinghy, you can no longer go spearfishing, snorkeling or diving. Our lives would be seri-ously altered until we got to where we could spend another $5,000 to buy a new dinghy and motor. Since we did not carry much cash aboard, we would have to find someplace that accepted credit cards. The inconven-iences went on and on... Until then, we would have to swim to shore, towing dry clothes, wallets, and anything else we needed in watertight Tupperware boxes.

Glen got quiet; absorbing the impact the dinghy loss would have on our plans and finances. He was silent and calm, not angry. Personally, I was devastated by my carelessness. My deck and line-handling skills were usually good, but this time I really let us down. A deep appreciation and respect washed over me for Glen's quiet, non-judgmental manner.

Squinting through my binoculars, I anxiously scoured the horizon behind us, hoping the dinghy had only worked loose in the last ten minutes or so and that it was still within sight. No luck. I studied the cleat for signs of remaining line, which would mean it had snapped and therefore not my fault. Again, there was no sign of the yellow nylon line I had used to tether the dinghy to our boat. Whatever knot I had used had worked itself loose during a day of motoring through the coral heads.

The sun was low and right in my eyes, but up ahead there appeared a rare marina. I looked longingly toward the marina, then behind us, desperately scanning for our little dinghy, or tender as the big yachts call theirs. The sight of nothing but blue water and coral heads in the wake behind our boat was a game changer for our immediate future. At least, with the marina ahead, we would have a dock to step onto that night. Once ashore, we could possibly borrow someone else's tender to look for our vanished dinghy—maybe all was not lost.

The marina and manmade harbor we entered was part of a failed development financed by a drug cartel which was busted by the DEA. With the investors in jail, the real estate developer had gone belly-up. This was not an uncommon occurrence in the Bahamas and we had seen abandoned projects on other islands. We pulled alongside the unfinished dock. A man from another sailboat told us it was free to use if we wanted, but there was no drinking water or electricity.

During the time it took us to tie up at the dock I worked myself into a high hover over the dinghy loss. I wanted to redeem myself by finding it, but there were 70 miles of possible search area behind us, not counting current, wind, drift, or the possibility that another boat had salvaged it. Reality painted a grim picture. As a relentless never, never, never give up kind of person, I told Glen I was going to hire one of the powerboats tied up in front of a waterfront condo nearby and go out looking right then before the sun set.

"In your pajamas?" he asked. I was frantic—the last thing I worried about was how I looked.

"It just looks like a dress," I told Glen.

Time was running out as the sun was setting so I jumped off the boat and burst into the unlocked door of the first condo I saw. Four startled men looked up from a game of cards.

I pleaded, "Can you please help me? I lost our dinghy. Can I rent your boat to go out and look for it before the sun goes down?"

The men said nothing, looking nervously at each other, one with a card he was playing hovering in midair. Thankfully, one of the men stood up, all business, and asked, "Was anyone in it?"

My degree of desperation must have exceeded what they thought reasonable for the loss of a small boat. I noticed the other three card players sizing me up—they looked a little scared. Besides my abrupt entrance into their card game, I looked down and realized I was barefoot, wearing a sheep-print pajama dress, a floppy hat, and a face contorted with anxiety.

Thankfully, the islands have different norms of behavior and another man spoke up, "Time's a wastin'. Let's go look!" Folding his cards and getting up he added, "If you have a husband, bring him. I'm sure my wife will want to come."

Our helpful ally in the quest was named Steve, and I ran to get Glen so the four of us could search for the dinghy in his 24-foot fishing runabout with a shallow draft perfect for the waters of the Bahamas. Steve and his wife lived in Eleuthera year-round and knew the waters well. After an hour of zigging and zagging through the coral, the sun truly set. With a heavy feeling of resignation, we called it a day.

Steve understood the severity of our dinghy loss and recommended we get on the VHF radio to announce our location and offer a reward. "The islanders are good people," he told us, "and if your dinghy turns up on the shores of Eleuthera Island, you will get it back." We returned to *It's Enough* with doubtful spirits. The dinghy and motor were practically new; such a prize would be difficult for both local fishermen and other boaters to resist. Back on the boat, exhausted from our long, hot day in the sun, we cooked fish from our little freezer, studied the charts of the area, showered, and dropped into bed.

The next morning, we were at Steve's house early with binoculars and a portable radio in hand.

"No pajamas?" his wife asked with a laugh.

After hours of searching the coastline and our approach to the island, we finally had to admit the dinghy was gone. But when times are bad, good people step up. Once word got out of our loss, two different residents from the condominium development offered us their old inflatable dinghies for free. Unfortunately, they were worn, full of holes, and not substantial enough to take a motor. If we couldn't find anything better, we would be able to repair the better of the two to paddle to shore until we could find a better alternative. We were moved by the generosity of those expat Americans and let them know we would get back to them if we could not find something more long-term in town.

We rented a car from someone at the condo complex and started driving around the island. A few minutes down the road, Glen and I spotted an islander hitchhiking. We stopped to pick him up and told him about our situation. We asked him to be on the lookout for our dinghy and told him we would pay a finder's fee for its return.

"Sure, I be on the lookout," he told us in the local patois, "but if you wanna 'nudder one, I knows where." A dinghy for sale? We might be back in business!

Sidney, our local hitchhiker, explained he and a friend had previously found a dinghy and motor when they were out fishing. They already sold the motor but the dinghy was still available. One drawback: the coral punctured one of the rubber pontoons before they rescued it. Glen and I looked at each other with hope. We had plenty of rubber patches and marine grade epoxy back on the boat. If this dinghy were sturdy and repairable, it would solve half our problem. We were pretty sure we would be able to find a new 15 horsepower outboard for sale on Nassau, the main Bahamian island.

We inspected the dinghy propped against the side of Sidney's friends' house. Though one of the pontoons seemed to be holding air, the other was punctured and torn in two large areas. On the plus side, the dinghy was a top-of-the-line Novurania; the Lexus of dinghy brands, often found in service on mega-yachts.

Tentatively, Glen asked, "How much?" Sidney and his friend conferred aloud, as though we weren't even there. Sidney was sort of advocating for us... "Dese folks driving this ole car, loss their brand-new dinghy and motor..." Finally, the two friends came up with the price of $750. That was tricky. If the dinghy could be repaired—and Glen was not sure—it would be a bargain. The only hiccup was we had only $500 in cash on the boat.

"That's all we've got," we hesitantly and truthfully explained. Both men broke into toothy grins, obviously thrilled at the deal.

Back at *It's Enough*, Glen's rubber epoxy repair job ended up curing nicely. Our new expat friends from the condos gathered round as we got our manual air pump in place and started *pumpa, pumpa*, pumping. The patches held! We now had an ugly but sound runabout for the foreseeable future. Our patched replacement dinghy was sturdier and of better quality than the one we lost. As a result of our misfortune, we'd been drawn into a unique and wonderful slice of the island community. Our sturdy Novurania dinghy was the silver lining. That night we celebrated for our new dinghy, luck, and the kindness of strangers.

* * * * *

We quickly established a morning routine in the Bahamas. After breakfast, we donned our wetsuits, grabbed our snorkel gear, and motored out in the dinghy to explore. At first, I found myself stunned by water color so intense it almost seemed a cliché. The depth of the water determined the shade, which could be anywhere from iridescent turquoise to a shimmering cobalt blue in the direct sunlight. And that was just the panorama from the dinghy. Once below the surface, it was as though someone had flipped a switch and the view turned from living color to brilliant high-def.

For my part, snorkeling was effortless, and I drifted from one coral head to another, amazed to discover that what appeared like deserted coral heads from the top were teeming with grouper and rainbow bright reef fish below. When the tide pulled out, the water was shallow enough to peer down as I stood on the bottom, taking care to avoid the stingrays with long dark tails that dragged across the sugary-sand ocean floor. Low tide also exposed the very tops of the reefs that from a distance appeared to be giant mushrooms sprouting in the sea. As I snorkeled, Glen worked on his freediving skills, a streamlined version of scuba except that instead of using air tanks, what are used are one's own lungs, a weight belt, snorkel mask and fins. Freediving is about more than the amount of time a diver's breath can be held. Neutral buoyancy must be attained so as not to expend too much oxygen getting down to the bottom or back up to the surface. Depending on how deep Glen wanted to go down, he worked to set the right amount of weight, often returning to the dinghy to slide lead on or off his belt to find the just right combination. His full freediving kit also included the all-important spear gun for catching dinner. The longer he could stay down, the greater the chances of catching dinner.

Glen could stay down on the sandy bottom holding his breath for more than two minutes. After one minute, the fish that vamoosed when he descended came out of hiding and swam near to inspect, curious about what strange creature had entered their environment. His technique was to wait quietly on the bottom until the fish returned, and then take his best shot for dinner. I was an avid supporter of Glen's freediving efforts because a freshly speared fish guaranteed a delicious alternative to our rice and canned goods on the boat. Glen was usually productive with his speargun and I worked hard to keep meals interesting: grilled grouper, grouper with butter and almonds, grouper with lemon and ginger, grouper with tomato and basil, grouper with pineapple salsa... searching for countless ways to cook the same fish.

Our agreement, however, was that Glen would hold off from spearing until I climbed back into the dinghy and was clear of the water. Sharks have such a sharp sense of smell, they appear seemingly out of nowhere seconds after a fish is speared. I did not relish the idea of getting caught by a shark in search of a meal.

One morning Glen and I rode out from *It's Enough* together, then anchored our dinghy far enough away from the reef so as not to damage the coral, but close enough for quick water exit in case we spied an unfriendly shark. By that time, I had adapted to the real and imagined dangers of paradise, and was accustomed to certain types of non-aggressive sharks such as black tip, reef, lemon, nurse… It was only the menacing hammerhead, tiger or great white sharks that I considered dangerous.

That morning I was snorkeling blissfully along when suddenly, in the normally silent waters, I clearly hear the *BZZZIINNGG* of Glen's speargun. I thought that Glen must be simulating a shot with his free diving practice, because I was still in the water! And far from the dinghy.

Startled, I raised my head and saw Glen doing an odd swim stroke with his spear high in the air, trying to keep the blood of a grouper from saturating the water. A second later I spotted a giant tiger shark gliding my way in a zigzag motion, as the regular black-tipped sharks also appeared out of nowhere, summoned by the vibration of the shot and the blood in the water. I spun around, looking for the dinghy, but it was far away. Afraid to look underwater, I did a gentle breast stroke toward the dinghy, because flailing my arms or making waves would mimic a fighting, convulsive fish. My mind flashed unproductively to the opening scene in the movie, Jaws, and I did not want to be that woman. With teeth chattering from fear, I kept my head high. A shark attack is one thing, but I definitely did not want to see its teeth coming for me. If this is *IT*, let it be swift, surprising and painless. But the sharks seemed to disappear once Glen heaved his speargun and bleeding grouper into the dinghy. I was beyond anger — more in shock — and pulled myself into the dinghy with superhuman strength and speed. Sitting in the dinghy with the spear and grouper on his lap, Glen looked nervous and his gaze could not meet my eyes.

Falling short of an actual apology he said, "It was a clear shot and a great looking fish. Don't those sharks have phenomenal smelling abilities?"

I couldn't stay mad for long with the teamwork required on a boat and as Glen cleaned the, yes, good-looking grouper, I took a shower to clear my head. We ate dinner watching the sunset and I thought about the new world we had entered. We were close to the circle of life where everything that lives is food for something else. In that world, humans are food too. Today wasn't our turn, but the experience had been a wake-up call. Sharks are all business when it comes to the food chain.

Early the next morning, with good visibility and what little wind there was coming from the south, we crossed the Bahamas Bank and then the Gulf Stream. Though sorry to leave the Bahamas, it was warming enough to make our way north for the short New England summer. In every way, the Bahamas had been more than we imagined. After three months of exploring countless islands, we knew that whatever doubts we previously had about our new sailing life, we were at that point true cruising sailors with only about 32,000 more miles to go...

ESCAPE FROM THE ORDINARY

Chapter 7

I want to travel the Ditch instead of sailing the Gulf Stream up the Atlantic coast," I announced, tracing my finger along the network of inland waterways on the navigational chart unfurled on the table and weighted down with a glass. "That route is dotted with small towns we could explore."

Glen and I were at a marina in Miami readying the boat to sail north. After several frustrating months of maneuvering in tight spaces with our still not-quite-right engine, Glen's annoyance was palpable. It wasn't the best moment to spring this new routing idea on him. With no consideration and no discussion, he shook his head. I, however, was of different opinion about traveling north by way of the Ditch, the nickname given to the 3,000-miles of Intercoastal Waterway (ICW) between Miami and Boston. We had been racing along as though we had somewhere to be and I was sure we were missing wonders galore.

I tried a different tack, "Rushing and sailing are two words rarely used in the same sentence, but that is what we have been doing. After our Atlantic crossing we sailed hard and fast from Guadeloupe to Miami to get the engine fixed. Now that we know fixing the engine is a search for the Holy Grail, let's do the Monty Python bit and be lighthearted." To myself, I made a silent argument: Who could feel uptight sailing up a body of water called The Ditch? To me it was a far better option than going back out to the Atlantic Ocean for a dash up to Maine as though we were being chased.

Glen, frustrated over the engine, believed his binary code type logic would win the day. "You can't sail the ICW—you have to motor through narrow waterways clogged with powerboats, and dozens of bridges—some too short for our mast to pass under. Our engine is still limping at half power and we'd be lucky to make 25 miles a day."

I slid from under the navigation station, reached out to Glen and put my arms around him. "But they'll be 25 enjoyable miles each day," I whispered while winking. Glen understood I was open to compromise, the wink reminding him of our third way rule. The third way was our tool for harmony when we disagreed on a point. It was our commitment to working together to find a third, and usually better way, to end a disagreement.

I tested a couple of ideas to myself and kicked in a third possibility. We could avoid the frustrating parts of the ICW by sailing up the Atlantic Ocean, then detour to the Ditch as we neared places that were historic and charming in ways that only small seaside villages can be. In first-mate speak, this meant shore trips whenever and wherever I wanted! After all, as first officer and galley chef, I was 49% of the vote as well as the person who did most of the navigation and all the cooking.

This third way was a good compromise and gave us more options to be spontaneous. Any time either of us would call out, "Hey... this place looks good," we'd take down the sails, drop anchor, and point the dinghy toward shore for a crab feast, a good movie playing in Beaufort (please, lots of butter on my popcorn), or a grocery store named Harris Teeter in Charleston. It was a sailor's dream: traveling anywhere from one to eight hours a day, no 24-hour watch schedules, and *It's Enough* as our base camp for the adventure.

Admittedly, there were a few snags. The Ditch was not as straight-forward as just pointing north. The lace of tributaries, inlets, outlets, creeks, and rivers along the Atlantic deceived me into navigating us up the wrong way more than once. This meant doubling back with a limping engine as the water became shallow enough to threaten the boat's bottom. We also shared more than one tense moment squeaking our mast under bridges, but eventually the rhythm of life slowed to match that of the meandering water.

Through late spring we made our way up the backwaters of Georgia and the Carolinas, and by early summer we passed Norfolk, Virginia, its massive boatyards crowded with Navy ships looking like grey war horses at a trough. Blowing our foghorn in greeting, I waved at sailors high on the deck of an aircraft carrier as it passed; the towering, steel behemoth dwarfed us like a minnow in the wake of a whale. We passed a large, vertical post piercing the water's surface, so I snapped up the navigation chart to be sure we weren't entering a marked hazard area. What a surprise when the post shifted and without a sound glided off in the opposite direction. I smiled and waved when I realized it was a submarine periscope. I figured someone not far below us was smiling back.

I laughed so much during those carefree months that new lines were developing around my eyes. "Or it could be too much reflected sun under your hat," proffered Glen, my ever-analytical captain. There were plenty of reasons for the new smile lines on our tanned and sun-warmed faces, not the least of which were the greetings from and the easy, casual conversations with the townspeople along our way.

"Americans seem to have gotten nicer since we retired," I noted one day, knowing full well it was Glen and I who were transforming. We were becoming the kind of people who take the time to talk with strangers and learn about the history and culture of the small, waterfront towns we visited. Aboard *It's Enough*, stress was at an all-time low and morale soared like the sea birds as we discovered wonderful places to explore and fresh local foods to sample. Even laundromats were a convenience to be relished. Overall, there was little to pose a threat as we sailed north through the protected waters of the ICW, eventually arriving in summertime Maine.

* * * * *

"LOBSTERS - $4 LB" at the lobster shack triggered instant salivation. We wanted our first dinner in Maine to be freshly caught lobster, so on advice from the ruddy lobsterman who sold us the still snapping crustaceans, I dropped a bucket over the boat's edge to draw seawater—the secret ingredient for boiling lobster. Whether it was the seawater, the garlic butter, or eating in the open air of *It's Enough*'s cockpit, the dinner experience was better and more memorable than any fine-dining establishment. As it turned out, the lobster preparation was the easiest part of what would become a steep learning curve in Maine.

Setting sail each morning in the fog-obscured islands made tricky business out of navigating. We shared the waterways with fleets of lobster and fishing boats plowing through fog at a fast and fearless clip. Our own careful progress convinced me the fishermen must have possessed a sixth sense to guide them through the mist. Their wooden boats were nearly invisible to our radar and after one frightening narrow miss, and a good cussing from the lobsterman, we learned to sit tight and let the mid-morning warmth clear the fog before moving onward.

* * * * *

SAILMAIL: IT'S ENOUGH

TO: Mom, Jeanne, Johnny

FROM: Julie Bradley

We just arrived in Maine and dropped anchor in a bay of what appeared to be old-fashioned, Victorian-era hotels, but are massive summer homes they call cottages in New England. The folks hereabouts seem standoffish after the super-friendly Southerners we met coming north, but they are probably jaded by all the seasonal visitors who, like us, swat wildly at the swarms of blackflies around our heads. These flies are tiny, quite vicious, and make mosquitoes seem like amateurs. The biggest caution is the tides. Yesterday, at high tide, we dropped anchor up a small river, then went ashore for a hike and picnic. When we returned to the boat at low tide, huge boulders were sticking up from the riverbed right next to the boat. Nothing short of a miracle that It's Enough wasn't hulled. We have taken to studying the chart carefully and dropping anchor in deep water. Our usual trick of diving down to check the underwater surrounding doesn't work here. The water is cold and dark with tiny organisms that fish and whales love.

We hear there are puffins, my favorite bird, on an island offshore and tomorrow we sail out to see them.

Love, Julie

* * * * *

Anchoring in Maine is not for the faint of heart; the tidal range is a staggering 24-foot rise and fall, compared to just 3 feet averaged across most of the earth's oceans. The partly accurate reason for the huge tides is Maine's proximity to the Bay of Fundy where 52-foot tides are among the highest in the world.

The extreme tides also create a metropolis of sea life. Like a front-loading washing machine, the cold, fast tidal flows swirl tasty critters from the ocean floor to the surface waters attracting legions of fish. There are countless seabirds as well, but to my disappointment, no sight of puffins—the bird I most wanted to see. Female puffins lay only one egg a year and live close to the open sea, so the species is rare and difficult to spot. They are so cute that it's easy to believe they just dropped out of a Disney animated movie, but their real life is much more difficult.

Once a puffin leaves its nest, it normally does not return to land again for two or three years. The best way to see a puffin would be at a nesting site such as Machias Seal Island, off the coast of Maine near the Canadian border.

"Puffins are like tooth fairies," advised the brochure of a commercial bird-watching boat with daily trips to the nesting island. "You hear about them, but our boat is your best chance to see one." With our own boat, we had the advantage over the tour boat crowd, and set sail to the nesting site the brochure claimed was the largest colony of puffins in the Atlantic. True to the marketing message, I spied puffins flying toward the nesting island. "Here they come!" I called, and Glen followed the line of my finger tracing their path. Three of them suddenly veered overhead, their little wings a blur at the sides of black and white bodies. A flash of bright orange from their large beaks was clearly visible as they sped past.

We anchored off the island and near the shore laid a vision of striped beaks, iridescent orange feet, and shiny black backs. Mothers cared for their newly hatched pufflings by filling their own parrot-like bills with fish, waddling like penguins to their babies, and spilling the food from their own large beaks into the miniaturized versions of their offspring. Those babies would need to bulk up in order to endure a couple of years of waterborne traveling to places as far away as Iceland and Scotland in the North Atlantic.

* * * * *

SAILMAIL: IT'S ENOUGH

JULIE BRADLEY

TO: Mom, Jeanne, and Johnny

FROM: Julie Bradley

I've eaten so much blueberry pie in Maine my tongue is turning blue. It is a short summer here. One week into September and we are wearing sweatshirts during the day and covering with blankets at night. Tomorrow we sail south to the Chesapeake Bay, then head offshore to Bermuda, on our way to the Virgin Islands. Tropical is sounding good to me right now.

Love you, Julie

ESCAPE FROM THE ORDINARY

Chapter 8

Eating popcorn in the cockpit, Glen called for me to come up and watch the sunset, but I stayed below decks hunched over the long-distance SSB radio, taking notes. The connection was scratchy so I donned headphones and held up my hand for quiet as Glen called me to join him.

Things on board had been light hearted and laid back since we departed Norfolk for Bermuda the day before. It had been a great summer in New England. We had become seasoned sailors and I looked forward to the coming weeks of Atlantic offshore sailing as we made our way to the Caribbean islands. To break up the monotony of the passage, we planned to head to Bermuda first, but if what I was hearing on the weather forecast was true, things aboard *It's Enough* would not be popcorn and perfect sunsets for much longer.

Herb Hilgenberg, a meteorologist and friend to boaters, was in the middle of a weather forecast that startled every sailor on the east coast. Herb had just predicted that Hurricane Mitch was heading towards us and its landfall in Bermuda would smack dab coincide with our arrival. Burdened with the news, I climbed the ladder's four steps to the cockpit expecting Glen to be as upset when I relayed the message.

"Julie, I appreciate your humor, but wrong ocean. I checked the weather before we left Annapolis, and Hurricane Mitch is in the Gulf of Mexico, downgraded to a tropical depression. At most it is a storm dying out in the Gulf."

As a late-season, mean-spirited category-5 hurricane, Hurricane Mitch had killed 20,000 people in Central America the previous week. The sailing community was abuzz about a Windjammer sailing ship lost with 31 hands aboard as her captain tried to run behind an island but was caught in a vise of 50-foot waves and 100 MPH winds. Hurricane Mitch had been a sledgehammer of waves and wind before dwindling to tropical storm strength. Now, just a week later, Herb Hilgenberg was warning vessels that the beast was not dead—far from it.

I sat next to Glen without the hint of a smile. Glen was our captain and interpreter of the weather. Once he realized I was not teasing, he would take it hard that we were once again sailing into a dire situation. But Glen also knows that no matter how much a person studies the weather, listens to expert forecasters and plans for what's coming, it's impossible to know if you've made the best plan until you get out there and are in the thick of things.

"Hurricane Mitch was downgraded to a tropical depression with disorganized remains, just as the weather office told you when we cast off in Norfolk." Continuing with my notes, "Mitch has regained tropical storm status near the Yucatan and is picking up speed. Hurricane Mitch (version 2.0) is veering to the northeast, and has decided to visit Florida, then Bermuda." I stressed, "Hurricane Mitch 2.0 will arrive at Bermuda the same day as we do if we keep this same boat speed!"

The look on my face convinced Glen it was no joke and he immediately began plotting coordinates and tracking speed. Sure enough, if all happened as projected, we would converge on St George Harbor,

Bermuda, about the same time as Mitch 2.0 with its pent-up and building hurricane winds.

I gathered myself and worked to stave off what felt like an approaching panic attack by trying not to think about the hurricane force storm we had endured during our first week on *It's Enough*. I never wanted to go through anything like that again. My only desire was to reach the protected harbor of Bermuda before Hurricane Mitch walloped the island—and us.

Uncharacteristically, I asked, "What do you think about letting out more sail?" Glen and I set to work as one, inching out more sail and adjusting course to maximum advantage. This increased our speed, but the faster, more direct course put us on an uncomfortable angle of heel. In the previous days I had been in pursuit of a better ride and set our heading a wee bit off course. Now there would be no half-measures. To try to beat the coming storm, we would head straight to Bermuda with everything the boat could handle.

Speeding along under full sail and sunny skies, it was all so hard to believe as there was no indication of a hurricane lying in wait. Knowing the reports were surely correct, it was easy to imagine how ancient sailing ships were often taken by surprise and clobbered by big storms, given the clear sky that arched above us.

The winds are the messengers of the seas. The next day a pronounced swell built in strength, and that night the winds foretold the presence of Mitch. The higher wind also increased our speed, and the ride became rough as our bow battled waters whipped to a frenzy. As the wind and seas continued to strengthen, we tethered our inflatable safety vests to bolts in the cockpit as we moved about. Cooking in the galley in front of a rollicking, gimballed stove proved too much of a challenge, so I pulled a frozen lasagna out of the freezer to last us for the next few days.

Months before, Glen had bought all the materials for a storm drogue and built it himself. He rummaged through the stern locker in search of the drogue in case Hurricane Mitch moved faster than projected. The drogue consisted of a series of cones attached to a long rope and was designed by the Coast Guard to prevent a boat from pitch poling end over end if overtaken by monster waves. He coiled the drogue close to the stern and I felt tightness in my chest—if we had to use the drogue we would be in survival mode.

The meteorologist had been correct so far in his estimate of how fast the hurricane was traveling. With our added speed, we had so far been able to stay ahead of Mitch. The winds blew at a steady 35 knots—gusting to 45. We were flying east under a deep-reefed main, head, and mizzen sail, but the ride worsened. Safety demanded we always keep to the cockpit with life vests tethered to the boat. The winds continued to strengthen, and 45-knot gusts had become a constant, buffeted by 60-kt gusts. Waves turned into hill-sized steamrollers as *It's Enough* plowed through at such a tilt it was a wonder we were able to move about at all. The quick change from sunny skies and light winds to approaching storm conditions was impressive to behold.

We made it, entering Bermuda harbor at night, just 24 hours ahead of the hurricane. Normally we would not risk entering a reef-strewn area after dark, but outrunning Hurricane Mitch called for extreme measures. By radio, we announced to Bermuda Maritime we were heading through the reef into the harbor and requested updates on any deviations from the navigational lights on our charts. St. George Harbor was designed for 24/7 operations with commercial ship traffic, so we were working with pros who monitored our progress on radar. Once safely arrived, we dropped anchor and grabbed a few hours of much needed sleep. At dawn we repositioned *It's Enough* to be protected by land from the strongest quadrant of the counterclockwise hurricane winds we knew were coming.

We assembled our gigantic 4-foot Danforth storm anchor—it would be our first use of the expensive piece of equipment we now rejoiced at having bought. To set the Danforth we moved far away from other boats that likely had normal-sized anchors, to avoid a situation where another boat could drag and ram into us or foul our storm anchor, causing us to crash onto shore. That humongous storm anchor and St George Harbor itself was a boost to my confidence that we could weather out Mitch 2.0. The harbor was well protected from extreme wave action and our large Danforth was set deeply into the harbor bottom.

We tried to imagine—and plan for—every worst-case scenario that could happen at anchor during the thrashing of a hurricane. Glen's plan was to throttle the still problematic engine forward at low power (though it was always at low power anyway!) to take strain off the anchor. We also tied all our available fenders (large air-filled rubber bumpers) to the rails on the side of our boat in case another boat dragged down on us. The fenders might protect us from a runaway boat, causing it to bounce off our side and not tangle our lines. *It's Enough* was our home; we would stay aboard and protect her from dragging to shore just like land-side homeowners who choose to stand their ground when their house is threatened by natural catastrophes. On top of all our other worries, we were not entirely sure our costly boat insurance would cover any damages since we were obviously in a vulnerable latitude during official hurricane season.

Hurricane Mitch approached, and we felt as ready as we could be. I brought up a thermos of hot tea and we huddled, sheltering from the driving rain under the hard dodger (fiberglass cover) at the helm. Bermuda maritime radio kept everyone updated in real time on the conditions out on the ocean. There was much concern for a large group of sailboats still at sea in a sailing rally called The Caribbean 1500. The rally sailboats had departed the east coast the day after we had, and the slowest of those boats had been caught in the open seas. I listened and tears filled my eyes as I learned of sailors, afraid of the brutal sea conditions, who abandoned their sailboats in favor of life rafts, thinking the Bermuda Coast Guard could rescue them.

Our own rule for abandoning ship was this: never leave our sailboat for a life raft unless we had to step up into the life raft. *It's Enough* would have to be sinking for it to make sense to leave a still sound, floating, large vessel to enter a flimsy, rubber raft in storm conditions. A sailboat is like a corked bottle unless it takes on too much water. Even if a boat goes end over end and loses its masts and everything on deck, she will still right herself and continue to float. Injuries will be a near certainty, there may be a heck of a lot of water down below, and she may float low in the water, but she will float. Tragically, some of those sailors from the rally were lost at sea and the perfectly good sailboats they abandoned were later sunk as hazards to navigation by the Bermuda Coast Guard.

As for the captain and first mate on *It's Enough*, the Bermuda harbor proved itself to be so protected that the extent of the winds we recorded was in the 60-knot range. Glen powered the engine through the worst of it, and the muddy harbor bottom firmly held our Danforth storm anchor. Several boats around us did drag anchor, but the owners powered their engines to reset them and did not lose control of their vessels.

It was a tense day—I wish I could say like none other. By night, I was a mix of emotions: relieved we had managed our own survival so well but saddened by the loss of the sailors who had abandoned their boats.

We were now veterans of two hurricane-force storms. The first encounter could have been avoided with more experience and better judgment, but no weather expert or computer-based forecast had predicted the resurrection of Hurricane Mitch. With two Force 10 storms added to our *sailing credentials*, we felt wiser, and, were thankfully unscathed. I made a mental note of lessons learned, which would surely grow in length before our world voyage was done.

The biggest factor in our safety and survival was our boat. Amel's sturdy construction and design are renowned. *It's Enough* possessed three watertight bulkheads, ensuring that even if we were unlucky enough to hit a floating container or a reef, we could seal off that section and the boat would still float. We bought the best boat possible, and she never let us down.

Almost as important as the boat, was our attitude and teamwork. Glen and I learned to work together and do that extra thing to lessen each other's load. Glen was the better sailor, so in heavy weather I tried to handle things as much by myself as possible, letting him get some sleep and be fresh if the situation got beyond my ability. At times I was miserable and afraid on watch but held off rousing him with the thought that if I could just hang on a while longer by myself, the conditions would get better. Sometimes they did.

Glen is not easily influenced by outside forces or *groupthink*. After misjudging the weather forecast in the Bay of Biscay and entering into our first Force 10 storm, he became a serious student of weather. He downloaded weather-fax predictions long before our intended departure, learning the patterns for that part of the world. His track record gave me confidence and I never pressured him to leave with the fleet or change his mind. We made our own decisions and lived with them, for the better. After all, we were a team, and each problem that we solved together brought us closer.

* * * * *

Hurricane Mitch 2.0 moved quickly south and by early evening, the weather had settled. The next morning, we motored the dinghy to shore to check in with the authorities. We saw minimal damage among the sturdy houses in Bermuda. Disaster-response crews were already removing debris from the streets and restoring the power grid. We stayed a few days to see what we could of the island and to allow the oversized waves from the hurricane wake to subside.

Chapter 9

S ailing south from Bermuda required a sharp lookout for debris generated from the storm. During night watch I spotted a fully enclosed metal life raft so large it must have come loose from a cruise ship or commercial vessel. I woke Glen and we approached the life raft to see if we could salvage it. As we got closer and saw it was almost as long as our sailboat we steered clear. It was too dangerous to approach the drifting vessel or deal with in any way. It was painted a bright orange and with a flashing light, was easily avoided, but the thought of hitting something that sizable and solid prompted me to bring out our night-vision goggles and scan for other hazards loosed by the storm.

As the days passed, the Atlantic weather warmed and nearing the Caribbean islands we shed our polar fleece for T-shirts and shorts. On night watch my thoughts went to the ups and downs of our voyaging dream we had made come true. Our early retirement, a great boat, endless places to visit, daily adventures…all were very real. Everything I had left behind now seemed unreal. I traded a camouflage, bulletproof vest for an orange safety vest, biting winters for sunny warmth, and nuclear-weapons inspections for… thankfully there was nothing in my present life to compare.

ESCAPE FROM THE ORDINARY

As we wended our way down the Caribbean chain of islands I kept a journal, and the daily entries recorded my surprise at how paradise was different than I expected. The dream that I conjured all those years had one-size-fits-all islands with white sand, waving coconut palms, welcoming islanders, and pristine reefs for snorkeling. I had since learned that each island has its own personality and geography—mountainous volcanic islands, barren atolls, white sand (yes, and black sand), and rocky beaches... more island varieties than Baskin-Robbins has flavors, and like ice cream, everyone has their own favorites.

The former British islands were like orphans to me: still in shock at their sudden independence and lack of financial support. For centuries the islands had created fortunes in sugar and rum trade for England, until changing world markets and political pressures accelerated the mother country to cut them loose with the lofty notion of independence. Just like real life orphans, some islands were able to flourish despite tough odds, while other islands still had not managed to overcome the past. After visiting a half dozen or more Caribbean islands, we learned that if we did not feel welcome, it was best to pull anchor and move on to the next one.

Our island explorations became routine: drop anchor, take our dinghy to shore, check in with customs and immigration authorities, then walk around town to get a feel for the people and place. We walked or caught rides to historic or interesting attractions. Depending on the pantry situation in the galley, we might eat lunch in town, then visit the local market to replenish our food stores. Long walks, talking to islanders, socializing with other sailors, and snorkeling the reefs filled our days and many evenings. If an island was especially welcoming, we might stay a week or even more. On others, one or two days were enough before we resumed our exploration of the long chain of Caribbean islands.

* * * * *

"You owe me $20 for saving your boat." The dripping-wet islander in cutoff shorts could not look me in the eye as he tried to extort money with a fanciful tale. "I should charge more than that, but you seem like a nice lady and all… you would have lost your boat during the night and ended up on shore but I reset your anchor. That might still happen if I unfix it."

This was a first—an island scam artist!

At anchor on one of the British orphaned islands, Glen had taken the dinghy out to spear fish for dinner while I read in the cockpit. I snapped out of my book when I heard someone shouting insistently, "Hey lady, lady, lady…" The call came from the bow and I walked forward to see what was happening. The yelling was persistent but not desperate—no one was drowning.

The request for $20 came from an island man who was hanging on to the chain leading to our anchor while wearing dive fins and a snorkeling mask pulled up on his forehead. I kept cool, as playing the righteous Anglo would only inflame this situation from bad to worse. But I had no intention of playing the fool. In a second the scam unfolded with clarity. The man had noticed our dinghy was gone, and saw me, a woman, reading alone in the cockpit. In his mind I was an easy mark for a quick $20. I knew it was a setup but needed to handle the grift with at least a minimum of diplomacy. I had no concerns about our anchor. Glen was compulsive about setting and testing to ensure it held by reversing the engine. He then would snorkel down to visually inspect the anchor, giving us one less worry. He was careful to the point of obsession.

With a mind toward de-escalation and giving the islander an easy out, I told him it must have been the anchor from another boat; my husband had visually inspected our holding and it was firm. With that I bid him a good day and returned to the cockpit. The islander swam around to the stern and offered anchor insurance for the reduced price of $10 to make sure no one stole our anchor during the night. Breathing deeply to stay on the safe side of anger, I firmly asked the islander to move on, but his departure did not erase my concern.

When Glen returned wearing his dive suit, I told him the story of the island extortionist. Just to be sure, he dove to check our anchor, which was just as he had left it. We decided there were plenty of islands ahead with a potentially warmer welcome and departed the next morning.

Each island is as varied and culturally unique as every state in America, and I came to realize the happiest islands were the ones still supported by rich French and Dutch parents. Not surprisingly, happy places were where we wanted to be.

* * * * *

Nothing attracts a crowd better than the possibility of a 3,000-pound engine breaking the sling and falling through the bottom of a boat. We were at the Amel boatyard in Guadeloupe, and our broken Volvo turbo diesel motor had to be slung out of our engine compartment and the new replacement lifted in to replace it. This gave double the possibility of an exciting mishap. The tense maneuvering attracted 30 or so sailors to gather at the dock for the action.

It was finally happening. We had a fully functioning engine for the first time in more than a year since we bought our boat. Along the way, people who had admired our uncommon and well-designed French boat were surprised when we started our old engine and it hobbled along at a slow pace, coughing and wheezing as Glen tried all his tricks to get enough oomph out of an engine that puttered loudly but lacked muster.

Ironically, our engine problems had opened unexpected doors in our voyage planning. What started out as an annoying problem turned into a gift, causing us to visit places we might otherwise have missed. Our engine troubles started on our Atlantic crossing and the engine parts replaced in Guadeloupe more than a year before had not resolved the motor issues. Volvo, a Swedish company with no major presence in the Caribbean, thought that U.S. mechanics at the Volvo Marine dealer in the USA could figure it out, so we had wasted days, then weeks with them, in Miami, then Charleston, and finally Maine. We had made long sail passages on the promise that some elusive mechanic would finally solve the mystery of the broken, brand new engine. It was through Amel, our boat builder, that Volvo finally agreed to replace the entire engine. But, because the broken engine had come from a French Volvo supplier, the new one had to also come from Volvo France. Bureaucracy this confounding can't be made up.

After spring and summer on the east coast of North America, we had made our way south along the Caribbean island chain, returning to the French island of Guadeloupe, where the engine was first serviced.

The engine change took only one day and happened without drama or incident. Glen beamed as the new engine came to life at full power. The previous thousands of miles of motoring (albeit slow miles) on the old engine were history and we finally had a brand-new engine on our 18-month-old boat. It would be a welcome change to power up in low-wind situations instead of having to hear the sails flapping and banging.

We were ready to take on the world—again!

ESCAPE FROM THE ORDINARY

Chapter 10

After voyaging for nearly two years, something completely under my control was troubling me, but it took a long time before I recognized it and chose to do something about it.

Island by island, we had worked our way down the Caribbean, exploring ashore and socializing with other sailors at countless sundowner happy hours. I could not say exactly when it had become serious enough to cause me concern, but somewhere along the way since crossing the Atlantic, I realized I was drinking ever larger quantities of alcohol, developing a strong craving for red wine. What started out as social drinking had begun to feel like a nutritional requirement. By mid-afternoon I would start thinking about happy hour, and one small glass at sundown turned into half a bottle, sometimes more. Most days, I felt proud if I could hold off until 4 PM to uncork.

This was a notable shift. Early on in the Army, I hardly ever drank alcohol. There was little leisure time then and five-mile runs in the darkness of the morning were not enhanced with a fog-filled head. In those days, I easily waved off drinks when offered—without the need for explanation.

That is, until I worked in Russia. I remember that first deployment when my Russian counterparts pulled out a bottle of vodka to toast our arrival. I had turned down the liquor and toasted instead with a bottle of water. Right or wrong, my American mentor told me that taking a social drink was the diplomatic part of the job. By the ninth week of my first deployment, the vodka had become downright tasty. For the three years I thereafter spent in Russia, diplomacy drinking was the norm. And wine consumption became a daily occurrence while at home in D.C.

Moving from land to the water only made it worse. It's a fair assessment to say the liveaboard sailing community has a culture of drinking. A person can feel very isolated traveling and living on a boat, and we looked forward to gathering socially with other sailors at every opportunity. After only a few months on our boat, I went from drinking a glass of red wine every night to glancing at the clock to see how close we were to four o'clock happy hour, then having several large glasses. Every day on the boat seemed to provide a reason for celebration: a pretty sunset, bringing in a fish on the hand-line, snorkeling over pretty coral, sighting a whale, reuniting with friends we met two islands to the north.... There was no lack for causes to celebrate.

I slid from a fit and disciplined Army officer to someone who thought a lot about drinking. Looking back, addictive behavior of a different kind had served me well in the military. I used to call it a positive addiction, but it was compulsion nonetheless. Why run five miles when I could run 10? Why do 15 push-ups if I could pound out 50? More is better. On the boat my extreme tendencies had taken on what I was slow to realize was a bad turn. Physical performance and working crazy hours to succeed in the Army was one thing but sailing across oceans and through storms with alcohol-dulled brain cells could put our lives at risk. It was neither healthy nor in my best interest.

It grew to an ugly head one night off the island of Antigua. We had been sailing in the company of another couple, and instead of dinner one Saturday evening, we ate snacks, drank wine, and talked into the night.

The next morning, I woke with a throbbing head and an unsteady feeling. I wasn't quick to realize the bells in my head were those of a church on shore. My reflection in the bathroom mirror caused me to cringe and I stumbled to the cockpit where the night before I drank large quantities of wine with our friends. Empty red wine bottles were lined across the cockpit floor and there were red wine stains on the deck. In Russia, empty liquor bottles are called dead soldiers. I counted five dead soldiers consumed by four people.

With an inexplicable clarity, I knew this had to be the end of the line for my drinking. If I did not quit now, there would be no going back. We were still in the early stages of our voyage and I knew that my addiction would be completely unmanageable by the time we got halfway around the world. I wanted to feel as though I could do anything in life, both now and when we completed our circumnavigation. Knowing myself, and being honest about the situation, I had to stop drinking. Immediately. I picked up the five dead soldiers, scrubbed the red stain out of the floor… and never drank again.

After that firm decision, when I craved alcohol, I distracted myself with physical labor where I could see progress and feel accomplishment. I cleaned the boat, scrubbed algae off the boat hull, or cooked a complicated, time-consuming meal. In that way I found the key to my release. I began a journal as a form of distraction and writing every day turned into a different, but harmless, addiction. Writing became a form of therapy for me, giving voice to and then filling whatever ached inside me. Yes, it is an addiction of another sort. But I am stronger knowing I am able to look at words from which I can draw strength instead of gazing on a row of depressing dead soldiers.

ESCAPE FROM THE ORDINARY

Chapter 11

A man wearing a safari outfit stretched out and grabbed the tether as we beached our dinghy on the island of Dominica. Far too fashionable to be a sailor, he introduced himself as a tourist and nodded toward the cruise ship anchored in the distance. His wife had returned to the ship because the people of Dominica scared her: she had been insulted by a large islander with a machete hanging from his waist. A crew member on the ship had planted the seeds of concern when he warned the couple that theft and robbery had frightened off many passengers from coming ashore at all. The tourist, dressed as though heading out to stalk lions, was nice enough but we needed to check in with Dominica immigration and offered farewells as we headed to our destination. Having arrived at the island a few hours before us, he offered a bit of cautionary advice. "Don't leave your dinghy here unattended. This island is aggressively poor and someone is going to take it."

Merely the fearful thoughts of an inexperienced traveler, I told myself. However, minutes later I glanced back toward the beach and saw a towering, broad-shouldered islander, dressed like my image of Robinson Crusoe, trying to jimmy the lock securing our outboard motor to the dinghy. I yelled and—with my heart thudding and pumping legs powered by a surge of adrenalin—ran back. When he saw I was a woman, the robber dismissed me as a threat and continued trying to work free our precious outboard motor. Fortunately, once he saw Glen was hot on my heels, the would-be thief gave up and sprinted away empty handed. Breathless, I bent over, hands on knees, and considered what I had just done, wondered what I could have done if he had stood his ground. Having already lost one dinghy and outboard in the Bahamas, I was determined we would not lose another, and I had given chase before the thought of a real confrontation with a huge, angry islander entered my head. I decided the lion-hunter wannabe tourist was wiser than I had given him credit, and I stayed with the dinghy while Glen checked us in.

Not wanting to miss the island or risk losing our valuable motor, we later asked a sailor from a neighboring boat to drop us off on shore for exploring.

After having already visited a dozen more-predictable islands in the Caribbean, the roughness and unique beauty of Dominica appealed to us. It was a rare, misshapen, black pearl—but not for everyone. There are few beaches, and those that do exist are black volcanic sand. The mountains jut 4,000 feet above the ocean surface and the summits are lost to hovering clouds. There are active volcanoes that boil in the lakes and old-growth rainforests are laced with more than 300 rivers cascading down slopes creating a fine, swirling mist. Most villagers did not seem to have much interest in tourists, but some were friendly enough and returned our greetings not with a "Hello," but an amiable "OK!"

Cruise ships had just added Dominica to their itineraries, and it seemed the government was more interested in tourism than were the Dominican people. There were signs of the government's new focus as we saw men working on hiking trails for the expected influx of cruise ship visitors. We attempted to navigate one of those trails, but the rainforest made things confusing and slippery enough that we decided that a guide was needed. John—a dreadlocked local—could have carried Glen and me one under each arm for the entire day, but despite this ability, he declared it was better to go by boat. On board a wooden *cayuca*, a rough-hewn dugout canoe, John effortlessly paddled the three of us up the Indian River. We glided under giant, gnarled, old-growth bloodwood trees, named for their deep red color. The massive roots were spread out like spider webs laid atop the soil looking like long, thin toes dipped into the river's water.

John was talkative and regaled us with facts about Dominica. We learned there were 172 bird species, some which fussed at us for disturbing their peace, flying from the trees as we paddled quietly beneath them. Every so often John would stop the *cayuca* and while Glen and I held the boat steady near an exposed root, John would spear 10-inch *crapauds*—big frogs or mountain chickens—that he bagged to take home as dinner. During one such stop, a blue-green Amazon parrot, unfazed by our presence or the spearing of frogs, glided across the clearing on three-foot wings to land on a branch ahead of us. Apparently, a religious omen, John touched the large, leather-bound cross he wore around his neck. Dominica, John claimed, was Eden before the fall.

John, proud of his knowledge and eager to share, told us the Dominican names for different varieties and species of trees, snakes, birds, and flowers. Many varieties of spice plants grew wild in the jungle. It was a place where nature's life force is so strong and the black soil so rich, that coconuts left lying on the ground took root. We shopped our way through the forest, John using his machete to chop banana stalks, and filling a sack for us with grapefruit, cinnamon bark, nutmeg, mace, cloves, bay leaves, and lemon grass.

John was Carib; a descendant of a fierce and cannibalistic tribe that dominated the Caribbean islands until the Europeans came. The Caribs easily conquered the peaceful native Arawak tribes on the island and then imprisoned them in corrals like cattle. Like food in a pantry, the

Caribs would pull Arawaks out of the prison corral, cook and then eat them.

At the end of our tour, John, the perfect host, offered us one of the giant frogs to fry up on our boat. With every attempt at graciousness, we declined and told him we were happy enough with our fruit and spices.

The following day, we asked another sailor to take us to shore, and from there hitched a ride to Boiling Lake, a cauldron of bubbling, gray-blue water simmering around 200 degrees Fahrenheit. A well-trodden trail dropped through a half-mile wide moonscape of sharp volcanic rocks, hissing steam vents, and hot springs—unfortunately much too scorching for soaking tired muscles.

I don't know if Dominica will ever be pasteurized and appealing to the kind of genteel visitors we met on our first day, but I do wonder about it. Of course, the islanders will have to leave dinghies and outboards in peace if they have hopes of attracting the tourists' dollars. But even if Dominica stays wild and rowdy, there are sights and experiences such as the Boiling Lake that were unique in our travels and will remain in our memories. I like a little quirkiness and thought Dominica a misshapen pearl worth wearing.

* * * * *

After the edginess of Dominica, I looked forward to visiting its southern neighbor, the island of Martinique. From the deck of *It's Enough*, Martinique looked much like any other volcanic island with black beaches spread at the foot of rising mountains covered in what appeared to be blankets of green fur. As we drew closer, the fur became lush forests fed by the abundant rain and warmed by the equatorial latitude. Back in French territory, I raised the small French courtesy flag on our mast spreader before checking in with the gendarmes (police in France and

French territories). Ashore, signs read Patisserie, Pharmacie, and Bar-tabac as though we had been transported instantly to France, halfway across the world.

Fort-de-France, the capital of Martinique, was decorated with ornate wrought iron balconies and was like a laid-back version of France, but with a New Orleans twist. The people were descendants of African slaves and colonial planters who spoke Creole—French mixed with a bit of African and English. Culture, language, and history aside, Martinique had something of even greater interest: long-absent foods and flavor. It was shallow to use food as a measure (surely, I'm better than that). However, it had been a long time since we had been able to bite into lettuce, tomatoes, spinach, or broccoli and I was missing the enjoyment of eating crisp and fresh vegetables.

"Why doesn't anyone here garden?" I asked myself on many previous islands where I was left to make salads of onion, canned beets, and corn. In the islands, people tended to cling to the food they grew up eating and were content with cassava and manioc root tubers cooked in coconut milk or roasted. I had not adjusted well to tubers and I never wanted to eat another yucca or cassava root. The universe must have heard me, because on Martinique, our limited diet of canned fruits and vegetables was officially, and thankfully, on hold. On Martinique, an abundance of real food, flown in regularly from France, called to me.

I tugged at Glen's hand and bounced on my toes, "Come see, they have broccoli and cauliflower!" We had sailed through a mist between Dominica and Martinique, but it must have been fairy dust for it gave way to a fresh-produce wonderland. Inside a small market, Glen pushed the cart down the aisle and waved me over to fresh-looking chicken and meat displayed behind a clean, refrigerated glass case. Rivaling grocery stores in France, there were apples, spinach, tomatoes, cheeses, spices, croissants—leg of lamb for goodness' sake—all at subsidized prices from Mother France.

"Allons enfant de la Patrie…" Wheeling our folding shopping cart back toward the dinghy, I sang La Marseillaise, the French national anthem. In my mind I was already planning a real dinner, with grilled chicken, fresh vegetables, and salad accompanied by crusty baguettes slathered with double crème butter. We had arrived at the market too late for the French pastries but I knew where to find them the next morning.

After our delightful dinner and a good night's sleep, it was time for exploring. It was our intention to dinghy over to a neighboring boat to speak with sailors who had arrived before us and could advise us on the sights. In preparation, I studied our stack of reading material and picked out some books we had both already read. It was a common practice among sailors to trade for fresh reading material at any opportunity. But before we could climb into the dinghy, I heard British sailors conversing over the radio and tuned in for a listen.

Whatever meaning the term "party line" may have today, it originally described a non-private arrangement of sharing one telephone line among two or more houses. Each house sharing the party line could join or listen in to what was intended as a private call. Sailboat radios are similar except the communication is over a marine VHF radio that can be heard by anyone within about 12 miles tuned to that particular channel. At sea, boats keep the VHF radio on channel 16, the international hailing and distress channel, but at anchor the radio becomes a way to chat with other boats. If you are at anchor and want to announce a fish grill and potluck on the beach, you can spread the word to other boats on the chat channel—often channel 67. If you wanted to converse with a friend on a nearby boat, you would call them on channel 67 and ask the person to switch to another undesignated private channel of choice. Depending upon what was going on, it's likely any boat that hears you—

and every villager ashore with a VHF radio—would follow you to the private channel to listen in on the conversation. It was through such a call that we learned something important during a conversation between sailors on S/V Lollipop and S/V Sailing Home.

"Lollipop, this is Sailing Home, over."

"Lollipop here."

"Lollipop, switch to channel 63."

Lollipop and almost everyone else switched to Channel 63:

"What's up, Sailing Home?"

"Did you hear what happened to Dragonfly? It just got towed back yesterday by a local boat. The owners had to pay thousands of dollars to get it back."

"Whoa! Tell me everything from the beginning."

"The owners of Dragonfly dropped anchor and left for a day on shore. They hired a car to see the volcanic ruins of St. Pierre and hike the Beauregard Canal. While they were gone the wind picked up and they didn't have enough anchor chain out for the winds and steep bottom. Their boat dragged anchor and floated out to sea. The owners returned just before nightfall and freaked out when they got back and their boat was gone. They thought someone had stolen it so they went to the police station. The French gendarmes told them, "No one steals 50-foot sailboats around here—this is France. It probably dragged anchor. It's happened before."

The French police put the word out on 16 (the distress channel), that there was a sailboat drifting around. It was too dark to find a missing boat but at daybreak an islander motored out, found the boat and claimed it as salvage. The islander found a key in the ignition, started the sailboat engine and towed his own small fishing boat back. The islander demanded $100,000 to return the boat. The couple accused him of stealing the boat and got the police involved. A real mess. The police ended up helping with a settlement. In the end, the owners paid a few thousand dollars finder's fee. They were lucky this is a French island—some others—the finders might have been keepers. End of story."

Without the least bit of embarrassment about eavesdropping, other sailors from other boats broke in and started asking questions and conjecturing about international salvage laws. The channel got crowded with comments and I turned back to the hailing channel. Glen and I talked about what had happened. Could someone really claim your boat if the anchor dragged, it floated out to sea and no one was aboard? Concerned, we played it safe and let out a longer scope of anchor chain to accommodate for the steep and deep ocean floor. For good measure, Glen powered in reverse to set the anchor securely and we waved to other sailors on deck doing the same.

From my own eavesdropping, I learned a variety of useful information, including: there was a car rental place in town, Martinique had once been destroyed by an erupting volcano, one could hike the Beauregard Canal, and we should lengthen our anchor chain to compensate for the sloping ocean floor.

The next morning Glen and I found the car rental company situated in a tourist hotel. The agent asked if we wanted a driver who could also act as a guide. We shrugged—just like the French do—and said, "Sure." Normally, only the passenger gets to enjoy the scenery, so having a driver would allow us both to take in the green, beautiful island. Local knowledge would make the trip even more memorable.

The rental agent made a call and in a short while a man in a long-sleeved white shirt arrived breathless, ready to guide and drive. Laurent was a descendent of slaves and European planters and had the *café au lait* colored skin of one from such lineage. He wore a planter's hat that shielded his eyes and gave a mysterious look because only his quick smile was un-shaded by the brim. His slow, clear French was laced with English, so we understood most of what he said.

A retired schoolteacher, Laurent supplemented his retirement pay by providing guided tours. He instantly endeared himself to us by proclaiming we were not tourists since we were not at all like the 3,000 or so cruise ship passengers let loose on shore for four hours. No, Laurent declared instead, "You are travelers!" We were flattered by his distinction and to this day we refer to ourselves as travelers.

I asked Laurent to guide us on a non-touristy trip around the island. "Where you might take visiting friends… that's where we want to go… no rum distilleries or shops of souvenirs made in China." We wanted the insider look at Martinique.

Laurent steered with one hand and glanced often at Glen in the passenger seat. When he craned his neck to me in the backseat and allowed the car to drift, I encouraged him to return his eyes to the road by assuring him that I could hear him clearly.

The French ruled Martinique since the 1600s, when they killed off the native Arawaks, and brought African slaves to toil for long, back-breaking days on their sugar plantations. According to Laurent, Africans were better suited to working in the heat of the sugarcane fields. A century later, during the French Revolution, the British took advantage of the war and occupied Martinique, providing asylum from the guillotine for wealthy French planters. In a park, Laurent pointed out a headless marble statue of Josephine, hometown girl and daughter of a wealthy planter who became the wife of Napoleon Bonaparte. Opinions of Josephine must have been complicated. Vandals had made off with her head and Laurent explained, "Some blame Josephine and claim she influenced her husband to continue slavery even after the French Revolution because her family owned a plantation."

As we drove up the coast toward St. Pierre, Laurent told stories in his French/ English *patois*. St. Pierre was at one time called (what else?) the Paris of the Caribbean. Unlike Paris, however, St. Pierre was wiped off the map in the early 1900s. Here, Laurent provided sound effects. The Mt. Pelé volcano erupted with a deafening roar (RAAAAH!), expelling superhot gas, ash, and rock travelling at more than 100 miles per hour. This wiped out St. Pierre with a force that must have seemed equal to that of a meteor falling to earth. Thousands of barrels of rum stored in the city's warehouses exploded, sending rivers of flaming alcohol through the streets and into the sea. In the harbor more than 20 ships were destroyed. The city of St. Pierre was buried within minutes, and most of its 30,000 inhabitants died instantly. Only two survived: a shoemaker and a prisoner (who claimed to be innocent). The prisoner discovered that his jailers were dead and walked out of his decimated cell. He was later pardoned by the French government and left Martinique to join a sideshow at the Barnum and Bailey circus as one of only two St. Pierre volcano survivors. St. Pierre was no more, so the capital was moved to Fort de France, and according to Laurent, "Now St. Pierre is a tourist place. Except you two are travelers, not tourists," he laughed as he corrected himself.

* * * * *

"Are you afraid of heights?" Laurent asked. "The Canal du Beauregard is very steep in parts and quite narrow." Glen and I assured him heights would not deter us. "I climb to the top of our 63-foot mast," Glen told him. Turning to look at Glen, Laurent said with evident unease, "Are you sure? I will not come with you because heights do bother me."

Hanging atop the mast, we were to discover, is far different from walking along the Beauregard Canal, or Canal of Slaves as the islanders call it. Our hike was like clinging to the edge of a skyscraper's roof line with no safety hook. "Don't look down. Just put one foot in front of the other," I told myself over and over, surprised at the depth of the drop. For much of the hike, the walk is along an 18-inch wide stretch of rough slippery concrete that forms the outer edge of a two-foot-wide canal. The mountainside forms the inner boundary of the canal. If brave enough, you can lean over the canal and touch the mountain on the other side for support, but in other places the foliage forces you to lean out and over the deadly drop to the valley below. A slip could mean a 200-foot free fall, before crashing through steep foliage, then finally sliding down more sloping cliff—to a place from which it would be very difficult to retrieve bodies.

Islanders still call it the Canal of Slaves rather than Canal du Beauregard because slaves built it in 1760 with stones transported on their backs, likely motivated by whips and a promise of being fed. It took a tremendous amount of effort to bring water to a small valley, which unlike everywhere else on the lush island of mostly rain forests, did not have its own source of water.

Despite the danger, the path offered unrivaled vistas of beautiful valleys, bordered by steep, jagged mountains and cliffs with a very high, though low-volume waterfall. The trail was just three miles each way, but before we reached the end, a group of Dutch hikers walked towards us head-on at a particularly steep drop-off. Even though the hikers offered to crawl through our legs in order to pass, the deadly nature of the path convinced us to turn back.

As Laurent drove us back to the boat I thought about all the reasons I love the French islands. The reasons were far more than the food, wine, fresh vegetables, and first-world conveniences. There on Martinique, as well as most French islands, there was the allure of France softened with a friendly, homey island culture. Martinique was our fourth and last French island in the Caribbean. We would not be in France again until we sailed the South Pacific, where we hoped to find dozens more well-stocked French islands.

Chapter 12

Thus, I give up the spear!" Ahab shouts
as he hurls his last harpoon at Moby Dick.
— Herman Melville

W e were almost two years into our voyage and Glen and I had become part of a community of liveaboard sailors cruising the Caribbean. We often traveled in the company of other sailboats, trading information about islands we visited along the Caribbean chain. Bequia, one of the 32 islands that make up the nation of the Grenadines, often came up as unspoiled and yet undiscovered by cruise ships. We looked forward to exploring the small island, but as we approached, shared uneasy glances. Something was amiss; the harbor was jammed with other sailboats. Glen and I were stunned when we discovered that once or twice a year, Bequia hosted a whale hunt. Today was one of those hunts.

Japan and Norway still took whales, but why would the people of this tiny island take part in what, for me, was a gruesome pursuit? I made an effort to keep my tone neutral and rein in my brimming emotion. "I thought hunting whales is illegal," I said to a British expat shop owner in town. He explained that the International Whaling Commission had granted permission to the fishermen on Bequia to take two humpbacks a year. The international rule permitted "aboriginal people to harvest whales in perpetuity, at levels appropriate to their cultural and nutritional requirements." Though a handful of native cultures around the world were permitted to legally kill whales, I was surprised that a tourism-based Caribbean island opted to take advantage of such an exception.

Between 1880 and 1920, there were six shore-whaling stations on Bequia that killed 10 to 15 whales in a year; not very large numbers. It did not sound as though whaling was a bedrock of the local history, and the expat shop owner explained that the whale hunt was not really about cultural tradition. He claimed it had more to do with the Japanese government donating millions of dollars to the island of Bequia in solidarity as whaling brothers. I can't say if monetary gain was the reason or even if it played a part, but it was easy to see on the faces of many Bequia citizens they were as sad as Glen and I were about the whale killed that day.

For a so-called whaling festival, it was a silent, grim crowd watching as a beamy, wooden fishing boat cast off from the beach and motored out into the surf. I asked a Bequian on the beach why they didn't use sail-boats to at least give the whales a sporting chance.

"Dey jus use dat engine to find 'em. For harpoonin' da whale, dey got no engine," answered the man in his island *patois*. We nodded respectfully, but I knew their modern equipment and motoring into place set the odds heavily against the whales. That's not to say the hunt was without danger to the men involved. Herman Melville related in his classic novel, Moby Dick, that harpooned whales bolt at such speed, the rope could catch fire as it ran out through the blocks. A line caught around a man's limb could yank off his arm or pull him overboard. In harrowing accounts, the whale would sound and then come up through the bottom of the boat at full speed. Even a slack line was something to fear; harpooners would peer anxiously into the depths and try to see from what angle their own death could come.

None of that type of Moby Dick drama would happen that day; Bequia hunters were looking for an adolescent whale. Convinced the motor-assisted whale killing did not come close to even odds of a traditional whale hunt from past centuries, I found myself pulling for the whale.

Glen and I stood among the crowd on the beach watching the boat full of harpooners motor away until they vanished offshore in search of their prey. The calm day made it easier for the hunters and I wished the humpbacks Godspeed as they cruised past Bequia on their annual migration south. If there is one species to best represent sensitive, intelligent sea creatures, it's the humpback. These are the same astounding creatures one might see breach for whale-watching boats or sing for marine biologists. More than 90 percent of the humpback population has been destroyed in the last 100 years. Those that remain spend the summer at feeding grounds in the North Atlantic before migrating south through the Caribbean islands in December. They winter in the Caribbean islands mating, calving, and raising their young. In the warm water, the newborns grow at a rate of a hundred pounds a day. When the new calves are strong enough, the entire pod journeys north. That is, those who survive the Bequia whale festival.

While the whalers hunted we walked up a small hill to a tiny whaling museum where the caretaker described the best way to kill a whale. He told a reluctant audience that the hunting party would sight and single out a mother and her year-old calf from the pod of 20 or more whales. The fishermen would kill the engine and row to approach silently. The calf would then be harpooned and secured, but not killed. The mother, hearing the cries of her baby, would circle until she too was harpooned and killed, along with her calf. Gunshots to their hearts would be the coup de grace.

Glen and I stood on the beach a few hours later along with a group of other sailors and watched as the Bequia whalers returned with their prize. In this case the mother was not taken, but the calf's carcass was winched up a concrete ramp, the blubber removed and boiled into oil, then the meat cut into slabs for islanders to take home. The sight of the magnificent animal reduced to meat-by-the-pound left many Bequia islanders quiet and the queue for whale meat was short. I examined the faces of the crowd and it was clear the whale killing did not bring joy to most of the islanders, only embarrassment.

Early the next morning Glen and I were both quiet and thoughtful as we lifted anchor and headed south following the humpbacks' pod reduced by one treasured youngster.

* * * * *

On a boat, mystery meals are the norm when you have been out at sea long enough to run low of supplies. If you want to simulate menu planning after months away from real markets, try this little exercise at home.

Open your food pantry and scan the shelves for a minute, taking careful note of the *sell by* dates, then find the oldest item in your inventory. Expiration dates? Ha! Dates are for sissies! The only rule of Mystery Meals is the can must not be breathing. Eating the contents of a swollen can sets off a kind of nuclear reaction of bad events potentially culminating in your death, or at a minimum, you might be wishing for your death.

In this culinary game, you get extra points if the oldest can is also missing its label. If it is label-less, don't fret about the ingredients. It might be condensed cream of celery soup or black beans, olives, beets, peas, chickpeas, artichokes, or even a can of miniature corncobs. Let's take the mystery can, get creative, and turn it into a memorable feast you can share with friends at a fish BBQ on the beach.

Beach parties typically start in the afternoon with an invitation shouted from a neighboring boat's dinghy coming alongside. Inside the dinghy is usually another sailor with a snorkel, fins, and spear gun who asks something along the lines of, "Can your husband come out and play?" Before long, husbands are piled into two or so inflatable dinghies heading for the reef. A couple hours later they return with fish—grouper, sea bass, or red snapper—to be cleaned and taken to the beach for a grill and potluck. The potluck part is where your mystery can gets committed. Put some rice on to boil and open that old, unlabeled container. If you're surprised when you open it, all the better! Let's pretend you found a can of olives. As soon as the rice is cooked, pour the can of olives into the pot of rice, add a goodly amount of ketchup, some hot pepper sauce, cumin, and voilà, you're bringing Spanish rice to the potluck.

Sunset is an hour away—it's the time of day sailors get into their dinghies and head for the beach. Husbands hold up the cleaned and seasoned fish each has speared and offer it to the grill like paying homage to a god. The women place Mystery Meals in the categorized space at the potluck. First come the appetizers, followed by a long line of rice-based courses, and finally by desserts. Bets are that at least one dessert will be made from rice, coconut milk, and chunks of coconut meat gathered earlier from the palm trees along the shore. You might have added mandarin oranges if you were lucky to have those as your oldest can. Everyone is completely at ease with their contribution. There is no fretting or second-guessing. You all are sailors on the earth's ocean and—pardon the pun—in the same boat. Fresh fruits and vegetables have long since been eaten, though you might have an onion or potato or two squirreled away beneath the floorboards of the boat, which you are saving for a special occasion. It's expected for you to keep it for private consumption. No one shares their secret morsels at a potluck on an island in the middle of the ocean.

At the potluck everyone shares new ideas for seasoning canned goods and picks up recipes from others to use at the next one. Those resident gatherings in the wild, blue yonder are more about community than food. From them I have learned to appreciate the importance of being a relaxed and happy hostess who can serve rice and peas instead of stressing myself in pursuit of unattainable perfection.

Before you come to dinner at my house, you might ask me, "What's the oldest can in your pantry?" Right now, it is a can of coconut milk. Hmm…. That goes well with curry and rice!

Chapter 13

Glen and I had become so accustomed to not having a working motor that our restored ability to power up in windless conditions filled us with profound gratitude. Strangely, once we could power up, we were rarely becalmed, and the further south we sailed, the more boisterous the trade winds became. Stopping a few days at each island, we headed down the Caribbean chain with an eye to getting to Tobago and Trinidad—far enough south of hurricane latitudes to satisfy our insurance company.

It's Enough was heeling at such a sharp angle I had to hang on to prevent being thrown about or tossed down the stairs leading to below deck. "No way we can make Tobago," I called from the navigation station in order to be heard over the din of the boat crashing through rowdy seas. "We have to change course for Trinidad!" Though I was looking forward to visiting Tobago and its abundant wildlife, butterflies, and bird species, the direction of the wind was working against us. We'd been beating and tacking back and forth against 30-knot headwinds, making little discernible progress. I attempted to calculate our Estimated Time of Arrival (ETA) in Tobago using our present course, but the navigation program flashed an ominous: NEVER. That settled it.

We altered our course for Trinidad. Within minutes, the stiff winds and crashing steep waves were left in our small wake. Though disappointed to miss Tobago, the now-quiet ride offered quick consolation. Our new course provided smooth trade wind sailing at its finest, verified by a pod of 20 to 30 dolphins jauntily escorting us to Chagauramas, the main harbor of Trinidad. I believed the dolphins were a sign of welcome and shifted my thoughts to what we would find in Trinidad. Just seven miles from Venezuela, Trinidad is as much a part of South America as the Caribbean, and it felt like real progress in our voyage.

I was lying on the deck with my head over the water, enthralled by dolphins riding our bow wave. I felt a real connection to those lovely creatures, making eye contact and laughing at their cavorting just beneath me on our bow. They abruptly veered off as we neared land, and surveying the harbor, it was easy to see why. The oil port of Houston, Texas had nothing over Trinidad's Port of Spain. There were oil tankers at anchor in the harbor and a large refinery spewing black smoke into the air in an effort to obliterate the sun. I had complained to Glen at other ports that cruise ships wrecked the nature of the islands at which they docked, but this industrialization of the ocean's edge shocked me to silence.

Motoring to our marina, I realized we were no longer in piña colada territory, and it took considerable effort to reframe my thinking. Throughout much of the Caribbean, the rampant cruise-ship tourism and indifferent natives left me jaded, so the bright side in Trinidad was that it already looked to be an authentic, non-touristic experience.

I had heard about the great marina facilities of Trinidad, and it was true. The marina area was a hub for sailors who want excellent workmanship and good value for boat and engine repairs, and even major overhauls. The first-class boat facility in Trinidad was expected, but what took me by surprise were the stunningly beautiful, friendly people. I had never seen people with such distinctive looks or heard such lilting accents. The people of Trinidad exceeded the Creole fusion of forebears from Africa and Europe. Trinidad had an attractive mixture of African, East Indian, Chinese, and European descendants, creating an exquisite blend of customs, cultures, and physical features.

The East Indian influence prevailed, with Bollywood music playing on the radio and dress shops selling saris. Larry, an American expat who had been living on his boat at the marina for more than nine years, explained the strong Indian influence. When slavery was abolished in the British colonies, the English governor of Trinidad made the decision to bring over tens of thousands of laborers from India to work the vast sugar plantations and produce rum for export. I raised my eyebrows at the enormity of the number… "Tens of thousands?" Larry confirmed the number and went on to say that in previous centuries, most of the island was planted in sugar cane, producing huge profits for a small number of British landowners.

"Rich as a Trinidad planter," was an eighteenth century saying, Larry claimed. "Native Caribs and Arawaks could not be coerced to work in the fields, so imported workers were the only option. The British governor figured that India, a colony with an abundance of hard working, cooperative people who could withstand tropical heat, was the ideal source of the needed manpower. The British shipped thousands of Hindu-practicing Indians to Trinidad and their descendants have since built temples, newspapers, radio stations, clothing stores, and restaurants while clinging to their native language. There are now as many Trinidadians of Indian as African descent, with a smattering mix of Chinese and Europeans."

It was the sugar and rum that brought the East Indians to Trinidad, but oil grew to be the new commodity. The island country was a melting pot of cultures, and Indian food the main culinary thread on the island.

While authentic Indian food can be spicy, the Indian food on Trinidad was a different kind of piquant; more like a fusion of Jamaican and Indian food. It had been years and many sea miles since we had been lucky enough to find an Indian restaurant, and now we were spoiled for choice.

Larry stopped by one evening and knocked on our hull to invite us to the Bat Cave for dinner. "Super cheap and really good," he promised. The name alone was enough and out we went, only to discover later the title was merely Larry's pet name for the place. With or without the catchy title, it was a simple roadside café next to a food truck. The place did not have an actual name, so there was no sign. Once they sold out of food, the place would fold up and disappear down the road. That was our first encounter with Trini street food and the chalkboard menu left us laughing with its simplicity and frankness.

Bake and Shark: Lightly breaded shark meat, fried and eaten in a chewy bun dressed with salad and pineapple.

Doubles: Bara (a purely Trini bread) sandwich of curried chickpeas finished with a spoonful of tamarind or mango and a kick of pepper.

Corn Soup: Not what you think. A thick soup filled with meat and vegetables, can include surprises at the bottom such as corn cob pieces, figs, or sweet potato. (In Glen's bowl was the biggest surprise: a literal pigtail! I wish I hadn't asked.)

Trini food is not for the timid. Like the people, it is spicy. Trinidadians move with a jaunty, positive, friendly, good humor vibe. After a couple of weeks among them, I decided their enthusiastic attitude was because Trinidad was always either getting ready for, or celebrating, Carnival. Preparations for the months-long festival took all year, and I saw evidence of it everywhere. The streets were lined with fabric and sewing shops making skimpy, outrageous, and elaborate costumes.

Locals and visitors alike vied to join Carnival band groups and attended *Mas Camps* (Mas was short for masquerade) where they created elaborate feather and sparkle costumes as well as practiced together on steel drums.

One evening, months before Carnival, Glen and I took a taxi into town on a Saturday night to hear calypso and steel drum bands practicing and playing music that forced us out of our seats to move to the beat. The music and atmosphere were contagious. Caught up in the steel drum rhythm, we dance-walked past bars, restaurants, and slow-moving traffic. We dipped into places called pan yards where we could listen to the music for free and they sold beer at small counters, barred like an 1800s bank teller's window. A gripping sound was Chutney Calypso, music with Bollywood-inspired steel drum music bubbling up through the melodies.

The first time I heard Calypso music I was just a kid. My parents had a vinyl album by Harry Belafonte called Calypso and my sister and I would sing along with Day O and Jamaica Farewell. I saw a poster for a Calypso (sometimes called Soca) competition at a bar in town where we heard songs delivered in fun melody. Some of the messages and titles were political, such as, *Take Ah Rest Mr. Prime Minister*, and *Last Elections*. Other songs such as *Carnival is the Answer*, and *Party*, were clearly written to lift spirits. Great flashbacks to the time with my sister and those timeless Belafonte songs.

During a break in the program, a man came out and told the audience Calypso music originated with West African slaves who told their story through slightly veiled songs mocking the slave masters or other slaves. The slave owners were so worried that the gatherings of music and drumming would result in an uprising that British authorities banned drums. The answer was steel-pan music, initially consisting of frying pans, dustbin lids, and oil drums. I assumed that the steel drums we saw came from the local oil industry, but the announcer said the United States had a large military base on Trinidad during WWII and when the base closed, the Army left thousands of oil drum barrels that islanders turned into musical steel drums. Groups drummed across Trinidad in backyards, parks, bars … our marina. Someone might even block off a street at night for the drummers to gather and play.

Trinidad at Carnival time sounded like a level of fun above anything I could even imagine.

* * * * *

Trinidad is one of the largest islands in the Caribbean and we had only seen the area around our marina. We were torn between exploring on our own with a rental car or hiring a guide and car. Glen preferred to rent since neither of us had driven a car in a long time and he missed that open road feeling. Thankfully, we listened to good old expat Larry—our man in Trinidad—who recommended we forego the rental car bit. On Trinidad, everything and everyone was on island time except drivers. Speed limits were largely considered suggestions, turn signals only for the naive, and drivers zoomed through traffic lights red enough to burn corneas. What's more, the roadsides were a hazard as locals were inclined to pull to the shoulder for any number of reasons. Snacking, potty breaks, taking a nap, and mixing drinks were all valid reasons to pull off without warning and park at the side of the road.

Even Newton, the guide we hired, did not drive in Trinidad; we rode with his driver. Newton was a nature guide, possessed a wonderful sense of humor, knew exactly what to show us, and where to find it. We brought binoculars from the boat and both pair got a workout. Newton pointed out dozens of the more than 460 species of birds. Some of the hummingbirds were no larger than a bumblebee. There were also more than 650 butterfly species and 200 orchid species, but that would take more time finding than we had on the island. After a long day of flora and fauna, Newton's driver took us through a white-knuckle driving experience, before arriving intact at the Grand Riviere turtle nesting area on the far side of the island. Darkness was descending as the sun melted into the ocean horizon, so we followed closely behind Newton. He stopped abruptly, blocking our way with his arms outstretched. "Is this close enough to see your first leatherback turtle?" Newton asked in a hushed tone.

The largest turtle I had ever seen was lumbering slowly past as though we did not exist. She had a large teardrop-shaped body covered in skin and oily flesh—not the bony shell of all other sea turtles. "You will see even larger turtles here tonight," he promised, "some as large as six feet in length and weighing more than 1,000 pounds. They are the gentle giants of the turtle world."

As the day grew darker, Newton pointed us down the beach where we could hear waves rushing across the sand. In the moonlight we could barely make out the large, dark shapes. Moving slowly like an invading armada, a group of female turtles trudged slowly forward, leaving the water that normally supported their enormous bodies. Watching their labored progress, I thought the poor mother turtles looked exhausted as they left the surf and slogged onward. Each turtle searched for what seemed to her the best place on the sandy beach to build a nest. One momma turtle came within five feet of us, then began digging and pushing the sand with her powerful flippers. It took her about an hour to dig a nest that was two feet or so in depth, and then lay 80 to 100 eggs. She spent an additional 45 minutes covering them up, tamping down the surrounding sand to hide her clutch before shambling back into the sea.

In a low voice, so as not to disturb the turtles, Newton told us that the number of leatherback turtles had declined by as much as 90 percent in the past 20 years. Trinidad was something of a stronghold for them and the Grand Riviere beach had so many nesting leatherback turtles that it claimed the world's densest leatherback population. At first that all sounded great, but Newton pointed out, "Turtle nests are so thick here that by the middle of the nesting season, nest-digging females accidentally dig up eggs laid by other turtles. The beach is too small for the roughly 3,000 females who nest here each season. Each female turtle lays at intervals of several weeks, about six clutches per season. That's just too many nests for a beach only half a mile long, and so narrow that on the full-moon tides (as on that night) the surf reaches almost to the jungle."

The confusion of unearthed turtle eggs was a boon to the dozens of vultures who would hang around the beach in the daytime to eat the eggs and any hatchlings lucky enough to have survived the incubation period but unlucky enough to hatch after sunrise or before sunset. For those hatchlings, even getting to the ocean did not ensure their safety as fish and seabirds are just as predatory.

Newton told us that the males never come ashore—only females did in order to lay eggs. Between nesting years, they wandered the ocean, mating, eating, and preparing their bodies for the next round of egg laying. Turtles can live to be 80 years old, but the odds are not in their favor.

After a couple hours of discretely watching mother turtles doing their best to ensure the safety of their offspring and the future of their species, we reluctantly climbed back into the car where I closed my eyes and prayed for the survival of the nests we had seen. The resilience and determination of those turtle mothers reminded me that sometimes you just do what you can and hope for the best.

The near-spiritual feelings of the turtle nesting experience left us sedate to the point that we almost skipped our plans for the next day as being too mundane. Thankfully, I listened to my adventure mantra: "ALWAYS SAY YES!"

Pitch Lake, the natural feature we were scheduled to see did not lend itself to an enthusiastic rally, and Newton was such an understated type of man, he did nothing to sell us on the outing. Measuring 100 acres and an estimated 250 meters deep in the center, it was the largest natural asphalt lake in the world.

At first sight, Pitch Lake looked like an erupting parking lot, bringing to mind a 105-degree day that I spent in St. Louis. I was about eight years old and walking to the cool, air-conditioned library (our home was cooled only by fans) to read for the day and return a stack of books. It was so hot my flimsy flip-flops stuck to the oozing asphalt of the road crossing, and I was glued to the middle of the busy street. Thankfully, a nice person wearing real shoes scooped me up, grabbed my tar-coated sandals and set me down on the sidewalk in front of the library. The smell of that experience overwhelmed me at Pitch Lake. I was not as keen as Newton and Glen to see how long I could stand on the semisolid surface before sinking.

"It's quick-tar," Newton declared, standing on the slowly moving, black surface. "Like in those Tarzan movies where people drown in quicksand." No one has yet made a movie of people drowning in tar, but I bet someone has suffered that dreadful fate. The asphalt moves with a stirring action like a food processor on its lowest setting. Prehistoric trees, skeletons, and other objects have been known to appear, disappear and reappear.

Newton told us Sir Walter Raleigh discovered Pitch Lake in 1595, and in addition to using the sludge to caulk his ships, he took some of the asphalt home with him, where it was used to pave Westminster Bridge for the opening of Parliament. Since mining of the lake started in 1867, an estimated 10 million tons of asphalt has been extracted.

According to the interpretive signs, tar from Pitch Lake paved streets in more than 50 countries including the USA, England, India, Singapore, Egypt, and Japan. The sticky lake was estimated to contain reserves of around 6 million tons, which could last 400 years at the current rate of extraction.

True to form, Newton continued to understate the balance of the tour. After Pitch Lake, the four of us squeezed into a pirogue canoe and motored through the rich birding area of Caroni Swamp. A man from a nearby village paddled as Newton pointed out blue herons, iguanas, a boa constrictor curled tightly around a thick branch, fast-moving crabs, oysters, egrets, a four-eyed fish (which have two eyes to see above water and two eyes to see below water), and more... so much more. As it turned out, Newton's actual objective at Caroni Swamp was for us to see scarlet ibis, the national bird of Trinidad.

We spent an hour observing wildlife in the swamp before heading to the roosting area of the ibis. Newton had planned the day so we could be there at dusk when thousands of the red-feathered, migratory ibis returned from feeding in nearby Venezuela to roost for the night. We landed our boat near a 40-foot-tall wooden tower and climbed up to be close to the birds when they returned to their roost. Pointing west, Newton told us to get our cameras ready because the return of the flock would happen fast. In the day's last light, the ibis swooped in from the direction of Venezuela, landed, and settled within just a few minutes. The birds chatted with neighbors—perhaps discussing when we would leave—and preened. The deep-green mangroves were suddenly alive with scarlet ibis dotting the higher branches, the white egrets staying below.

The entire scene was like a Christmas tree decorated with animated crimson ornaments that became black as the night deepened. The roosting ibis grew quiet as darkness quickly settled.

I wished for a headlamp as I felt my way down the tower ladder, rung by rung. By flashlight we all crammed back into our narrow wooden boat to return, gliding through the mangrove-lined swamp.

* * * * *

The sign on the food stall read, "Hottest Peppa Sauce in The World," and the name on the bottle read, "Underwear on Fire," which was fair warning. We were visiting the market food stalls in Trinidad, and a man with a mischievous twitch pulling at the corner of his smile offered me a bit of Trinidad red scorpion chili from his gloved hand. "You a redhead—try this red chili on for size."

"No!" exploded his wife, probably concerned her husband might kill a tourist with hot pepper. "Stop Child! Hold it right there. He funning you," she warned. A few drops of Louisiana hot sauce are as spicy as I get, so there was no chance of this redhead munching down on a raw chili called scorpion pepper. When I relayed the story to Newton, he set me straight on the power of that hot pepper. His response was terse, bordering on angry, that a fellow Trini would try to trick a visitor.

"To say the Trinidad scorpion is hot would be like saying the surface of the sun is hot. This is a chili so hot people have to wear latex suits and gloves just to work with it. If there were a category on the Scoville scale titled Sweat Just Thinking About Them, the Trinidad scorpion pepper would be listed first. These things make a jalapeño look like child's play," he said. "Trinis do not eat them. Everyone on the island avoids them."

I made a case to stay an entire year in Trinidad so we could join a steel drum band group, attend Mas Camp, and have costumes made for Carnival. I was thinking to go as a scarlet ibis, a vision in red boas. However, Captain Glen reminded me that we probably had plenty more adventure ahead in Venezuela.

After one last round of spicy eating (still no scorpion peppers, though), I agreed it was time to move on. We sadly said goodbye to the many delights of Trinidad, home to some of the best wildlife, food, skilled labor, and most beautiful people we would experience in our circumnavigation.

Fickle me. Once we sailed out of the harbor, all I could think about was the wild, untamed Venezuela just ahead.

Chapter 14

For some reason the day sail from Trinidad to Venezuela made me happy way out of proportion to the simple act of moving on to the next stop of our voyage. That was probably because we had been traveling and living aboard *It's Enough* for over two years, and of late we had been receiving emails from family and friends asking when were we going to start sailing around the world. Really. Sailing across the Atlantic Ocean must not have counted, nor exploring the East Coast of the United States. Perhaps visiting most of the islands in the Caribbean chain was too tame for the armchair travelers back home. Well, to all our detractors and naysayers I could finally write and tell them we had departed North America. Okay, it was just a few hours day sail from Trinidad, but we had arrived in South America, a whole new continent.

Before we ever set foot on our exciting, new continent, a 30-something Venezuelan with a broad, white smile and a shotgun slung over his shoulder waved us into our dock space. We soon met Luis and the other armed guards who kept vigil over the upscale marina where we would live on *It's Enough* during hurricane season. The plush surroundings of Marina Mare were adjoined to a five-star hotel in Puerto La Cruz, Venezuela. Not a bad hideout; our boat insurance required us to stay below 13 degrees latitude during hurricane season, which technically had already begun.

As Glen likes to say, everything is a tradeoff. On the upside, we would base out of an inexpensive country in South America that was free of hurricanes, and where we could practice our Spanish on a daily basis. The downside was that we would live in a politically unstable country with a dictator who hated America. In other words, we chose to avoid the unpredictability of hurricanes for the daily clear and present danger of Venezuela.

A sailor we met in Trinidad got us there. He raved about the Venezuelan luxury marina, claiming it was, "Even better than Trinidad." The favorable exchange rate made the luxury affordable, but it wasn't long before I discovered what the male sailors liked best about our five-star, marina; the thong bikinis!

The hotel and marina operated as a sort of country club for wealthy locals. It was a place where my critical eye was better left shut to the idle, pampered folk. Indulging in judgmental behavior at Mare would be to risk drowning in it. While affluent Venezuelan husbands worked, wives lounged in *bikini central* around the pool, being rich together. Every so often a reclining, bikini-clad beauty would rouse herself from magazine reading long enough to stretch her legs and strut through the hotel grounds and along the marina docks, teetering on stiletto heels. A proud and attractive member of this group informed me that Venezuela had produced a dozen Miss Worlds and Miss Universes—more than any other country. Yes ladies, the bar was high in Venezuela.

"Skip Venezuela!" was the advice we had received from both family and friends (they have different metrics than sailors). "It's dangerous and the government leaders don't like America." Their warnings, the newspaper headlines, and advice from the beauties at the pool were delaying (or deterring) our desire to explore other parts of Venezuela, a trove of unspoiled nature. Weighing sage counsel against the rare chance to see a still-wild country with commonplace violence, theft, and political unrest... Well, striking out did sound dicey, but doable.

How could we be based in Venezuela for months and not explore that area of world-class wonders? A full fifth of Venezuela was untapped wilderness with vast grasslands leading toward countless *tepuis*, isolated, flat-topped mountains full of biologically unique creatures. Some species are found only on one or several tepuis, thriving but stranded there for eons. Last but not least was Angel Falls. With a 3,212-foot drop, it is the world's tallest waterfall.

Much of Venezuela is unspoiled partly because getting to these areas on one's own is an exercise in futility. The country has not made much effort to become more tourism accessible or to provide remote travel options. Venezuela lacks the early America "Go West" encouragement to pioneers that was needed to settle much of its territory. Venezuelans were not drawn to conquer their vast wilderness as our early Americans had been. Ninety percent of their population lived in cities or towns. Dangerous cities and towns.

We heard many warnings, some more often than others. Don't carry all your money in one place; don't go anywhere at night; don't travel on side streets at any time of day; don't hire cabs in the streets; don't leave your car doors unlocked at red lights; don't accept drinks because they may be laced with drugs and lead to rape or robbery; don't wear a fanny pack, backpack, or carry a purse; don't dress fancy or wear a watch; don't travel with your passport, or without a copy of it... Like the bikini beauties had learned, it was safe only at the pool. All I needed at that point was a pair of size 10 stilettos and I'd be all set.

It was not in my nor Glen's nature to be complacent or fearful, so after a couple weeks of Spanglish with the elite by the pool, we tired of the easy life and were eager to experience more of Venezuela than the occasional taxi ride to a restaurant or grocery store. We wanted to discover the *authentic* Venezuela.

* * * * *

"The best way to explore a country is by taking public transportation," I insisted. Glen, whose Spanish is wobblier than mine, wasn't so sure. "A friendly, bikini-clad lady at the pool recommended we hire a car and driver," he argued. I was tired of all the fear talk and disgusted with myself that I'd been too afraid to venture out of our posh space. "How can they live like this?" I blurted. "Let's go see for ourselves!"

Glen was persuaded. We left *It's Enough* safely in the marina and took a taxi to the Puerto La Cruz bus station. We bought tickets and boarded the bus for the nine-hour ride to Guacharo Cave National Park— touted as one of the 10 top things to do in Venezuela. The cave itself, over 10 kilometers long, is the longest in the world and home to more than 10,000 nesting oilbirds, a rare bird that echo-locates like bats and at one point, was nearly killed off as a cheap source of oil for lanterns.

The bus traversed the roads with the agility and comfort of a toppled refrigerator on skateboard wheels. The driver pushed the vehicle's limits with a sense of urgency so intense that we often passed cars around blind curves on the narrow mountain roads. There was no apparent cause for the hurry; he simply seemed compelled to overtake every vehicle in our path.

Having survived the trip, we were the only passengers to exit in Caripe. As we stood on the side of the road at the edge of town, Glen gave me a look that demanded, "What Now?" I flagged down a passing car for help and learned that there was an old estate turned guesthouse nearby. It was sunset and darkness was bleeding in from the outer reaches of the sky. With scant light remaining, Glen and I grabbed our daypacks and ran-walked the mile or so to the opposite outskirts of the town where the promised inn waited. Not wanting to give way to a flood of pessimism about our situation, I pointed out the bright side. "This is working out perfectly. We needed to stretch our legs after the nine-hour bus ride and that's just what we got!" I couldn't see Glen's face in the dark, but his answer conveyed his expression well enough.

"Maybe by the time we get back to Puerto La Cruz you'll be so good at positive thinking you'll think positively about hiring a car and driver for our next trip." Feeling guilty, I was happy for the distraction of other travelers at the guesthouse, all backpackers from Europe. English being the official language of backpacking, we were able to compare notes about Venezuela with the young travelers and found something interesting: each person in the group had been robbed, mugged, or ripped off in Caracas, the capital of Venezuela. Note to self: Caracas was out.

One young man, with a posh British accent added, "Venezuela is full of incredible beauty, but they make it really hard to get here. Once here, you are a prime target for people who have a huge chip on their shoulder about how their country has fallen from oil wealth and luxury to rationing. There are shortages of some food products, despite the fact the nation is rich with oil. It's a tough adjustment and the people are angry." The bikini-clad, poolside ladies in Puerto La Cruz were seemingly right to stay put.

The backpackers had toured Guacharo Cave and considered it *interesting*, said in a way that was purposefully vague. Glen, never a good whisperer, told me hoarsely, "That's faint praise for one of the top 10 things to see in Venezuela. I hope it's worth that loopy bus ride." With the Brit's peculiar assessment in our thoughts, we ordered a hearty soup from the guesthouse kitchen and retired early for our big day of exploring.

We arranged for a ride to the cave through the guesthouse and left early to beat the large crowds we expected to be waiting to see the world wonder. As it turned out, the only visitors to the cave were the two of us. With my ever-increasing Spanish vocabulary, the entrance signs said that we needed to wait until there was a party of 10 or more for a guided tour. With no one about, or likely to come soon, Ricardo, the one and only park ranger agreed to guide us.

The high-ceilinged, pitch-black cave hovered uncomfortably as Ricardo proceeded into the darkness armed only with a flickering Coleman lantern. Glen and I followed closely behind while bringing up the rear was a little dog that somehow managed to follow us in from the street. Ricardo used a combination of English and Spanish to point out formations of stalactites (coming down from the ceiling) and stalagmites (coming up from the floor). Most of the rock formations had been named for religious figures, such as Virgen del Carmen, and others that sounded like a Spanish-accented roll call of the Last Supper. With the only illumination coming from the guide's dim kerosene lamp and a small penlight Glen always carried in his backpack, it was nearly impossible to see the formations through the blackness, much less discern the vague shape pointed out by Ricardo. Using my imagination—and squinting my eyes—I could barely make out shapes slightly lighter or darker than the surrounding blackness.

Given the darkness, the oilbirds were more heard than seen, and it was difficult to get a feel for the size of the birds as they flew and nested far above us. Ricardo, in respectable guide parlance and tone, said that oilbirds have a wingspan of more than three feet, and estimated 10,000 or more of the large birds roosted above us in crevices. It was easy to accept the number as gospel given the ruckus they made. Oilbirds use echo-location in order to maneuver and produce shrieking louder than that of any creature I've ever encountered.

We were relieved after crossing a narrow passage to enter a second chamber known as El Silencio. It was much quieter here, but our ears still rang with the high-pitched screaming of the birds. If pitch black has shades of darkness, the second chamber was even blacker. Being blindfolded and held captive in a box in an underground vault couldn't have been any darker—it was that kind of black. As if the darkness weren't creepy enough, the cave was also home to numerous large and bold rats. As our small arc of light reached the floor, we found a sizable rat enjoying an oilbird meal at our feet. The rodents were fearless as they crouched and stared at us brazenly, practically daring us to enter their territory.

Feeling more than a little uneasy, we stayed close to Ricardo and his lamp as he moved along a narrow stream filled with blind fish. We passed through the second chamber and moved deeper into the cave. Suddenly, we heard frantic yelping.

"Where is your dog?" Ricardo demanded in alarm. Glen and I looked at each other and then at Ricardo, "It's not our dog," we said in unison. The barking escalated and was now braced with panic.

Ricardo's voice was tight. "The rats are attacking the dog!" and ran off with his lantern in the direction of the cries. Glen and I were left half a mile up a cave in total darkness sliced by nothing more than a penlight.

Glen moved the narrow sliver of light around on the ground only to find the numbers of rats were multiplying—seemingly from the moist, stone walls. Holding the tiny beam between us, Glen and I yelled and stomped with outward bravado (and inner fear) at the creepy vermin as we rushed to find our way back along the narrow stream of water filled with blind fish.

For several minutes we stumbled alongside the trickle of stream, among rats, bird guano, and eerie fish. I squeezed Glen's hand and exhaled with relief when I finally saw the dim vision of the guide approaching, his lantern shedding soft light on the small dog sticking close to his side. *"El pero* (the dog) is OK now," the guide told us and started back in the direction from which we had just come from. *"No es necesario,"* I told him. *"Bastante*—no more—Guacheros."

We had seen enough cave, oilbirds, and rats to last several lifetimes.

Chapter 15

Lying in bed that night, Glen and I both felt sick. We had eaten different things for dinner at the only café in Caripe, so it was hard to guess the cause... food poisoning... giardia... amoeba... cholera? Every traveler's nightmare is getting sick in a foreign country with no access to good medical care. I felt a little better by the next morning, but Glen was so sick he dared not lose sight of the bathroom. We were skeptical that we could find help in the village and Glen preferred to get back to the boat in Puerto La Cruz. Surely there would be doctors there who tended to the wealthy clientele at the hotel. With the help of the innkeepers, we boarded the bus and steeled ourselves for a repeat of the previous nine-hour harrowing experience. The good news was that there was a bathroom in the bus. The bad news—neither Glen nor I could stomach the stink of it. The packed, cold bus had individual monitors playing telenovelas; Spanish-language soap operas, cranked up at full tilt. Between the screaming TV, frigid air, and mountainous, looping terrain we both grew even sicker. Eventually we sat on the stairs by the driver to let him know when he needed to pull over so we could be sick outdoors.

The occupants of the bus became involved in our illness, offering sips of their drinks through their straws (*"No, gracias."*) or parts of their sandwiches ("*No puedo* [can't]) and sharing their home remedies for the *bichos* or intestinal virus we had surely acquired. While Glen and I slipped behind the trees with our Handi-Wipes, every face in the bus was watching us through the windows, but we were too sick to care. We had literally nothing left in our system to slow the passage of liquids on a straight route in and out. We, the *gringos enfermos*, suffered those nine hours as though prepping for a colonoscopy. When we finally and thankfully reached our boat, we liberally self-medicated from our extensive onboard medical kit.

Glen, worn out in body and spirit, asked with a weak voice, "Did we just have an *authentic* experience?" Smoothing my hand down his feverish forehead I agreed maybe it had been a bit too real.

By morning, my health was improving and I was able to keep down liquids, then crackers, then food. Glen, however, did not improve; days passed and he got worse. The hotel had a doctor on staff who came to the boat to check on him. After the third day of strong antibiotics with no results, the physician wrote down the name of a private hospital and helped me get Glen into a taxi. The private hospital looked and smelled clean—always a good sign—and the emergency-room staff was friendly and attentive. The ER doctor spoke some English and had Glen give a sample to analyze under the microscope in search of the *mikrobios* making him sick. I asked them to give him stronger antibiotics. It was too big a coincidence we had both gotten ill after a meal out in a village at a dodgy café. He clearly contracted something from unwashed or tainted food, or so I thought. The physician, however, had his own ideas and wanted to make sure it was not something more serious.

"Like what?" I asked, fearful of malaria, dengue, or yes, cholera.

After a few hours, the doctor came back shaking his head and saying, "We didn't find anything wrong. You can go home now. Probably just food poisoning and he will be fine tomorrow. *Lo siento*," we were told. "Sorry!" And we were sent home.

Glen did not recover the next day and lay on the bunk closest to the bathroom. He was getting weaker and weaker from weight loss, malnutrition, and dehydration. He had no appetite and forced himself to eat a few bites to keep his strength.

After a few more days of this, Glen was getting too weak to walk without fear of passing out. I resolved to fly us immediately to the U.S. after rehydrating him at the hospital. My unvoiced fear was that Glen could not survive much longer at this rate. He could not keep food or water in his system and the electrolytes he was drinking went right through him. He felt no hunger or thirst but forced himself to hydrate. His clothes were loose and his face gaunt. He protested feebly when I offered him food and insisted he could not force himself to eat. It seemed his body was shutting down; I was fearful Glen would die in that godforsaken country.

I was going to do everything within my power to prevent the worst from happening, no matter what the cost. My plan, I briefed Glen, was to get him on the airplane despite looking too weak and emaciated for the flight. I would book first-class tickets because travelers in that category get to board right away and the bathroom would be close. Glen (in a wheelchair) and I would arrive at the gate just as they were preparing to board, and we would hold an upbeat and cheerful manner—as though nothing was wrong. The explanation for the wheelchair: a bum knee.

I feared I might have waited too long to get Glen back to the United States and tortured myself with thoughts of the worst-case scenario: Glen dying in Venezuela before I could get him to the States. His electrolytes, gauntness, lack of nutrition for... how many... nine days? How long could a person live without eating and minimal hydration? I did not plan to find out.

All our savings had been put into our boat. Ever practical, in spare moments I worried what I would do if Glen did not recover. I would have to hire someone to help get *It's Enough* back to Miami. I would sell it at a loss. I would go back to work. Back to square one but without Glen. Our marriage had been saved, and even flourished, on the boat. I refused to believe Glen would be taken away right when everything was so great in our life.

I woke up the next morning determined to take charge of the situation; take the hill in Army parlance. I bundled Glen into a taxi and returned to the hospital where I persuaded the doctor to hook Glen to an IV for a couple of days so he could hydrate, regain some strength, and rebuild his electrolytes. That accomplished, we would fly *el pronto* to Miami for some first-class medical care. I knew he needed an IV or we would risk the airline denying us a flight in his degraded condition. Glen was a familiar face in the emergency room. I held his hand as he was hooked up to the IV and forced a smile to cheer him. Inside I was distressed. Waves of fear washed over me, in a foreign country where we had neither family nor friends. Mentally, I already had Glen in Miami.

Glen lay fully clothed on the hospital gurney in the emergency room, with the IV pumping nutrition and fluid into his body. "You okay?" I asked, stroking his forehead. "Yeah. Just…. worn out." After a silence, I said, "I'm sorry." Glen met my eyes. "Sorry about what?" Still stroking his forehead, "Everything from the moment we left the marina. I risked our dream to see some caves." Reaching for my hand, Glen said, "It's not your fault, but please, let's not try to save money anymore by taking public transportation and eating in dicey places." My eyes teared with sadness and guilt.

The ER doctor jauntily returned, practically skipping up to Glen's gurney. "*Muchas dysenteria amebas*!!! Maybe they naughty—sleeping before and now awake. Big sorry not find before." Finally—the answer!

At long last, Glen was admitted to the hospital and treated for what they called a resistant strain of amoebic dysentery. We were so relieved at the lab results and so amused at the doctor calling amoebic dysentery "naughty," that we laughed and cried at the same time.

After numerous apologies from the doctor, Glen had his own room in the special wing of the hospital. This was the first time Glen had ever stayed overnight in a hospital, the experience expanding us into the realm of medical tourism. A resistant strain of amoebic dysentery was definitely not among the list of the top 10 things to see and do in Venezuela, and frankly, it's not an adventure we would recommend.

With his hospital room came a new doctor—a woman with long, red-polished fingernails, a short skirt, no white lab coat, and big blond hair. She did not speak English, and her visits involved hand gestures with a heavy use of our Spanish-English dictionaries. Glen and I each had our own dictionary, which proved handy in what turned into a Spanish language and cultural immersion course. Glen received lots of attention at the hospital, maybe because he was an American, but probably because he is a really nice guy who needed help. The nurses went out of their way to look after him, taking vital signs and plumping pillows. There was no shortage of attractive nurses, their long fingernails polished a vibrant red, displaying cleavages threatening to burst from the low necklines of starched, white nurses' dresses. They wore pert, little white hats with the obligatory high heels—greatly resembling the outfit worn by Nurse Barbie when I was a kid.

The professional environment in the Venezuelan hospital was cheerful and social; nurses and doctors took time for small talk. One nurse spent her spare time giving Glen private Spanish lessons. When I walked into his room, she was sitting close on the hospital bed, trying to teach Glen correct pronunciation in a totally nonstandard instruction format, helping him form the words on his lips with her fingers. Obviously, this was a Miss Universe approach to teaching Spanish. She jumped up as I entered, but I had to laugh because it looked like a sitcom skit. I figured it would help Glen recover faster; he deserved a little cleavage after his weeks of dysentery.

Hooked up to the IV cocktail of antibiotics and nutritional fluids, Glen was getting stronger by the day. After four days, he eased real food into his diet, and the doctor eventually announced he was ready to be discharged. The entire time I had never asked the cost of anything. Glen would get well if it bankrupted us. I went to the office to pay the bill for Glen's medical care and private room for four days and three nights.

Offering my trusty credit card, the accountant broke the news, "We only accept credit cards from Venezuelan banks, but you can change dollars into bolivars at any bank." I studied the bill; it was in the hundreds of thousands of bolivars. Inflation in Venezuela was crazy, but it still looked like a lot of money. I went back to the boat, emptied the small, onboard safe of our dollars, grabbed a backpack to carry the thousands of bolivars, and caught a taxi to a Venezuelan bank to see if we had enough money to make it work. When I showed the bill to the bank teller, it turned out that those hundreds of thousands of bolivars equaled about 1,300 U.S. dollars. Suddenly there was a whole new meaning to affordable medical care.

With a mix of debit card charging and currency exchange at the bank, my bag bulged with bolivars that were not worth an extraordinary amount but most certainly could catch the interest of a mugger. The last thing I needed at that point was to get hit over the head and end up in the hospital myself. I slipped out of the long-sleeved shirt I wore over my tank top for sun protection and stuffed it on top of the bag to make it look like laundry. The bank manager was quick to understand my attempt at camouflage and arranged for a driver to take me to the hospital.

"*Lo Siento* (sorry)," I told the cashier back at the hospital as I put the bulging bag full of bolivars onto her desk.

"*No se preocupe* (don't worry)," she said. "Normal in Venezuela."

When I returned to Glen's room, he was standing in clothes that were loose and hanging off his 15-pound lighter frame. Glen's doctor and nurses showed up to hug and bid him farewell. We were touched.

"*Cuidado* (careful)," they told him. "Venezuela is *muy peligroso* (very dangerous)."

Eating healthy, safe food, Glen grew progressively stronger over the next few days. Soaking up sun by the pool, we told our tale to the bikini bunch who raised their eyebrows knowingly, falling just short of saying, "I told you so."

* * * * *

Glen had regained much of his weight and strength. Life in Venezuela was feeling a bit like the movie Groundhog Day where our daily routine duplicated itself repeatedly. Every morning we read the English-language newspaper deposited on the boat deck by our marina guard and ate breakfast in the cockpit with the occasional greeting to attractive Venezuelan women arriving for a pampered day at the hotel gym. After breakfast—before the steamy summer temperature became unbearable—Glen and I walked or cycled the vast hotel grounds or exercised in the gym, then read or wrote in the shade until it was time to join the 4:00 p.m. happy hour crowd at the pool. It may sound like an idyllic life, but neither of us had it in our personal nature to enjoy being idle or lack purpose. I, for one, was ready to do something outside of the hotel area, even though our last trip into the real Venezuela had not gone well by anyone's measure.

Relating a newspaper article to Glen, "I thought Angel Falls was a religious name, but this newspaper for gringos says it was named after

American aviator Jimmie Angel, who crash-landed his plane on the mesa where the falls originate. Angel, his wife, and two traveling companions walked for 11 days to reach civilization. The falls were named in his honor after word of his adventure spread."

I was quiet for a few minutes. "Let's go to Angel Falls. It's one of the seven natural wonders of the world. Hugo Chavez wants to change the name because it's named after an American pilot." Handing Glen the news article, I added, "I promise we will either go first class or not go at all."

President Chavez was not fond of the U.S. Venezuela had already nationalized and taken U.S. oil company property as well as anything else U.S. companies or citizens owned in Venezuela. Like possibly our boat! The time to get the heck out of Venezuela was fast approaching, even though there were two months left in hurricane season.

Despite all we had been through on our last trip outside the marina, I wanted to visit Angel Falls. Surely a wonder of the world was worth seeing. But like everything else in Venezuela, getting to the falls would be a challenge. What's more, time was running out. If Venezuela decided to seize even small American assets, we might lose our boat and be trapped there by politics. If we were going to Angel Falls, we needed to do it soon.

One of the ladies at the pool owned a travel company and spoke of an outfit that ran an ecotour into Gran Sabana, the location of Angel Falls. She described a trip that toured the vast and remote area of Venezuela and departed from Caracas, the capital. Caracas was a show-stopper; almost everyone we met who had traveled to the gritty city had been robbed, mugged, or assaulted. The five-day tour would have us spending two nights in Caracas, canoeing up a river, hiking through mud, climbing steep hillsides, sleeping in hammocks… It sounded like a week of misery from the travel gods.

We studied the map, saw an airstrip close to the falls and inquired about small airplane flights. Glen and I are both pilots and love the convenience of small planes. The travel expert at the pool told us that, yes, if we did not mind a dirt airstrip, she knew of a man with a twin-engine airplane, and we could make the trip with only one night at a primitive lodge run by the native Pemon tribe. She finished with a reasonable price, so we decided to go for it.

Our American expat pilot set down the old twin-engine Piper smoothly at the Puerto La Cruz airport to pick us up. We told him we were also pilots and he motioned for Glen to sit next to him in the right seat of the cockpit while I had the luxury of the backseat. The pilot talked as he pointed out terrain features, banking suddenly and steeply in whatever direction his fingers were pointing. I did not have headsets and heard little over the engine noise, so I just nodded and smiled every now and then. After a couple of hours in the air, we got our first glimpse of the rugged, eerie, flat-topped tepui mountains, draped in rain-forest green with a circle of clouds around them. In all there were 115 tepuis; long, dramatic mesas, some as high as 10,000 feet in elevation. Tepuis look like islands in the sky and are home to more than 2,000 unique, one-off species—mostly plant and reptile— marooned as the surrounding land eroded. It was lost-world territory, shrouded in mystery and exquisite beauty. There were no pterodactyls flying overhead but it was easy to picture them cruising in front of the misty falls. The water gushing out of the top of the tepui did not drop from a shelf as it does at Niagara Falls, but fell uninterrupted more than 10,000 feet to mist-shrouded pools at the base of the falls. Like a scene from a Jurassic Park movie, the view left me breathless.

Our destination was Canaima National Park, created to protect the tepuis and Angel Falls, which flows out of a crevasse in the tallest tepui.

A native Pemon village within the park would be the staging area for our canoe ride and where we would spend one night.

After a gutsy flyby of the top of Angel Falls, my ears popped as the plane descended rapidly. Our pilot greased the landing on the short dirt strip, burning rubber from the braked tires. We climbed out of the plane and stretched our legs on the deserted airstrip. The three of us grabbed our backpacks and hiked to the primitive tribal village lodge. I looked askance at the rows of hammocks strung up along a covered portion of the porch, but our pilot assured us we had rooms reserved with actual beds.

We ate a quick sandwich lunch, then boarded a 38-foot-long dugout canoe driven by a 50 HP outboard motor. It would carry Glen, a guide, a bowman, the driver, and me, along with an extra engine lower unit, and two extra props. That alone should have been indication that we were in for a rollicking ride. We hovered close to another canoe loaded to the gunwales with Venezuelan tourists and proceeded to bump our way up the Carrao River.

In the beginning, the river was fairly wide and slow moving, but after a while the canyon narrowed and the rapids increased. The extra engine hardware made sense when I realized that most of the way we would be powering the boat up harsh rapids. At one of the raging whitewater points—a likely section for capsizing—the guide had Glen and me exit the canoe and walk along a trail while the plucky Pemon crew motored past the challenging area. Once we got back into the canoe, the rapids increased and the canyon narrowed further still.

Showing considerable skill, our boat driver steered and walked the boat up, around, and over the rocks and rapids. My knuckles were white and now, understanding the extra motor parts, I hoped we had enough spares.

Finally, we reached a large pool at the base of a what looked like a mini-Niagara where other canoes of tourists gathered. Our guide directed us to walk underneath a towering shelf of water, called Sapo Falls. He pointed out a ledge at the back of the water flow where we could inch and shuffle from one side to the other. This gave me pause. I left the canoe but inwardly moaned at the thought of hiking beneath a gauntlet of water powerful enough to sweep our bodies downstream. I could easily imagine being tossed like a Raggedy Ann doll by the roiling water, bones shattering on jutting rocks.

The Venezuelan tourists from the overcrowded canoe were just ahead and we watched as they crept along the ledge with focus and apprehension. The Venezuelans were not too keen and I was flooded with uneasiness myself. A fall into the shooting water would be cause for another hospital visit—or worse. As token gringos, we could have stayed in our canoe and headed back down river, but Glen and I nodded to each other and silently agreed to forge on. Shuffling slowly, we followed behind the Venezuelans. Behind the falls, we leaned against the slimy wall for stability. I slid my feet sideways through a mist so thick I had to hold my hand up in front of my nose to be able to breathe; it was like walking through the deep end of a swimming pool. The entire passage I clung to the rock wall behind me as tightly as a fly with my free hand, and eventually came out soaking wet at the far end. Gratefully, we climbed back into the canoe, shivering from the cold.

"Another a-a-a-uthentic experie-e-e-ence," Glen stuttered through chattering teeth. The canoe ride back downstream was fast, but both of us were too cold and wet to worry about hitting the rocks or losing an engine. We sat close to each other for what body heat we could provide to the other and hoped for the best.

Once back at the village lodge, the happy and beaming Pemon bowman proudly held up a bent and misshapen propeller he must have replaced during the time we walked through the Falls. This had not been their first rodeo.

After toweling my hair in the sun and changing clothes, it was time for dinner in the rustic family-style eating area. The chicken, rice, and beans on our plate was the hot meal we needed to stave off hypothermia and hunger from our exertions. I enjoyed sitting family style at long tables and speaking Spanish with Venezuelans from the other canoe, but my head bobbed as I tried to stay awake. Giving in completely to exhaustion, we excused ourselves early and, in the comfort of our own room, were asleep within minutes.

The next morning, Glen, the pilot, and I tiptoed past the rows of sleepers cocooned and snoring in the hammocks. Flying the small plane off the dirt strip went smoothly and the early morning sun was like a spotlight shining onto the falls offering us a picture postcard view. Our pilot was quiet. He had stayed up late drinking a native alcohol concoction and was too hung over for aerial dives. I leaned forward to get Glen's attention and with a shared look, we agreed the excursion had been successful and we could now leave Venezuela, having seen its most wondrous of wonders.

When we returned to *It's Enough*, we began making a checklist of everything we needed to do and buy in order to get the boat and us ready to leave in a couple of days. We had done our best to see something of the country, but it was time to leave the harsh reality of the mainland and head to the part of Venezuela where crime would have a harder time finding us.

Next stop: the islands of Los Roques.

* * * * *

JULIE BRADLEY

SAILMAIL: IT'S ENOUGH

To: Jeanne

From: Julie

Hey Jeanne, we just left Venezuela and it was risky even up to the very last minutes. We were ready to drop anchor in a river off the mainland coast when dodgy looking men in a small powerboat circled us several times, giving us the once over and perhaps sizing up the situation to rob us. It was a likely scenario as we've heard of other sailboats here being boarded and robbed. While the men circled, Glen put our small engine into fast gear and I raised the sails for even more speed. Adios mainland Venezuela! That was close.

Don't worry, the Los Roques islands are technically part of Venezuela, but tiny, sparsely inhabited, and surrounded by ocean too rough for small fishing boats from the mainland. Things should be calmer and safer.

Love and miss you, Julie

* * * * *

It was still hurricane season, but we waved goodbye to the leisure ladies and our luxury surroundings. We sailed 70 miles offshore to Los Roques, an archipelago and national park of more than 60 islands barely large enough to have names. Not included in that number are an additional 200 plus unnamed islets and coral reefs.

There was not much on Los Roques beyond turquoise blue water, sunshine, and fish. In Gran Roque, the only town, the streets were made of sand. We had more food on our boat than was displayed on the shelves of the one small market, that aspired to serve 1,500 residents. The day we arrived the tiny shop had less than the usual inventory because the old landing craft that sputtered in every so often to deliver food was a few days late. The people of Los Roques were friendly and told us they, too, were afraid to travel to the mainland. I felt free and safe; paranoia about getting hit over the head and robbed was becoming a distant memory.

Furthermore, the islanders seemed to feel the same as we did about the politics back on the mainland. We met a German expat living in Los Roques who was not afraid to speak freely, "Chavez (anti-American president of Venezuela) has talked about plans for large, floating tourist cities in Los Roques and promised a 5,000-mile oil pipeline across the Amazon. He wants to go to war against the Netherlands over the Dutch island of Aruba, and our clocks now run half an hour ahead of Washington D.C. He's totally loco, but everyone is running scared because he has informants and anyone who complains disappears."

There may have been a lot to like about Venezuela, but we felt lucky to have gotten out of there pounds lighter and a lot wiser. Still obliged by our insurance to stay below the hurricane latitude for two more months, we headed for Bonaire. Though located on the outer edge of the prohibited latitudes, it was close enough to Venezuela to scoot back to our posh marina should a hurricane head our way.

Chapter 16

L et's see if they like oatmeal!" Smiling to the unseeing fish, I dropped the leftovers from breakfast into the ocean. So far, the fish had not been picky eaters. Sure enough, our little, striped sergeant major and angelfish buddies attacked the cereal as it sank through the clear, turquoise water to the ocean floor. I was contributing to the delinquency of these beautiful reef fish by giving them food scraps on a regular basis. At first it was just bread, but then escalated to cover all the major food groups. The transparent ocean surrounding our boat was like a special and private aquarium—one where when we rapped a spoon on the side of the boat, they would come. The shimmering water was liquid crystal and we could see the shadow *It's Enough* cast on the sand 20 feet below, and fish appeared out of seemingly nowhere to enjoy the bounty.

The Dutch island of Bonaire was a culture shock—the good kind. As much as we enjoyed improving our Spanish in Venezuela, the safety concerns in that country were exhausting. In Bonaire, language was no problem even though the islanders were transplants from the Netherlands or descendants of Dutch and mixed island ancestry. Nearly every person, regardless of income or education, spoke English, Dutch, Spanish, and Papiamento, a local Creole language. Dutch order and cleanliness combined with stunning underwater marine life made us glad we had bailed from Venezuela. We quickly assessed that Bonaire offered the best diving and snorkeling in the Caribbean—period. The island possessed some of the most abundant, thriving, and accessible reefs in the world, and not far from the shore, the water abruptly became deeper, by thousands of feet. We were told the rapid drop-off was the reason for such little sedimentation in the water, offering divers 60 feet of clear visibility.

To test the waters, we donned our snorkel gear and swam out 50 feet or so. Aware it would be coming, we were still surprised by the sudden change in depth. What began as turquoise blue water over a white-sand bottom gave way to a steep slope where the water became a darker blue and visibility tapered to an infinite, black void. A few reefs were shallow enough to snorkel, but it became obvious we would need to haul out our scuba gear to really enjoy Bonaire.

Glen was already a certified diver when we met. Later, while stationed in Arizona, I decided to also learn scuba in preparation for our then distant, ocean voyage dream. My training took place in a big swimming pool at Fort Huachuca, and our class traveled to the Sea of Cortes in Mexico for open water certification dives. My instructor was a retired Army Special Forces NCO, who obviously forgot he was retired, and set physically tough standards. Before each lesson, the class had to swim ten laps up and back an Olympic-sized pool, then dive down 12 feet without fins ten times to retrieve our masks. By the time the actual instruction started, I felt like sludge. I am not one for quitting, but the over the top rigor in addition to certain attitudes toward women during that class made me want to throw in the towel on more than one occasion. I was tempted to stick to snorkeling, but Glen thought it vital we both have the ability to dive during our planned circumnavigation, so I stuck it out for certification.

Once we were living out our plans, reality threw some kinks in the works. It was difficult to find safe air refills for our dive tanks, and even when they were available, the scuba equipment was so heavy for our medium-sized selves that lugging it around was not usually worth the effort. Glen almost always went free diving (snorkeling with a weight belt to 40 feet down) and I was happy enough to snorkel the reefs near the surface.

So, it had been awhile since we had gone scuba diving and our skills needed a refresh. Bonaire, with its abundant reefs and sea life, had instructors for currency training. It did not take long for us to get accustomed to our bulky gear, which did at least feel lighter underwater. What waited on the reefs of Bonaire was worth the effort. Just offshore, a couple of fin kicks from the beach, magnificent coral formations offered plentiful food for the sea creatures. The Dutch government protected the marine life and had installed more than 100 moorings for boats and dinghies to safeguard the fragile coral. It was against the law to anchor, catch fish, take souvenirs, or even wear gloves (so one would not be tempted to reach out and damage the reef). We thought the no-gloves rule was excessive but with the underwater forest elegantly swaying around us, we had to restrain ourselves. It was easy to be enticed by the beckoning, breathtaking beauty.

The entire island of Bonaire was geared toward diving. We were able to leave our sailboat on her mooring, pile air tanks and gear into our dinghy, putter out to the named and numbered dive sites, and attach our dinghy to a floating mooring line. The dive site names were descriptive of wonders that awaited below: Small Wall, Alice in Wonderland, Thousand Steps, Cliff, Forest... waving purple sponge tubes that were so slick they seemed molded from plastic. Fluorescent orange coral could have been pool toys and green gorgonians looked like luxurious, lace ladies' fans. Truly, it was nature in all its perfection.

An entirely different world welcomed me each time I squeezed into my tight, form-fitting wetsuit, strapped my heavy diving tank to my back, and fell into the aquamarine depths. Other than the occasional reef shark, it was a friendly place where fish and other sea life swam around me. The colors were a continually moving and changing kaleidoscope. Dive after dive, I saw something new, and the promise of something new the next day, and the next, and the next...

I thought doling out food scraps from *It's Enough* was an original idea but soon discovered we were not the only ones feeding fish in Bonaire. It had been going on long enough to give the reef fish a strong sense of entitlement: yellowtail snappers and angelfish came right up to our faceplates, as if inspecting the new additions to the neighborhood. I spotted the largest parrotfish I had ever seen—even common reef fish grow to be big boys and girls when they are protected. In Bonaire, fish have the law on their side, enabling them to grow larger and friendlier than on reefs in the Caribbean where villagers eat anything with fins. The fish had it all figured out and blatantly exploited their protected status, approaching humans without fear, some demanding offerings. Fish were so accustomed to their feedings that they rushed toward any human who merely stopped swimming. Unfortunately, when the morsels were gone, the reef fish made kamikaze runs at divers. It could be annoying to have fish bump up to my faceplate or poke my body to get attention, but I was willing to trade that for shark activity any day.

With each day I felt more comfortable diving, and I felt more at home underwater gazing at schools of colorful, shimmering fish rushing and darting along the coral reef. Rolling over on my back, I could see the sunlit surface 30 feet above—the only sound was the thunder of my breathing.

I glided through the water as a two-foot long grouper stared at me, his mouth agape, while a parrotfish and a zebra-striped sergeant major played hide and seek among the purple tube sponges and orange coral. All of it—the fish, the coral, the crystalline waters, and the bright sun sending glimmers in every direction like a disco ball — made me appreciate the supreme loveliness of Bonaire.

* * * * *

Though I enjoyed the beautiful conditions in Bonaire, I was skittish when sailing friends invited Glen and me for what would be my first-ever night dive, but I summoned my courage and agreed to join them.

The entire experience tested my nerve. Fumbling underwater in the near pitch-black darkness while fiddling with weak underwater lights pushed me right out of my comfort zone. Diving at night you only see what is in front of the narrow beam of your flashlight, which reminded me all too much of a certain Venezuelan cave. Shine the light below and there are sea urchins crawling onto a rock. Shine the light above and there might be a three-foot barracuda hovering overhead with threatening jagged teeth. Shine the light in front and a tiny clown fish darts into, then out of the beam. I simply did not have the personal constitution for the dark phantoms that appeared and receded outside of the narrow band of light—or what I imagined lurked close by that I would never see until it was too late.

Sitting with Glen over coffee in the cockpit the next morning, I came to the realization I needed more land time. "Let's take a wee break from the underwater stuff. After that night dive, I need a couple days on land to get grounded. If our bikes still work, let's get them out and explore Bonaire on land."

Our folding mountain bikes, new though rusting, took up precious storage in the stern locker and I had been vowing to give them away. Clearly, they were a bad investment considering how seldom we had ridden them. But flat Bonaire finally offered the perfect place for cycling.

After digging the bikes out from the bottom of our stern locker and assembly, getting our bikes to shore was a whole project in itself. Glen motored the dinghy around to the side of the boat, I handed down the bikes, hopped in, and we motored off toward the town dock, barge style, with our bikes and selves standing upright.

Biking on Bonaire was like riding through a flat area of Arizona, except the cacti and scrub brush were surrounded by turquoise blue water. Pedaling the shoreline, I signaled to stop when a great white mountain came into view. It was salt. Long, large pans holding shallow ponds of evaporating seawater provided explanation. The enormous mounds of snowy white sea salt were lit so brightly by the sun it hurt my eyes to stare at them.

Beyond the saltpans, thousands of pink birds strutted and roosted on nests. Informing Glen of the obvious, I said, "Flamingos, pink flamingos." Straddling our bikes, we watched them, taking in the striking contrast of pink birds on white salt. Later we discovered those very salt ponds cause the flamingos to become pink from eating tiny red brine shrimp in the water. Note to self: eat more carrots to keep your red hair from going gray!

Funny how once you become aware of the existence of some things, you start to see them more frequently. From that point on, it became a daily event to see flocks of pink flamingos flying overhead, commuting between Bonaire and Venezuela. No matter what we were doing; reading, walking, working on deck… our eyes would be drawn upward to a pink blur that looked to be a single body pulsing against a clear blue sky. "There they go!" one of us would sing out, looking upwards to trace their daily commute.

* * * * *

Places as wonderful as Bonaire are dangerous to sailors with world-voyaging ambitions. I could have stayed for a long time, but hurricane season was nearly over, and it was time to depart for Cartagena, Colombia. We picked a date for departure and discussed taking down our grand porch awning a few days in advance, but in the end decided to leave it up for sun protection until right before we sailed. That would turn out to be a bad decision.

* * * * *

Since Trinidad, we had endured torrid, tropical summer heat. Sometimes the sun and temperature made it too hot to sleep in our beds below decks, so we chose to sleep on cushions in the cockpit. To make it livable, in Trinidad we had a vast canvas awning built that we called our porch. The porch ran from the bow to the stern, creating another layer of living space while blocking the equatorial sun. It made such a difference that at midday we could lie on deck beneath the awning and read a book. The extra insulation also made it cooler for sleeping below decks in our stateroom (bedroom) at night. However, the porch was a gigantic stack of multiple canvas awnings, which took a good two hours to put up and connect. We only erected the porch when we would be at a location long enough to make the investment of time worthwhile. What a difference it made in steamy Venezuela, where little breeze came into the marina, as well as in Bonaire, where it was a drier, but nonetheless scorching heat. In Bonaire, we treated our deck like a real porch, leaving cushions and even our bikes beneath its protection from the sun. That complacency was almost our undoing.

Bonaire is somewhat boomerang shaped with the western, lee side providing shelter for boats. Trade winds normally sweep across the island from the long side, but the island protects sailboats on moorings from wave action. Ordinarily that made for a comfortable and safe anchorage, but Bonaire is only 40 miles from Venezuela and its rainy season. Normally we were not affected, and storms stayed close to Venezuela. It was an evening pastime for Glen and me to sit high and dry under our canvas porch, eating popcorn while watching the lightning storm pass across the distant sky. Every once in a while, a storm over Venezuela moved a little too close and caused a wind reversal that affected Bonaire more than I would have expected.

Wind reversals are rare but terrifying events for sailboats in Bonaire. Many a boat at anchor has been driven onto shore by those powerful winds that push the moored boats toward land. There was little, and often no warning of those dangerous wind shifts.

Just as Glen and I were preparing for bed one night, we felt the winds gust to over 40 MPH, and *It's Enough*, with its huge awnings creaking and swaying, tugged at the anchor from the wrong direction. "I think it's a wind reversal! What else can it be?" I shouted, throwing on a long shirt of Glen's as I rushed up to help.

Our mooring was set to hold against wind coming from shore, but that storm-strength wind was coming from the ocean, and now our stern (back) was 50 feet from land. At any moment the mooring line could work loose, and we would be driven aground, trapped onboard by the pounding of successive waves. The other 40 or more sailboats down the line were in the same predicament, and the entire lot of us was scrambling to make for the open sea, away from the dangers of shore and other boats. It was chaos.

I detached the mooring line, while Glen maneuvered the engine to keep us off the shore. In the pitch dark I stowed crazy deck items such as bikes, mats and cushions while keeping an eye out for and alerting Glen of other boats. Driven by adrenalin, I tried to declutter the situation.

Dozens of sailboats, all making a frantic midnight exodus from a confined space, were buffeted by wind and waves intent upon forcing us all onto shore.

In the black, overcast night we could just make out other boats' sail silhouettes as we all pursued more sea room. It was nothing short of miraculous that none of the boats fouled a prop on moorings lines. I had not been able to stow the bicycles but had managed to wrap them together on deck under the canvas porch with massive amounts of bungee cords. Unlike our neighbors, we could not raise sail because of the wraparound deck awnings. Not only could we not raise sail, we could not motor effectively. The massive sheets of canvas cloth became horizontal wind foils, creating havoc on our attempts at steerage.

"Keep away from *It's Enough*," we heard boat captains yelling in the night. "They can't sail or steer with all that canvas on deck!" I would have been embarrassed if I hadn't been so frightened. After nerve-fraying hours of fighting the sea and getting blown sideways in the storm tearing at our horizontal sails, the winds died down and the waves finally lessened. It was the wee hours of the morning before we could get back to the anchorage and jockey for mooring space with the 40 or so other sailboats caught in the same mess.

Once back at anchor we were so jittery from the experience, neither of us could sleep. In the scant moonlight, we worked on deck, removed our awning, disassembled and stowed the bikes, and counted ourselves lucky to have survived the wind reversal.

Our departure would be one day early, but it seemed the right time to once again become real sailors and say farewell to otherwise perfect Bonaire and its occasional dangerous winds.

ESCAPE FROM THE ORDINARY

Chapter 17

Motoring the last 100 miles into Cartagena, the wind was dead calm and the water oily flat. I was happy to motor and not fiddle with sails. Glen and I were both worn out; our four-day passage from Bonaire had been one of torrential rain and dramatic lightning storms. One bolt had struck so close I could smell the ozone in the air.

Living in foul weather gear, my night watches had been the stuff of nightmares. I called out, "Glen, you need to come help me up here. I hate to wake you but I need help to avoid hitting these floating islands of debris... I just saw a roof float by. I'm trying to slow down to get a handle on it, but the wind is pushing us fast without any sail up."

Joining me in the cockpit, Glen saw that the deluge of rain we endured the past four days and nights had obviously caused severe damage on mainland Colombia. Mammoth logs and branches from the mouth of the Magdalena River traveled right into our path. What we saw could only have come from major mudslides inland. Floating logs, branches, and the occasional tin hut formed mud islands that forced us to steer further and further off course. With Glen at the helm and me on lookout with night-vision goggles, we skirted the edge of the waste to avoid fouling our propeller. Finally, we got past the mess and aimed for Cartagena.

A couple of hours yet from Cartagena, there was a piercing, whining noise in the sky. We looked up and an American fighter jet was zooming toward us, flying right at our boat as if dropping munitions on a target. The roaring aircraft cleared us just above mast height—70, maybe 100 feet above the ocean—creating a volume and decibel of roaring, deafening noise. Glen and I had been on the military side of such events, but never the receiving side.

An American voice over the VHF radio blared through on the hailing and distress channel, "Sailboat identify yourself!" Glen was at the helm so I ran down to the radio as the plane again passed deafeningly close over our boat.

As former military, Glen and I understand the mindset as well as the monitoring of drug trafficking between Colombia and the USA. I said into the radio, "This is the American sailing vessel *It's Enough* (spelling our boat name with the NATO phonetic alphabet according to military protocol: India, Tango, Sierra new word, Echo, November....). We are stopping in Cartagena to refuel en route to the Panama Canal. We have two souls onboard. Glad to see friendly presence in these waters." The fighter jet immediately banked away from our boat, cautioned us to be careful, and flew out of our sight.

Whew! Spotter jets have the power to call in United States Navy and Coast Guard ships to board boats and do a search at their own discretion. We had no drugs aboard but still would have hated being boarded for a search. A boat can incur major damage—literally be torn apart—if the Coast Guard inspectors have any suspicions that drug trafficking may be involved. It is a judgment call on the part of the local commander. Being evasive, defensive, or non-responsive is the best way to strike concern and raise suspicion. We had dodged a bullet. A team in combat boots tearing up the deck and ripping open the cushions and interior of our boat was unthinkable. On the other hand, it was good to know help was a radio call away as we were traveling into drug cartel territory.

By the time we neared Cartagena harbor, I forgot about the lightning storms, debris field, and fear of a Coast Guard boarding that would leave our home looking like we had hosted a frat party. We were about to vault back through time as Glen throttled back on the engine and we entered the historic shortcut into the city. During the 1700s, the narrow entrance to the main harbor had been blocked by massive underwater links of chain as protection against invasion from the British fleet and pirates. Cartagena had been home to a Spanish Armada responsible for protecting the vast wealth accumulated from pillaging South America. The Spanish ships and fort guarded the gold-and-silver laden transports that gathered to sail in convoy to Spain. Today, several hundred years later, the passage was well marked as we made our way through the once-secret entrance.

During the past months in Venezuela and Bonaire, we had grown soft as sailors. Our 500-mile passage from Bonaire was not especially long but seemed harder because we were out of practice. Visiting Cartagena allowed us a chance to de-stress from the rigors of the past week, but we would not be able to completely let down our guard. As U.S. citizens, it was necessary to remain careful and keep a low profile. The powerful drug cartels had major wars raging and Americans were prime ransom bait in Colombia.

Visiting dangerous countries is a calculated risk. State Department warnings, insurance restrictions, and concerns of various family members all had us wondering if stopping in Colombia was the right course of action. Besides the normal garden-variety crime such as theft, mugging, pickpockets, and scam, there loomed a different, greater danger visiting the country. Kidnapping was a top concern for any American who ventured outside the cities.

Our plan was to attract as little attention as possible during our short visit and then leave unscathed. Half-jokingly I said, "I hope we're doing the right thing coming to Colombia. After all the warnings and dire predictions from our families, they would not be too keen on paying a penny of ransom."

Despite real and imagined concerns, circumnavigating was a once in a lifetime adventure for us. The whole idea was to voyage to places we would not otherwise visit. If we obliged the concerns of others, we would have lived their version of the voyage instead of our own. It was our personal mission to use good judgment, but risks and hazards ran through the very nature of our travels. I did not think it wise to inform worried loved ones back home that, on a daily basis, we had even greater concerns than they imagined: rogue waves that could knock our boat over, lightning storms that could disable our radios and navigation instruments, possible impact with floating containers or an unlit vessel, dismasting, man overboard at night—those threats were far more real and present dangers than the horror stories friends and family conjured up concerning foreign countries. We kept our fingers crossed that our visit to Cartagena would be worth their angst—and ours.

Historically, Cartagena is beyond compare with many cities in Latin America. It was founded in 1533 and managed to preserve much of its original Spanish colonial charm. It had not been much of a tourist attraction because of all the drug cartel related crime. Most people would not put Cartagena at the top of their lists for a vacation destination, but it deserves to be. The walled city was virtually free of post-1700s architecture and still showed its history that started with Columbus.

Cartagena's natural and well-protected harbor made the city a vital warehouse base for all the gold, treasures, and spoils that were discovered by the conquistadores between Peru and Mexico. The vast riches were hauled to the city by slaves and donkeys over land from the Pacific Ocean and by ship from the Caribbean. The vast riches sat stored in warehouses awaiting ship convoy transport back to mother Spain.

Pirates, privateers, and British invaders—Sir Francis Drake among them—were attracted to the caches of gold and frequently attacked the city. Tiring of the ongoing threats, Spanish conquistadores built a series of fortifications to fend off the sea-borne pirates. Engineers were brought from Spain and stone barriers were sunk across the inner harbor entrance, protected by forts on both sides and a huge chain that barred ships from entering. By the 1700s, Cartagena was impregnable and completely walled. In 1740, a Spanish force of 500 soldiers, with 2,500 native slaves, repulsed a British force eight times larger. The precautions worked.

We sailed over that very same once-secret passageway, knowing that somewhere beneath our keel lay an ancient rusted-out chain and remnants of the stone barrier. The shortcut took us directly into the inner harbor of Cartagena, and we headed straight for quirky Club Nautico, a marina owned by an expat Australian sailor and his Colombian wife. They had converted their small patch of Cartagena into an inexpensive mecca for liveaboard expat sailors.

As we got closer, I got a better look at the facilities. "I don't know about this marina. It looks so run-down, I would say it was in ruins if it weren't for all the boats at dock." Approaching the berth, we discovered that pulling up to the dilapidated docks was riskier than crossing the narrow, stone-lined entrance to the harbor. Chunks of rebar and upended concrete blocks masqueraded as piers with ragged edges, threatening to gouge an unsuspecting hull. Hooking up to the frayed and tattered wires on the dock's electrical post seemed dangerous, with the potential to lead to a shocking end. The cracked, floating concrete dock sunk down when I stepped off the boat. We were just getting ready to find the only other marina in Cartagena when a helpful dockhand intercepted our departure and offered to show us to "the best dock space" there. Other sailors encouraged us to overlook the physical drawbacks, pointing out that this marina was within the historic, walled city and everything was within walking distance.

Our dock neighbor, on S/V Next Life, had been at the marina for months replacing electronic equipment lost in a near lightning strike. "It doesn't look like much but it's safe," he said. "We've heard that the drug cartels have unofficially declared Cartagena off limits for violence because of its UNESCO World Heritage designation." It was a comforting thought—true or not.

Though decrepit, Club Nautico was brimming with friendly sailors who told us the reason for the poor shape of the marina was the absence of the Australian owner, who had been in jail for years for a drug-related crime. Hard to say what level of drug involvement was required to offend the Colombian government at that time, but it must have been something noteworthy. Our dock neighbor invited us to join him on a unique outing, "Hey, come with a group of us to visit the Aussie owner of the marina. Even though you don't know him it's worth the experience to check out a Colombian jail." We opted to skip that adventure as more paranoia was the last thing I needed.

* * * * *

SAILMAIL: IT'S ENOUGH

TO: JEANNE

FROM JULIE

Hey Jeanne, just read your email. Yes, we do feel nervous here in Colombia. In our favor is the fact that Americans rarely visit Cartagena and people here think we are from Canada. When I walked into a store, the shop owner asked where I was from in Canada. I wasn't ready for that question and said, "How do you know I'm from Canada?" The shopkeeper said, "Americans would never come here." We got the same comments from people in grocery stores and restaurants that thought we were Canadian. So, we have that going for us!

I hope one day soon the drug wars here finish and it's safe to visit this incredibly historic and beautiful city. Maybe we can return together one day on a sister trip.

Love, Julie

* * * * *

The dodgy cartel situation gave our boat insurer pause. The fine print of our insurance coverage specified we could only stay in Cartagena long enough to refuel and provision, and our three days in the city stretched the interpretation of that clause. On the fourth day, we sailed out of the harbor the same way we had come in, through the secret shortcut. I was happy to have had even that short time in amazing Cartagena. The stop was worth rough seas, lightning storms, islands of debris, and a bit of paranoia to visit the magical, walled city. Once the drug cartels get sorted out, Cartagena, frozen in time, is too special to miss.

Next stop: Panama.

ESCAPE FROM THE ORDINARY

Chapter 18

One night, while making bread, I had an epiphany. Earlier that day I had made soup from scratch and as I pounded the bread dough, considered, "I would never, ever have made bread or soup from scratch when I was on land!" In fact, on land it was rare for me to cook much beyond grilled meat and salad. My slow cooking insight made me think about all the other ways our seafaring life was different. At sea, when we did not have an ingredient, we substituted or left it out. We thought nothing of a dinghy ride to shore and a three-mile walk to get supplies. The slow, adventurous, and physically demanding life on a sailboat expanded me in ways I never imagined. Creativity and resourcefulness were honed to new heights. Instead of television, we read. Instead of long, hot showers, we took efficient, quick ones. Tasks that would take an hour on land took double or triple that amount of time onboard. It was the new sea-cruising math! Every action became mindful and at times Zen-like.

The extra effort required to do common, daily tasks produced a satisfying feeling of accomplishment. Even minor tasks became a significant part of my day, and I found myself appreciating the small things. I had grown to love our minimalist lifestyle. It's the only way you can live happily aboard a sailboat—adapt or get out of the water.

* * * * *

No people, no restaurants, no beach condos, no jet skis, and no bands playing Jimmy Buffett songs to tourists covered in oil. The San Blas Islands of Panama floated in an aquamarine ocean that blended lazily with a clear blue sky. It was rare to have such exquisite white sand islands all to ourselves and my first impulse was to rush ashore and walk the beach. We opted instead to nap first and catch up on sleep lost during our sailing passage from Cartagena. The cockpit seemed an ideal place to doze, until a wooden *cayuca* full of native women unexpectedly bumped the side of our boat.

I jumped as the leathery, brown face of a woman popped up into view and asked, "*Compra molas?*" (Do you want to buy molas?)

The Kuna Yala people of the San Blas Islands had found us. There were four women and one man with a paddle crammed into a single, narrow cayuca. The women had long, black hair and wore brightly colored full-length skirts like the finest of plumage. The man wore cutoffs and a necklace of barracuda teeth around his neck. Unbelievably, they all fit in the slender, hand-carved canoe. Granted, they were small people— around five feet tall—but piled between them was a stack of fabric artwork embroidered with the brightest blues, oranges, and greens this side of a box of crayons.

I was excited by their visit. Sailors told us that throughout the entire world they had never been anywhere like the San Blas Islands; an archipelago of coral islands, many uninhabited, with a primitive culture and native people maintaining their customs and isolation. I recalled the words of a sailor we met in the Caribbean, "My only regret from my entire circumnavigation is that I did not stay longer in the San Blas Islands. I was so eager to get to the Pacific, I did not realize the gem that was right in front of me. Imagine beaches with pristine white sands as fine as flour, deserted islands with waving palm trees, crystal clear blue water inhabited by countless fish, and a primitive culture and people who make you feel like you have traveled back in time. That kind of place doesn't exist anywhere in the world except the San Blas Islands."

Our plan was to linger and experience the San Blas islands as long as possible before sailing through the Panama Canal to the Pacific Ocean. When we first dropped anchor, Glen and I wondered aloud how we could make contact with the Kuna peoples. Just a few hours later a canoe full of Kuna settled that question.

Although we were technically in Panama, you would never know it. The Kuna people rebelled against the Panamanian government in 1925 and were given autonomy within the nation of Panama. The Kuna would say there are upwards of 380 islands in their realm, but it would be hard to count because some of the islands were so small there was only room for the five or six coconut trees crowding each other for the sandy beach. The islands were primitive and undeveloped, but the people seemed to get everything they needed using traditional methods of fishing, hunting, and growing basic crops.

The Kuna woman leading the delegation to our boat stood up in her wobbly canoe, waving a handcrafted mola. From the waving fabric, it looked like there was a parrot embroidered in a complex mix of fabric, thread, and colors. Yes, indeed, I would like to buy a mola. As it turned out, that would be the first of a dozen or more of the distinctive, hand-sewn items I would acquire from these hard-bargaining Kuna women. Surrounded by water, sailors are a hopelessly captive audience.

It is nearly impossible to describe the unique molas. I saw one framed in an art gallery with a card describing it as "reverse applique embroidery," which may mean something to you but did not explain a lot to me. Every design is a work of art, made using up to five pieces of layered fabric. Every mola I have ever seen depicted geometric patterns or something in nature: birds, iguanas, shells... The nature themes were endless, and the hand embroidery was intricate and executed with per-fection. I have trouble threading a needle with the help of reading glasses, but no matter how tiny and elaborate the workmanship, I never saw a Kuna woman of any age with any kind of spectacles or magnifying glass. Throughout the San Blas islands, I saw Kuna women making delicate stitches in front of a village hut or in a wobbly cayuca as her husband or son paddled her across waves from island to island selling her creations. Until our visit to the San Blas Islands, I had always figured most artwork looked best from far away, but the embroidery and sewing of a mola was so meticulous and fine, it needed to be examined up close to fully appre-ciate the work that went into it.

Traditionally, women make molas, but we saw some fine ones crafted by Kunas called *omegit*. Omegit are Kuna men dressed and raised as women. From what we saw, the omegit enjoy a high status in Kuna society.

A couple of times, the same transgender man, dressed as a woman, paddled up to our boat with some exceptionally fine molas to sell. One time, after striking a bargain, she asked, in her deep voice, if she could come aboard. Once aboard, she wordlessly stepped below and looked around until she saw our tiny bathroom. She closed herself off from us in there, and I heard her opening cabinets and drawers, pulling out toilet-ries and makeup. When she emerged, she wore lipstick, eye makeup, smelled of anti-mosquito lotion and one of my barrettes pinned back her long, thick, black hair. An omegit makeover! Her lipstick-painted smile was wide and happy. She held herself regally and appeared quite proud as she delicately climbed down to her canoe and paddled away.

I had bought enough molas to last several lifetimes; they were spill-ing out of cubbyholes in our limited storage below decks and I now needed to hide when a canoe of Kuna natives came with stacks of them to sell. They clearly understood their irresistible force was stronger than my immovable-object act. Understandably, I respected and loved the beautiful works of art.

* * * * *

There was not much to do on the uninhabited islands of the Kuna nation. There were few boats for socializing, so I mostly read and walked the beaches, leaving behind a solitary trail of footprints that were soon erased by the gentle tide. Glen immersed himself in free diving and spearfishing within the vast system of reef surrounding the islands. Though already an accomplished free diver, he learned to add extra weights to his dive belt so he could go deeper, holding his breath for more than two minutes. He became part of the reef in the same way as the native fish. As his skills improved, he also became more particular about what to spear for dinner. He hunted rather than fished. He no longer speared the first edible specimen and took pleasure in announcing at breakfast what delectable fish we would have for dinner. At times he speared a second fish to gift to the Kunas or the rare sailboat sharing our anchorage. There were times he stayed out so long in search of the right fish, I used binoculars to ensure he was still alive and had not stayed down so long he passed out and was carried away by the tide.

Weeks in the San Blas flew by with our sedate daily routine of fishing, snorkeling, boat maintenance, and visiting with Kuna women in passing cayucas. Eventually we ran low on staples and sailed to a larger island in search of fresh fruit, vegetables, and fuel. We were both excited for the trip. Not only would we get to replenish our stores, we would get to see a real Kuna village.

We pulled anchor and sailed to an inhabited Kuna island and were directed to their congresso building where we asked the chief's permission before visiting. A diminutive woman stood before us. Small even by Kuna standards, she stood only about four and a half feet. Walnut-colored, with a gold ring through her nose, and smoking a miniature pipe, she was the village chief. Trussed up tightly in her mola blouse and skirt, she looked like a Native American woman you might see in 1800s Wild West photos. She was adorned with treasures from ancestors, in what appeared to be an attempt to wear as many remnants of her personal history as possible. She spoke through an interpreter, and we asked to buy produce and jerry cans of diesel. She welcomed us, levied a fee, and explained even the Kunas must pay to travel, whether to another village or other town in Panama.

In the market we met an English professor who had been staying at a primitive Kuna-run hostel. The woman was writing a paper on albinism among the Kuna people. Though we had seen blonde, light skinned Kunas, we had not known what to make of them. The scientist told us that because of their small gene pool, the Kuna exhibited the world's highest rate of albinism, which they explained through folklore. The Kunas' legend claimed that if a woman looked at the moon during pregnancy, she would give birth to an albino, known as a child of the moon. For every one in 200 Kuna births, it was a prophecy that came true.

After picking up the supplies we needed in the Kuna village, we walked to the small, village airstrip. Glen's daughter, Dawn, and her husband had flown in for a mini-vacation visit in the San Blas islands and perhaps to help transit the Panama Canal. We were all excited and psyched about transiting the Panama Canal, though it is no easy feat for a small sailboat to make the crossing. Dawn and her husband also felt the magnetism of the Kuna nation, and were torn between staying longer on the picture-perfect islands or moving ahead to the canal. We let them make the decision, even though it was still too early for the Pacific trade winds. We could not depart the Americas until we were sure the trade winds had set in, and if we transited at that time, we would need to wait for a month or two at a marina on the Pacific side of the Panama Canal. After only a few days in the islands and with only a week remaining in their holiday, Dawn and her husband chose to sail on to mainland Panama to participate in the extraordinary event of taking a sailboat through one of the greatest engineering feats in the world.

ESCAPE FROM THE ORDINARY

Chapter 19

All ships, even sailboats, are required to have four crew to handle the lines; two on either side of the bow and stern, plus an official pilot to guide the skipper through the locks of the Panama Canal. With Dawn and her husband on board, we would need only two additional line handlers. During the journey, sailboats transit with the big ships. All have to be lifted 85 feet, cross a 31-mile freshwater lake, drop 85 feet and traverse a mile-long lake to reach the Pacific. It takes two dams, five locks, and 53 million gallons of fresh water to get a boat from one side to the other. Small boats like ours would be crammed into any spaces left by the big Panamax ships, the term for vessels that fall within the physical constraints of the canal locks; 1,000 feet long and 110 feet wide.

In Colon, the gritty city on the east end of the Canal, we were told that dozens of sailboats had been waiting weeks to transit. The sailors we talked to were dealing with the Panama Canal transit office and paperwork on their own, yet it was possible to get processed faster by hiring a ship's agent. We had already been assessed more than $1,500 in canal transit fees, a bargain compared to the alternative route requiring thousands of extra miles and risk rounding Cape Horn on the tip of South America. "What was a little more money for a ship's agent if we could include Glen's daughter on this epic journey though the canal?" we asked ourselves.

I thumbed through my journal where I kept tidbits of information passed on from other sailors and found the name of an American expat ship's agent who was the uncle of a friend of a sailor we met in Trinidad. Amazingly, the six degrees of separation seemed to hold sway, and the agent charged us a bargain price. On the spot, our agent made a call to a friend in the canal office and within minutes told us we could leave the next day for our transit. We were astounded at the results, but it might have been too good. We would have to find two additional line handlers and the hundreds of feet of line required to help secure *It's Enough* during the transit through the locks, and we'd have to do it fast.

* * * * *

True to form, a wrinkle surfaced in the last-minute planning. Before the agent left our boat, Glen asked, "What kind of marina facilities exist on the Pacific side?" Our agent's expression registered surprise, "None. The marina burned down and has not yet been rebuilt. There are some moorings, but you can't stay long—a few days."

That created a sticky situation for us as we explained to the agent, "We need to wait a couple of months for the trade winds to set in before taking off for the Galapagos Islands. Our plan had been to leave the boat at a marina on the Pacific side and travel by land in Central America until we knew we would have reliable winds for the start of our Pacific voyage. What do you suggest?"

Our ship's agent became worth every penny. "If you don't mind the old buildings and noise, I can arrange for you to keep your boat in one of the safest places in the world. There is a former boatyard right inside the last of the locks. It's called Pedro Miguel Boatyard, formerly owned by the U.S. Army. Since the American military pulled out of Panama, this boatyard has fallen through the cracks until the government figures out what to do with it. Plus, the price is right; a few dollars a day. When you're ready to leave the boatyard and transit the last lock, give me a couple days' notice and I will arrange things." He also assured us any charges for completing our transit would be included in his fee and not to worry about any additional payments. Sure enough, within hours we had aboard two sailors from another sailboat eager to gain the transit experience and our agent provided all the line we needed.

Taking in all that had happened in the span of a single day, we reeled at the speed of our progress. The next day, *It's Enough* would transit three-quarters of the Canal, stopping over in a boatyard within the Pedro Miguel Canal Lock, where we would be able to leave the sailboat and travel in Latin America until the trade winds set in. The boat would be safer there than in any marina, but to get to our temporary home, we first had to get through a nine-hour transit including three locks. The joy we felt at the great arrangements kept us from focusing on the real challenge: the transit of the Panama Canal.

The transit is a watershed event for any sailor. Filled with physical risk, there is a guaranteed extra dose of excitement for small boats. Cruise ships to canoes—everyone transits the canal with a pilot aboard to communicate with other pilot guides and canal personnel in case of problems. There is no real navigating involved, and it would be next to impossible to get lost in the Panama Canal, but one doesn't argue with the rules of a foreign country.

Jose, our stocky Panamanian pilot guide, and the two extra line handlers—with hundreds of feet of thick line—boarded *It's Enough* at 6:00 a.m. for the nine-hour canal transit adventure. Action began the moment Jose stepped aboard. He called Glen "Capitan" and asked him to assemble the crew for a briefing. Just like the supertankers!

Jose cautioned, "You all, even the Capitan, must do everything I say *immediatamente*! You are today in Panama what we call the *major league*. Yes, we play baseball here just like you do in the United States. If you do as I say, we will make it through with no problems." Jose had a sense of humor but was all business.

As sailors we quickly understood that small sailboat transits were a nuisance for the canal personnel. Our $1,500 boat transit fee was a lot of money for us, but Jose told us the big ships paid anywhere from $150,000 to $350,000. Winking, Jose conveyed what he called a fun fact, "If you want to swim through the canal, the charge is only 36 cents, but I have never seen a swimmer in the locks."

This is how it works for us small fry in the Panama Canal. Big ships tie onto the sides of the locks as they filled or emptied, and the smaller sailboats (us!) work their way in and around the cargo ships. Our sailboat would raft up next to other smaller boats or in front or behind the gigantic cargo and cruise ships. This caused Glen to liken us to bubble wrap or filler peanuts in mail packages. In concept, we would be safe from damage, but it was a dark thought to be a big ship's sacrificial packing material.

We were all worried as we approached the first lock. Everything around us was monster-sized and we were a toy boat bobbing next to gigantic vessels. Ships we dreaded at sea were suddenly right next to us, unimaginably more imposing than as blips on our radar. Jose directed us to line up behind the Nikkei Tiger, a 622-foot long, 103-foot wide cargo carrier. We became transit partners and called her our "Tiger" as we struggled to keep pace with her. As transiting ships go, Tiger was on the smaller side with room in the lock for the odd sailboat and tug. It took several attempts to heave our 150-foot lines up to the canal workers standing a distant 60 feet up on the topside of the lock. Once *It's Enough* was in place, the canal employees above held us steady with our lines as the large steel gates closed, and water poured into the lock lifting us higher.

In a textbook situation, once the water in the lock reached the level of the next lock, the gates in front of the ship opened and the *mules* (tractors on rails) pulled the ship in front of us into the second lock. In our particular case, that was when things went wrong.

Tiger started her massive engine to provide some power to go toward the tractor mules. Our little sailboat, with seven souls onboard, was tied up right behind Tiger's propeller. Everything happened in slow motion. All on board *It's Enough* fell quiet as we watched the giant propeller screw, only 20 feet in front of us, gain momentum, and start turning. Jose hastily reached for his radio when suddenly our boat began violently shaking with the force of a stray sock in a washing machine. Glen was at the helm, but we were still tied to the side of the lock. There was nothing he, or we, could do but pray our lines would hold and we would not get sucked into the ship's screw. Jose moved faster than his girth would have seemed to permit and stumbled up the tilting, quaking deck. He screamed into the radio he held in one hand and waved his arm across his neck in a kill motion. I raced to the crashing side of *It's Enough* with seat cushions and extra fenders to protect her fiberglass hull from busting against the steel side of the lock. In seconds—but what seemed an eternity—the giant propeller in front of us wound down and the water calmed inside the lock. Disaster had been averted, but it was not a good start for *It's Enough* and her rattled crew.

Jose's face was scarlet red and covered with sweat rivulets that streamed onto his shirt. "*Madre Dios!*" was the gentlest of words he used as he barked over the radio to the pilot in the ship ahead. Whatever it was those two pilots worked out between them, the Tiger moved forward using only the tractor mules. We were sidelined, like a time-out in kindergarten, then re-assigned to travel through the remainder of the canal with two large ocean-going tugboats being transferred to work the Pedro Miguel lock, our same destination.

From then on, our Panama Canal transit was textbook perfect. A series of two more locks lifted us 85 feet from sea level to Gatun Lake, which was 31 miles long. Glen pushed our sailboat engine as hard as he dared in order to make those long miles to the Pedro Miguel lock and boatyard before sunset. Towering container and cruise ships that outpaced us created waves in the otherwise still waters of the lake within the canal. Since no potential crisis loomed, we relaxed, ate, and sat surrounding Jose as he related stories of transit disasters he had personally witnessed in his seven years as a canal pilot. A number of those accidents involved sailboats colliding with large ships. It was like listening to a Stephen King audiobook: too scary to know more, but too riveting to turn off.

Completing the crossing of Lake Gatun, we readied for our three-lock descent to the Pacific Ocean. Pedro Miguel was our last descending lock, with procedures identical to the three ascending locks we had already passed. When the Pedro Miguel gates swung open, we were directed out of the canal traffic and got our first good look at the place we would call home for the next eight weeks.

As boat facilities go, Pedro Miguel boat yard was pretty bad. Its boatyard had dilapidated buildings from the era when the United States laid claim to and operated the Panama Canal. Back in the day, it had been a yacht club for the officers and soldiers stationed at one of five U.S. military bases in Panama. The grounds and buildings reflected the former grandeur of a colonial empire. The lush, green, but untended gardens; huge, shuttered jalousie windows; and creaking, hardwood, ceiling fans spoke of a different era and luxury living. Despite the present run-down condition of the yacht club building, we found it funky and charming—a shabby relic of better days. It was easy to imagine its former glory. There was still staff: a cook, a commodore who lived among us, and a paid cleaner, so it was run-down but clean. Hot showers, communal refrigerators, and unmetered electricity for the docks were bonus amenities. The cook served two-dollar lunches to sailors drinking 50-cent beer from a vending machine, and the upper floor offered a sweeping view of the ships transiting the locks. Despite the disrepair, or perhaps because of the quirkiness of the place, we formed fast friendships with other cruising sailors who, like us, needed a safe haven to leave their boat while traveling or waiting for the trade winds to establish in the Pacific.

The big setback to living inside the Panama Canal was the constant activity, noise, and ship traffic. We should have anticipated such a commotion since the canal operated 24 hours a day. The bulky ocean-going tugs were the rowdiest, working together to move large ships, creating agitation in the water surrounding our boat. At times, the wave action lurched our boat two to three feet left, then right, then forward and back. At night, the noise and sudden, violent movements startled us from our sleep.

The yacht club commodore fixed a drooping, wooden, 15-foot long (to allow for shifting) gangplank to the stern of our boat. During the daytime we had to be attentive about walking across the plank for fear of being tossed into the murky water. It was nerve jangling to have to warily scout the area for possible tug action as resident alligators lurked in the waters below. Peter Pan flew through my thoughts every time I ventured across that gangplank.

Though every day at our little yacht club was an adventure, the sleepless nights and constant commotion was all the excuse we needed to carry on with our planned land travels in Latin America. I always wanted to trek the Inca Trail from Cuzco to Machu Picchu, and it seemed like the canal gods were prodding me on.

We locked up *It's Enough* and left her to carry on as our sole witness to the nonstop action of the Panama Canal.

Chapter 20

Nauseated, sleepless, no appetite… a five-pound sledgehammer battered the inside of my head. Restless in bed, I got up to pop some aspirin for what was surely a case of altitude sickness, and force down water, water, and more water. I had been told fluids stave off high-altitude headaches, but so far, no relief; it was full-on agony.

Glen fidgeted next to me and I whispered, "Are you awake?"

Groan. Glen was also suffering. "My head is in a vise grip. We're leaving in a few hours. Will the Inca Trail be higher or lower than Cusco?"

I did not want to tell Glen that today was the first day of a four-day trek, and by afternoon we would gain another 2,000 feet in elevation.

"We should never have listened to United Mice. Those people are born at this elevation and we are coming from sea level. We need a couple more days to acclimate. How are we going to hike with such bad cases of altitude sickness?"

Glen and I had flown from the sea-level elevation of Panama to Peru the day before. Within an hour of our arrival at Cusco airport (elevation 12,000 feet), we were walking around the holiest city of the ancient Inca civilization. In the ancient Inca Quechua language, Cusco means *navel of the world*, which shows you how important it was to the Incas. In the 1400s, the Sapa Inca, their king, ruled ten million subjects over a 2,500-mile swath of the Andes Mountains. Sapa Inca was considered immortal, and his power came from both his family lineage and his religious status as the sun god.

Unlike Sapa Inca, Glen and I were feeling very mortal. We were a full 12,000 feet higher than our sea-level bodies were used to and it was hitting us hard. The owners of our six-room hotel said it would take three days for our bodies to adjust to the thinner air. I'm sure they were right, but timing is everything and it looked like our destiny was to start the trek that day.

Arriving during Inti Raymi, an Inca-era festival, was pure luck. Cusco was the place to be. Thousands of Andean villagers thought so too as they hiked through the mountains with their alpacas and llamas to gather for the festival the week of the June solstice. Inti Raymi celebrations still embraced the food, dances, music, and traditions of their ancestors. It was impossible for us to stay in our hotel room and do nothing but acclimate; there was so much happening. The Incan rituals and performances had a natural stage setting next to seventeenth century Catholic churches that had been built on top of Incan temples. Centuries before, Spanish conquistadors had laid waste to Inca monuments, thinking they needed to destroy the revered places in order to conquer the people. To build Catholic churches, conquistadores stole stones that had been precisely hand cut by Inca masons long before Columbus opened the floodgates to the Americas.

The festivities were too hard to resist, and we joined the throng in the city's square. During one of the many pageants, a man dressed as Sapa Inca was seated on a golden chair and carried to the famous ruin of Sacsayhuaman, on top of a hill overlooking the city. Brightly dressed villagers followed the procession playing music, dancing, and tossing flowers while women with brooms swept away the evil spirits. Costumed actors drummed while others danced. The entire town of Cusco was pulsating.

During a break from the pageant—before the altitude change had affected us—Glen and I strolled around and found a street with a dozen or more Cusco companies specializing in group hikes of the Inca Trail. We were drawn to the quirky company, United Mice, that had a sign in the window touting, "Daily Departures Inca Trail." We wandered inside to make reservations.

"We're interested in joining a trek of the Inca Trail to Machu Picchu that starts in three days," I told the United Mice tour operator. "We were advised to give ourselves a few days here in Cusco to acclimate before heading out."

The Peruvian United Mice guide shook his head and surprised me with, "No, you must leave tomorrow in order to arrive at the Sun Gate on the solstice. People come from all over the world to leave tomorrow. That's what the Sun Gate was designed for by the Incas." With a convincing smile he added, "We have a group of ten leaving early tomorrow morning and I can fit you both in."

The guide's strong assertion got my attention. We needed to take advantage of our unplanned and lucky travel timing. Why take the trek two days after the solstice if we could go tomorrow and see the very event for which the Sun Gate was built? That is probably why I then asked Glen the same question every delusional person does before his or her body starts protesting the lack of oxygen, "Even if we have a little altitude headache, how hard can the Inca Trail really be?"

That was before dinner, when the vise-grip headaches and nausea crept up on us, turning to full misery by nightfall. Despite the pounding, despite the nausea, at 5:00 the next morning, we stood in front of our guesthouse waiting for the United Mice van to pick us up. Our bodies were crying for oxygen and needed as little activity as possible, but the Sun Gate called to us.

In the van we met Fernando, our native Quechuan guide, as well as ten college-aged hikers with whom we would share the next four days. It was summer in Europe and the group was backpacking during their summer vacation from university. At first, they treated us a bit formally since we were as old as their parents, but once we told them our hike was a break from sailing around the world, the ice was broken, and we became fellow travelers.

The van wended up, down and through a succession of small villages. I took this as indication the hike too would be up and down. We finally stopped in a distant town where we all piled out of the van to stretch our legs and get psyched for the challenge. The camping gear we rented from United Mice was strapped on the roof of the van and would be carried by porters. We only needed to carry our daypacks. The hammering at the backside of my brow and the remains of the last meal that threatened to reappear left no room for guilty thoughts about allowing a porter to transport my supplies. Despite what might have seemed an uncaring attitude, I was thankful the small in stature, barrel-chested porters made it look effortless as they strapped our packs to their backs and, yes, foreheads, with thick ribbons of fabric. The burdened porters struck out ahead at a trot as the group excitedly filed in behind Fernando.

Twenty minutes into the walk, Fernando held up his hand and had us gather in a circle by a river crossing. "Come here, my family. Time to eat coca leaves," he announced, handing out bursting zip-lock bags of the dark green leaves. Coca is legal in Peru, and according to our guide, conditions required a medicinal application. Besides, according to Fernando, it would take much greater quantities of the leaves to make even a tiny bit of cocaine. Still gathered in a circle, Fernando instructed us to pick out the four best leaves, and we made an offering to the Inca mountain gods asking that they look after us on the trail.

After our ceremony, the guide gave us the Incan equivalent of a pep talk, "Please feel the energy of the nature, the mountains, the river, the Mother Earth," and requested we keep a positive attitude. "Machu Picchu is behind many, many mountains," he warned. Before we continued, Fernando encouraged us to stuff our mouth with as many coca leaves as possible, and following instructions, the dry leaves were processed with saliva into a wet wad tucked into my cheeks. On the edge of my tongue I was noticing numbness... I wasn't sure if Fernando's assessment of the lack of narcotic effect was right. However, all hesitation evaporated after chewing a couple of coca leaves. They immediately eased the impact of my altitude sickness.

"I prefer the tea over the leaf," one of the young Dutchmen declared, referring to the ever-present *mate de coca* tea we had been drinking to ease the nauseating symptoms. Coca tea is a mild, common drink in the Andes and helps greatly with altitude sickness. The tea did taste better but chewing the bitter coca leaves took care of my queasiness faster. Our group looked like a line of hiking chipmunks with wads of coca leaves mulching in our cheeks.

We started out too fast for comfort, as though a starting gun had fired and we were in some type of race. Hours later, we paused for a breather at the first Inca ruins on the trail, an outpost with neatly tiered terraces overlooking a river. Machu Picchu may be the most impressive of the settlements, but it's not the only one. In the coming days, as our legs jellified along the up-and-down trail, we would visit scenic ruins hidden by the mountains for centuries. Along the way, Fernando taught us about the precise stonecutting and masonry of his ancestors, as well as the original layouts and purpose of the structures. At the more-intact ruins we could make out what had been complex irrigation systems and sacrificial altars to the Inca gods.

The porters were the true heroes of our Machu Picchu trek. As sure-footed as mountain goats and, though small, each was able to carry a 50-pound sack on his back that contained most of our personal belongings, all the tents, food, and cooking supplies. As quiet as predators stalking prey, they padded up and down the trail at breakneck speed, their battered, swollen toes tucked into tire-rubber sandals. The porters chewed coca leaves in large quantities to stave off fatigue, wrapping the leaves in black, acidic potash for stronger effect. I tried that combination once—that was enough! So potent, it burned little ulcers into my chipmunk cheeks. The good-natured porters smiled at our headaches and prepared coca tea, which we all drank at meals. As unpleasant as the coca leaves tasted and felt in my mouth, I chewed a hearty wad before the steep climbs. The leaves made a huge difference in my energy level and continued to ease my headaches. There was no doubt, those leaves gave our group that boost we needed to keep the spring in our step on what would prove to be a very hard trek.

"You see how thin we are," our nimble guide jokingly told us and patted his flat stomach. I could feel my clothes loosening as well. Whether it was the coca leaves or altitude, I never felt hungry. Fernando encouraged us all to eat something at each meal in order to have the energy to take on the challenging terrain.

It was with great satisfaction that we reached the highest summit, Dead Woman's Pass, early on the second day. With utter amazement, I looked back at the distance we had traveled and hugged Glen, "We did it!" Looking toward the direction of the mountains between Machu Picchu and us, Glen offered, "Don't celebrate yet, we still have days to go."

My sense of triumph evaporated as we traversed down the mountain on baby-sized steps built of uneven stones that sometimes slid under our feet. Going down was far harder than climbing up. If the height and width of the steps were any indication, the Incans must have had truly small feet. When we finally reached camp that afternoon, I collapsed in the dirt next to my tent the porters had erected, too tired to unzip the door and crawl inside. Though exhausted, I woke several times during the night gasping for breath; the lack of oxygen in my brain felt like I was smothering. Propped up to relieve the pressure on my lungs, I was finally able to catch a few hours' sleep, but I dreamt in psychedelic greens and purples with strange themes. I don't know if it was the altitude or the coca leaves, but those visions and my raspy breathing were downright scary.

"Dress like an onion," we had been told at the United Mice office when we signed up. "Peel your layers as the temperature changes by the hour." June is winter in Peru and days on the trail were mostly around 65 to 70 degrees, but at sunset, it could plunge to freezing. We assembled for group breakfast and dinner at camp in frigid weather, sitting elbow to elbow for warmth, wearing everything we had packed. During the day we stripped down to running shorts and shirtsleeves as we sweated in the sun. The sun disappeared early behind the towering mountains and after dinner, Glen and I would huddle in our sleeping bags, reading books by headlamp and dressed in all our layers of onion skin.

After breakfast, our group would leave the camp as porters began packing. By midmorning they sped easily past us on the trail as though out for an afternoon stroll, their loads tied to their backs and heads with straps. Running ahead in order to find a good site to cook our simple, high-carb midday meal, they then hurried to the next stop to set up our tents at a campsite before we arrived. Around noon we would see them in the distance, squatted next to a stream, making lunch. Lunch for me was more of a break than a meal. None of our group had much of an appetite and Fernando told us loss of hunger was a symptom of altitude sickness. We forced ourselves to eat the bread, cheese, tomatoes and cucumbers.

During our days of pain and exhaustion, the normal barriers between 12 strangers quickly disappeared. Nothing seemed out of bounds to discuss and loose bowels became a normal topic of conversation. Our group tried to figure out what was causing the condition and how it could be stopped. We used iodine tablets to purify the drinking water from mountain springs that was boiled at camp for our pasta. Other than putting our bodies through strenuous activity, the exact cause was hard to pinpoint. However, we were eating food bought before we set out on the trail—carried heroically by our porters, but without refrigeration. By day three, we couldn't help but wonder: Why was there still chicken?

Between a decreased appetite and diarrhea, if you are looking to lose weight, a high-altitude trek is almost guaranteed to bring results. Fernando smiled and told us another week of hiking at altitude would toughen us up. No one piped up to volunteer. On the fourth and final day, we awoke to darkness at 3:30 in the morning. Fernando told us our goal was to reach the Sun Gate by sunrise. There we would catch our first glimpse of Machu Picchu. Soon after we departed camp, the porters rushed past our group, on the narrow, dark trail. Unlike their trotting gait of the past three days, it was almost as if they were running from something. It was the opposite, Fernando told us. The reason behind the 3:30 a.m. wakeup call was so our porters could pack up the campsite and race down the mountain in time to catch the early morning train back to Cusco. The porters would haul packs for a different group the next day.

Fernando led us, in the early morning darkness, on what could only be described as a mad dash through the last four miles to the ancient city. Our steps, previously slow and careful, came with a risky urgency in pitch-black conditions along a trail bordering a cliff. Glen and I fell to the back of the line and saw a very fit young man in front of us take a misstep in the dark—crying out as he disappeared off the trail. Our entire group stood stunned at the edge of the cliff. No one said a word as we all peered down the mountainside. The young hiker was surely a goner. But then, from about 15 feet down the cliff, we heard him calling for help. His daypack had snagged a branch and saved him. It was pure luck and sound stitching on his pack that kept him alive that day. Cutting through the dark with our small flashlights it took us a good half hour and some rope from our guide (had this happened before?) to retrieve him safely in the dark. Even seasoned and confident Fernando appeared a bit shaken over the incident, and we continued at a more reasonable pace.

Almost from the moment explorer Hiram Bingham stumbled, slack jawed, upon the ruins of Machu Picchu 100 years ago, experts have struggled to figure out why the Incas chose such a remote setting to build a temple. Even their descendants don't understand the remote location. Fernando believed the area was chosen because it is relatively open among the other mountains, and the buildings at Machu Picchu were designed specifically to interact with the sun, stars and surrounding landscape. Despite the drama on the trail, we arrived with plenty of time to join other trekker groups in witnessing the sunrise through the Sun Gate on winter solstice. On our fourth day of trekking, we were finally there. On that day of the year only, a beam of light shines through a window in the gate, forming a mysterious rectangle atop a granite slab.

What United Mice failed to mention was that Machu Picchu was usually misty at daybreak. Because of the thick haze, we could barely make out the ray of light. We knew that it must be there. I would like to say that the scarcely visible beam of light through the ancient, stone window was worth the altitude sickness. Since there are no do-overs with this kind of adventure, we agreed that, yes, it was totally worth it. At least memorable.

After a short rest at the Sun Gate, we continued our trek to the lost city of Machu Picchu where the magnitude of our journey came into focus. Our group was exhausted, but we possessed a kind of exhilaration that set us apart from the bored-looking tourists pouring out of the stream of tour buses and filling in around us.

Fernando noticed our dissatisfaction with the jostling crowds and said, "That's what happens when you've been on the Inca trail for four days. You no longer feel like a tourist." He nailed it. Arriving at Machu Picchu through the back door upped the experience. Though Machu Picchu was tremendous, for me, the journey far surpassed the destination.

Another two weeks in Peru convinced Glen and me that nothing either of us had ever seen or experienced equaled the range and diversity of that country. From 14,000 feet in the Andes to the indigenous Amazon River tribes, we did not have time to see all we would have liked or to process all we saw.

Eventually, no matter how fantastic a place, sailors have to bow to the wisdom of the trade winds. According to the weather forecasts, the Pacific trade winds were setting in and it was time for us to return to our boat in Panama and each begin our separate tasks to get ready for whatever the Pacific Ocean offered.

Chapter 21

L iving in the small space of a boat can be a challenge to relationships. The most frequently asked question about living aboard a boat has always been, "How did your marriage survive such close quarters?" The short answer is, "It takes a lot of work." Self-awareness and willingness to talk things out before they become issues are a great start. But what really helped me feel like a vital and equal member onboard was to embrace the clear division of labor practiced among cruising sailors broken down into what is widely called Pink and Blue tasks.

Ask any cruising couple about those two colors and they will describe their onboard division of labor. In the world of liveaboard cruising, men perform Blue tasks such as installing, maintaining and repairing everything mechanical and electronic on the boat. Women accomplish the traditional Pink jobs of provisioning the food, cooking, and laundry, just to name a few. Cleaning on board *It's Enough* was a shared duty according to personal preference. For example, I enjoyed donning my snorkel gear and scrubbing the algae and growth off the bottom of the boat. It was great exercise and I loved to clean things that showed a radical before and after improvement. Glen enjoyed washing the salt off the topsides of the boat, but since neither of us enjoyed polishing the stainless to keep the rust off, we did that task together.

Before we went sailing, I read about the Pink and Blue in the sailing magazines and it did not bother me. It made sense that two people living on a boat needed to keep out of each other's way space-wise as well as have mission areas to call their own. Plus there had always been a male-female division of labor in Glen's and my marriage. Though we never labeled it as such, we always had distinct Pink and Blue tasks.

Glen loved his Blue projects. No endeavor was too big for him to tackle and lack of experience was no barrier. The bigger the project the more likely it was to interest him. Some examples of Glen's project savvy included: building a 2,400 sq. ft. home with his own hammer and nails, restoring vintage cars, restoring a 1946 airplane, and other mechanical jobs too numerous to recount. Glen rocks in the area of Blue projects. What most people would never consider tackling are within Glen's considerable skill set. So the Blue tasks were well in hand.

But everything was not so smooth with my Pink tasks. Deployments aside, while serving as an Army officer, I was not pulling my weight in the household chores arena. In our home, the Pink task of cooking was performed half-heartedly. But before jumping to the conclusion that I am lazy, let me give you some background.

When I first met Glen, I was living in a bare-bones, studio-size Army bachelor officer quarters. My idea of an evening meal after work was a salad. I took sandwiches to work and ate at the field mess hall when deployed. There were times when I was known to eat cereal for breakfast, lunch and dinner. All that changed when I met Glen. I started doing all kinds of loving and frankly, very uncharacteristic things to make him happy. The most out of character thing I did was cook. I bought a cookbook, a slow cooker, special kitchen tools... I planned nice dinners, wrote up grocery lists for ingredients, and selected nice wines to go with meals, all lovingly prepared by yours truly. Along the way, I discovered that eating well could be a real pleasure and often worth the time involved to prepare and clean up afterwards. But I could not sustain it. After a while, and curiously, soon after we got married, sacrifices had to be made for work, and the first to go was my real effort at cooking.

Before sailing, I started my day early with exercise, was aggressive about laundry chores and tackled cleaning with gusto. I kept things tidy and organized like one might expect from a life in the military. But cooking rankled me as a female stereotype, partly because I came of age during the first wave of the women's movement. In those days, women who wanted to make it in a *man's world*, shunned female stereotypes. My mother, a commercial pilot, reinforced that. She went out of her way to mold my sister and me into professionally minded women who valued accomplishment. Mom would not let either of us sign up for home economics or typing classes (big mistake there) during high school. It worked—my sister, who holds a number of aviation patents, happily works 50-60-hour weeks as an engineer. And I am ashamed to say that the first time I realized the importance of said Pink tasks was about a year before Glen and I retired and went sailing.

The importance of Pink jobs first came home when a sailing friend named Dan asked Glen and me to join him as crew to reposition his sailboat from Los Angeles to Puerto Vallarta, Mexico. Dan and his wife had just retired, bought the boat and planned to cruise the coast of Mexico until they got their confidence up to cruise the Pacific Ocean. The plan was for Dan, Glen and me to sail their boat down to Puerto Vallarta as a delivery trip. Susie, the wife, was not so keen on the whole boat plan and wanted to be close to her grandchildren. She instead planned to fly down to Mexico and meet us once we had the boat safely at dock in Puerto Vallarta.

Though slammed with work, Glen and I took leave and signed on as crew, primarily because I wanted to experience offshore sailing and understand what it felt like to be alone on watch, solely responsible for sail adjustments, navigation and the safety of all aboard. Neither of us could miss work for more than two weeks, so Dan agreed on a delivery-type, accelerated passage. In what proved a lop-sided arrangement, Glen and I agreed to cover our flight expenses while Dan and Susie would provision the food for the two-week trip.

The couple sounded grateful and accommodating over the phone, "Just show up at the LA airport—we'll take you to the marina and depart the docks the next morning. That will leave you with a few days on the other end to enjoy Puerto Vallarta and preview the leisure life of a cruising sailor."

Imagine our surprise when Glen and I arrived on the boat and found that numerous major projects needed to be done before we could depart, and Dan had no idea where to start. Glen spent the first long day on boat repairs while I cleaned, and Dan organized chaotic piles of newly purchased boat equipment. Checking out the galley storage, I discovered that the only food aboard was Cups of Soup, Ramen noodles, oatmeal, candy bars, and instant coffee. No fruit, vegetables, eggs or hearty food. Army field rations would have been far better. I kept opening the cabinets and looking under the floorboards, figuring the real food must be squirreled away somewhere. When I finally accepted that Susie had dropped the ball on the provisioning, I told Dan and Glen the situation.

Embarrassed, Dan shrugged and told us to do whatever we wanted. Glen stayed on the boat to help with the last of the projects and I took a taxi to the grocery store, stocking up on cans of chili, pasta, ground meat, bread, onions, apples, bananas… and Oreos for scurvy. That two-week passage is still painfully memorable. Despite my last-minute provisioning trip, I had no meal plan and did not know how to properly store unrefrigerated fruits and vegetables. We ran out of some foods right away and others spoiled before we could consume them. All the *good food* was eaten or overripe to the point of being the home for fruit flies within days. That experience made me realize several key sailing musts:

Food is a big morale factor on a boat. Your crew will brave storms and the threat of pirates if they eat well.

Eat your best things right away. Saving the good fruits and vegetables for special occasions will cause them to be lost. Previously refrigerated fruits and vegetables ripen fast and will not wait.

Never, ever, skimp or try to be frugal when it comes to buying quality food for a sailing passage. It's important to make the extra effort and cook meals that are satisfying and appetizing. There will be long periods (weeks for sure) when there will be no other option but to eat your own cooking. And then you can only make meals from ingredients you thoughtfully provisioned weeks before and correctly stored for long shelf life.

I lost weight during that simple passage between Los Angeles and Puerto Vallarta. Psychologically, I was unsatisfied with meals that felt more like snacking. When we arrived in Puerto Vallarta, Glen and I both felt misused and could not wait to get off the boat. Looking back, I learned valuable lessons. On the plus side, I earned experience with solo watch-keeping on a 10-day passage. On the down side, what I clearly lacked was the ability to plan, provision, store and cook meals that mattered over long periods of time on a boat.

Another valuable lesson I learned carried over into all aspects of my life. When someone does something nice for you, be appreciative. Really appreciative. Glen and I vowed to never treat anyone with ingratitude and lean always in the direction of generosity and respect. Friends and family members have joined us on our boat all over the world and we emerged from those close living situations as better friends than when we started. Good feelings and respect make life aboard enjoyable, even under trying conditions.

The gift from that experience was the high regard I realized for the so-called Pink tasks. Afterwards I bought a couple of cookbooks for sailors with detailed instructions for baking bread, washing clothes in a bucket, and how to safely store foods that are normally refrigerated. Some of the information sounded extreme, but there were times when all that remained in the pantry were canned goods and rice. For the first year, I used the sailing cookbooks nearly every day. They taught me which spices can jazz up rice and mystery canned goods (sometimes labels fall off in the humidity). Plus, they also provided assorted hints such as how to use vinegar to make hard cheese last for months, how to make bread, how to prevent and get rid of mold on just about anything, and how to extend the life of unrefrigerated eggs. By the third year, I could have written an improved cookbook with all the tips I had learned from other *pink* sailors. Those included; how to buy and store fruits and vegetables to last longer, how to pick fresh foods with the longest shelf life (let's hear it for cabbage, onions and garlic), and working around limited refrigeration without poisoning all aboard.

Generally, the more effort I put into the Pink tasks, the better our life was in all respects. I started thinking of myself as a kind of sailing pioneer woman in all things related to cooking and eating at sea. And I never again considered the art and science of domestic chores beneath me.

Chapter 22

With Glen on his Blue tasks and me on the Pink tasks, it wasn't long before everything was ready for us to leave the funky boatyard inside the Panama Canal and set sail across the Pacific Ocean. Leaving the Americas was a big commitment. Turning back would be like trying to paddle upstream in a raging, whitewater river—maybe something like that day at Angel Falls. The southwest trade winds push sailors westward and the only way back was the long way, around the far side of the world. Supplies and fuel would not always be available in the hundreds of islands that lay before us, but we had done our homework on where to stop. Looking at a navigation chart of the vast Pacific Ocean, I was humbled and apprehensive. My eyes followed the countless specks of islands, many of which we would be happy to explore within the next seven months. After that time, we would have to vamoose away from the warmer latitudes to avoid tropical cyclone season. I could hardly take in the vast distance—a full 7,500 miles—between where we were in the Panama Canal and where we would end up in New Zealand, seven months later. Averaging six to seven knots under sail we could just make it on time if we did not linger too long in any one place. It was a tricky balance to enjoy the journey, only sail in good weather forecasts, while keeping our eyes on the tropical cyclone picture.

There was much that needed to be done to prepare the boat and ourselves. It was like graduating from sailing high school and showing up for graduate school the next day. The equipment and supplies required to voyage across the vast reaches of the Pacific Ocean were nearly endless. Glen was changing oil, replacing water desalinization membranes, and buying spare parts to stow on board. I was provisioning (*grocery shopping* in my former life) and attempting to find room to store enough food and canned goods to last for at least three months—the time it would take to traverse the more remote Pacific islands. We wanted to avoid paying triple the price for everyday food items if we could.

At the thought of our Pacific exploration, I felt like a thoroughbred at the starting gate pawing the ground in anticipation of them being thrown open. Glen, however, kept me reined in with the threat of dire consequences: "We'll be sorry if we don't fix this…" The repairs were small, but the maintenance and preparation lists were large. I became a daily customer at the Panama version of Costco, where I bought enough staples and canned goods to lower our boat in the water several inches. Glen left me to accomplish the pink tasks without question until one day I was rolling a small barrel container of olives down the dock and needed his help to get it aboard. Eyeing my burden, "Julie, you bought enough kalamata olives to get us around the entire world."

Looking up from the floorboards where I was trying to find room to wedge the barrel, "Ahhh, you say that now, but you will cherish them sautéed with freshly caught tuna." Point taken though and after that I kept moderation in mind—less so because of Glen's comment and more so because there simply was not much storage space left. I appreciated that spare parts take priority over olives.

After a week of intense scrubbing, stowing, repairing, and maintenance, we were at last ready to depart the unusual little haven inside the Panama Canal and navigate the last lock to open water. Our trusty ship's agent was as good as his word: a canal pilot, as well as line handlers with long ropes showed up for a pleasingly uneventful passage through the final portion of the canal. The buildings of Panama City and our life in the Americas vanished as we sought the open sea. The sails of *It's Enough* filled and billowed with trade winds off the port (left) rear quarter. She heeled ever so slightly and seemed to lean toward the Galápagos Islands with the same excitement we felt.

It was great to be back on the ocean. The unobstructed view of the constellations felt like old, familiar friends and the stars poked holes in the darkness with a bright, winking intensity—just as they would have appeared to earth's ancient sailors using stars to steer by. It had been months since we last sailed, but I flowed easily back into the feeling of being disconnected from the rest of the world. Interrupted only by occasional static on our radio, we were all alone.

Since Panama, our Single Sideband radio now possessed a wonderful advantage; we could send and receive short email messages. As one of his departure projects, Glen, a super-smart electronics engineer, had installed an improved modem that converted radio waves into digitized email messages. It was extremely slow and limited in message length, but the thrill of email on the open seas kept me busy writing updates to family and friends. We had been able to send expensive and short email bursts before, using an outdated satellite system. Now, at no cost, we could send and receive nearly unlimited one-page texts. It was the sailors' equivalent of using hot lead for early typesetting, but I found pleasure in those connections. I'm sure friends and family back home tired of my elated dispatches in their email inbox. I can just imagine folks saying, "Oh it's just another dispatch from Julie telling us what kind of fish they caught, how many ships they passed, or how many miles they sailed in the last 24 hours." What may have been humdrum to them, was bliss to me. We had experienced quite enough excitement so far, and I fully appreciated that things were so easy on our first Pacific passage.

An added advantage of the new email system was that we could now reliably receive weather faxes and forecast. Twice daily, Glen downloaded and interpreted the weather information, easing concerns about what the conditions of our coming days and nights would be like.

I was happy to be out at sea again. There is nothing like being at sea for days and weeks on end, in a small boat with someone you love and admire. I felt small in the universe, but vital in our own little world.

Quickly we fell into our boat routine, dividing the day into six-hour watches at the helm. I pulled the midnight to 6:00 a.m. shift, which allowed me to gaze at the stars. The wind at night was normally lighter than during the daytime, so besides adjusting the sails to minor wind shifts, my duties consisted mostly of checking for shipping traffic on radar and occasionally scanning the horizon with night-vision goggles. The quiet of night suited me.

Days were filled with cooking, cleaning, reading, and napping. One of us was always the designated watch person responsible for avoiding ships or large floating obstacles in our path. A couple times we were startled by big, weird floating objects, such as a sofa-sized fishing buoy trailing who knows how many miles of net in its wake. Our diligence and raw luck kept us free from the dangers of that giant expanse of ocean.

Long sailing passages cross deep ocean waters where fish are few and far between, so catching fish to supplement our diet was not something we could count on. Ever hopeful, we trawled a fishing line, and a day out of Panama hooked a small tuna, that started out as dinner that evening and ended up days later as fish tacos. We spotted a rare, leatherback turtle paddling its way to the Galápagos for what we imagined his spring migration. The sighting readied us for what was yet to come ahead in the Galápagos archipelago.

The quiet voyage was making me more self-aware and I found myself opening up to a kinder, gentler way of life. In contrast to my black and white military world, this was the full-spectrum color of truly living. I felt humbled and exhilarated at the same time, constantly close to the wonders and forces of nature.

Just as all the hardships, challenges, and rough spots in my life brought me to where I was, so had nature adapted and evolved man into the life forms we are today. It was fitting that the birthplace of Darwin's theory of natural selection and evolution would be our first landfall in the Pacific Ocean. I became more excited the closer we drew.

From Panama to the Galápagos Islands we sailed in sunshine, pushed by 15-20 knot trade winds. I hoped this implied a trend and explained why the ocean was called *Pacific*. A few days before reaching the Galápagos, I noticed the grid coordinates looked wacky: the latitude read south instead of north. Down was up! With no fanfare, bells, or whistles, we had crossed into the Southern Hemisphere on the bottom side of the world.

Days later during his watch, Glen called out, "Land Ho!" Startled awake from a nap, I squinted to see the first low island of the Galápagos archipelago come into view.

At sea, the waves and sun had lulled me into an unhurried contentment, but with the promise of the now visible island, I readied for arrival. Rummaging through the flag locker, I pulled out the yellow Q (quarantine) flag and continued to dig until I found the Ecuadorian courtesy flag. I unfurled those as well as the American flag, attaching them to the spreader and stern flag pole. We entered the harbor looking very official and correct, but I was overcome by less formal feelings. This was the Galápagos—we had arrived!

Anchored in the tiny harbor of Wreck Bay, San Cristobal Island—one of 13 islands spread across 17,000 square miles of ocean—we did poor jobs of reining in our enthusiasm. Driven by anticipation, we made quick work of launching the dinghy and motored to a public dock. Shiny brown sea lions, slick with drying seawater, had come ashore to enjoy an afternoon siesta in the sun. Beyond them, the beach was lined with hundreds more of their fat, bold cousins barking at one another as they jockeyed for position. Basking sea lions covered the decks of a sailboat unlucky enough to have steps on its rear transom, providing easy access for both humans and those impudent animals. Without land-based predators, the sea lions lacked fear and neither moved nor took notice as we stepped over them. Clearly, we humans were a mere postscript on the Galápagos.

Leaving the dock with our entrance permit, Glen and I were astonished at our good fortune. Instead of issuing the usual sailing permit for cruising only two islands with a guide required on board, we were permitted 20 days to visit four islands without a guide. Thinking back to other good fortunes on our journey, I should have been wary of that gift. A guide would have deepened our understanding of what we would be seeing, but Glen and I were not comfortable about having a stranger onboard for weeks in such close quarters. We decided to forego a guide and explore the extraordinary wildlife paradise on our own. It turned out to be one of the bigger errors of our circumnavigation.

* * * * *

Our first stop was an ATM in town to get Ecuadorian money. What a surprise when the machine spit out brand new U.S. dollars. We were unaware that the country had stopped printing its own money and switched to the U.S. dollar as their currency. Ecuador had just *dollarized*. It was befuddling how a country could simply decide to use another's currency, but it turned out to be —for us— financially beneficial. Perhaps because the conversion was new, the exchange rate greatly favored the American dollar. Everything we needed—fuel, restaurants, and food—were very affordable and we were glad for the break after the endless, unplanned expenses we had already incurred. Our first dinner ashore of pizza, beer, bottled water, and tip totaled less than three dollars—a bargain at twice the price! We quickly calculated it would be cheaper to eat on shore than cook the canned provisions we had bought in Panama. The olives would keep.

There was so much to explore, and we hoped our 20-day visa would give us enough time. With thousands of species of wildlife in the Galápagos, we felt a budding urgency to see as much as we could. The creatures on the islands lived without predators and showed no fear. Their tameness was eerie and disconcerting. The similarity to the theme of Jurassic Park, where the animals were emboldened to become the ones in charge, provided a reminder that not all is harmonious in a world where life seems to have forgotten the rules of evolution.

A real guide would have so enriched our understanding of all we encountered. With only a skimpy guidebook to inform, we tried to understand the wonders: a species of delicate, innocent-looking finches called *vampires* pecked at other birds and drank their blood; fluffy, masked booby chicks routinely killed their siblings to improve their own chance of survival; and the male albatrosses, with wingspans wider than a man is tall, gang raped their females as they returned from sea. The more we saw and read, the more we were weirdly reminded of Jurassic Park.

We beached our dinghy on an uninhabited island next to a sea lion that had just given birth, the afterbirth still dripping into the water.

Careful to avoid her and her baby, we then took care not to inadvertently crush underfoot some type of rare bird that might be standing on the trail—defiant of our approach. It was like a place where dinosaurs interacted with the other inhabitants.

As a child I was terrified by the movie *The Birds*, an Alfred Hitchcock thriller that turned the bird population into vicious predators of humans. I had to force those creepy images from my head as we approached thousands of breeding pairs of blue-footed boobies, masked boobies, and most of the world's population of waved albatross. The blue-footed boobies were engaged in a bizarre foot-fetish ritual foreplay, ever so slowly lifting each blue foot to show their prospective mates. I wondered about the evolutionary origin of such a strange mating ritual; could a naturalist guide have told us?

While swimming off the back of the boat near another of the islands, I told Glen I wanted to see the Galápagos penguins. "I think they're swimming right toward you!" he said excitedly and pointed to a small colony of aquatic, flightless birds approaching us. They had spotted me in the water and were coming to investigate the strange new creature in the neighborhood. On another island we looked forward to morning visits from a sweet, little goldfinch who would land next to us and offered a song in exchange for a bit of breakfast toast.

Everywhere we went, birds landed in bushes just a few feet away and scrutinized the new bipeds. Their interest in us gave ample time to thumb through our bird book to identify the peeping Toms. Iguanas, in shades of neon greens and blues, basked on rocks around the trails. Though we never stepped on one, their disinterest in our presence certainly made it possible.

The pesky sea lions possessed a strong sense of entitlement; several climbed aboard our dinghy on the beach while we walked and explored the island. We yelled loudly and clapped our hands until they begrudgingly left, but not without protest. In the end, they hopped away surprisingly fast on their flippers to find a quieter place to snooze.

Following a well-worn path through a parched forest of low, native manzanillo trees, we encountered four giant tortoises munching on leaves. Bumping one another as they fed, they moved at their turtles' pace, clanking shells sounding like coconuts being knocked together. Undisputedly, giant tortoises are the main attraction on the Galápagos. After all, the islands were named for them.

Galápago is an archaic Spanish word for saddle, a reference to the shape of the tortoises' shells. Darwin first documented the tortoises in 1835, and they lived there still—almost two centuries later. Once numbering as many as 100,000, the tortoise population had declined to critically low numbers. They were nearly wiped out during the old days of seafaring when they were captured and stacked upside down in the holds of ships to be used later as food. The tortoises survived for years in that manner and provided a source of fresh meat as the sailors harvested them, working through the layers. Darwin, the scientist who marveled at the giant animals, noted in his journals that not only did he attempt to ride atop their shells, but that "the young tortoises make excellent soup."

* * * * *

At the start of our voyage, we marveled at the number of people sailing around the world at any given time, even sailors and boats from land-locked countries such as Switzerland and Paraguay. The common pursuit established a bond between sailors, the type of bond that fosters concerns for one another and prompts you to offer aid when needed. When we set sail, we became part of a floating community of friends. In the Pacific Ocean, the bond was even stronger as we joined the ranks of others who made the same enormous commitment to leave the Americas and cross the vast Pacific. The odds were great our path would come across those same sailors with whom we once shared an anchorage in a remote bay. Galápagos, the first stop for most Pacific crossings, underscored that strong relationship among the community of sailors.

Nearing the expiration of our Galápagos visa and nearing departure, I was on shore buying last-minute food items for our upcoming non-stop, 3,500-mile passage to French Polynesia. Glen had stayed on the boat to study the weather fax, but when I returned to *It's Enough*, Glen was not onboard. Since I had taken the dinghy to shore, I was puzzled by his absence. That qualifies as a full-scale mystery when you live on a sailboat. I checked the water around the boat; maybe he had donned a snorkel and was scrubbing the algae off the bottom—but no Glen. I checked the engine compartment—no Glen. As I continued my search, I heard what sounded like Glen's voice on the boat anchored next to us. I reboarded the dinghy and rode over. Chaos ensued.

Jonathan, the captain of the neighboring boat, had gone to shore with his two young daughters and ordered drinking water to be delivered to their boat. The local Ecuadoran who brought the water was puzzled and complained in Spanish about being asked to deliver 100 gallons of water to a tank that took so little. The boat's fuel and water tank were both on the same side of the cockpit, and by mistake the workers pumped fresh water into what was actually the fuel tank. The wife, Caroline, alone on the boat, realized what had happened when she saw the oil and water overflow from the fuel tank. With her husband still ashore, she panicked and yelled over to Glen in hopes the situation could be fixed before her husband and daughters called for pick-up from their errands. Glen knew there would be no fast, simple solution, but he thought it likely they could extract the water without damaging the engine. I understood the gravity of their situation and hoped Glen's fix would work. The remote Galápagos was not ideal for finding parts for rebuilding an engine.

When Jonathan, the husband, returned with their two small daughters, he went into a mild state of shock and told us, "This isn't even our sailboat. It belongs to my brother. We are sailing it from Europe to Australia where he will meet us with his family and take it the rest of the way. I don't know how to fix this." Glen laid out the work intensive solution and together they spent close to two days inside that engine compartment in the equatorial heat. Glen saved their engine—along with the sailing dreams of two families.

That incident reminded me that there are 1,001 things that can go wrong on any boat, and this was a prime example of just one. A devastating one, to be sure—but not one I believed could happen to us—at least not going forward, not with that experience behind us. Though we desalinated our own drinking water onboard, we did need a fuel delivery for our upcoming passage. A lesson learned, Glen and I both monitored the refueling operation, which fell far short of the western-level safety standards to which we were accustomed. A large powerboat motored alongside *It's Enough* loaded with 55-gallon fuel containers on high platforms. The workers took turns inhaling on a long rubber tube to siphon diesel into our sailboat. It was unnerving to watch them, time after time, suck up a mouthful of diesel, spit it out, and keep fueling until our tanks were full.

* * * * *

The next passage would take about three weeks, so we needed as many fresh eggs, fruits and vegetables as we could store. It was time for a big food provisioning and the fresher, the better. We knew from experience that if a food item had ever been refrigerated, it would rot within days in weather and sun intense enough to crack the rubber on my Teva sandals. Produce needed to be picked while still green, then ripen gradually in hanging net baskets strung from the ceiling near the galley. Most produce arrived from mainland Ecuador already ripe or past its prime, but with the use of our limited Spanish, we found success buying fresh produce out of home gardens. We would return to the boat with crates of eggs, heads of cabbage, dozens of onions... though our stock of olives was still sufficient. I used our quantity of galley-sized string hammocks as a guide for purchase planning but wished for more netting, as the upcoming passage would be the longest stretch in the entire world without anywhere to stop. I filled the nets we had to bursting.

Leaving the islands, we visited Post Office Bay, simply a barrel for sending and receiving mail that was situated in the same place on shore for more than 300 years. Centuries ago, ships would stop at the bay, pick up any mail on their route, and leave mail to be picked up by a ship headed in the direction of the addressee. Visiting sailors like us kept the tradition alive. Looking through the barrel, surrounded by memorabilia dating back to the whaling ships of the 1800s, we found cards addressed to Colorado, Paris, Canada... connecting us to the lives of those whalers from so long ago.

Post Office Bay was our last stop. It was time to begin the next and longest leg of our circumnavigation, more than 3,500 miles from the Galápagos to the Marquesas Islands in French Polynesia. We calculated the trip would take 18 to 25 days, depending upon the strength of the wind. Radio contact with boats that had departed the week before helped set our expectations. Those sailors had not benefitted from wind for the first 600 miles and had been forced to motor a long distance. Though we carried enough diesel to motor about 1,000 miles, we hoped the trade winds would kick up and allow us to sail most of the way. If we were forced to use fuel, we knew replacement diesel would be very expensive and hard to find in much of French Polynesian—and not available at all in Fatu Hiva, our first planned landfall.

With my fruits and vegetables ripening at an alarming rate in the tropical heat, I was raring to go. Memories of prior impulsive departures helped me restrain myself, and we waited at anchor (not patiently) for Glen to download and study the weather fax. Finally, he gave our departure a nod, and we pulled anchor, steering south of our desired course to pick up reliable trade winds.

As we got underway, Glen shared the weather picture with a couple of other yachts also aimed for the Marquesas, and we arranged a nightly radio net with them. Good winds were with us as we plotted our course past the last island in the archipelago. French Polynesia—only 3,500 miles to go.

* * * * *

During the passage from Galápagos to the Marquesas Islands there was no possibility of stopping in that vast stretch of ocean. Years before, while priming myself for our early retirement and sailing voyage, I read an account of a woman who was so afraid of that great expanse of isolation, she had her appendix removed to have one less thing to worry about. At the time I laughed, thinking it an extreme act, but as we started on the same passage, I experienced random aches and pains and my brain spun out unproductive and fearful thoughts. On our first night, I had a nightmare that my appendix had burst, and I hailed a large ship in the distance to come save me. I woke crying and went to the cockpit in search of fresh air and comfort from Glen. My mental state must have scared Glen. Instead of comforting me he told me I was on dangerous territory with my mind; that kind of thinking could make it happen, and I needed to learn to control my thoughts, mind, and body. He was right, of course. When I ignored my pains, they spun away, and it was as if they never existed. When I focused on them, they worsened, and no amount of internal conversation lessened what felt to be real. Keeping my mind in check during that long passage became part of my job.

We were making good time—our hull sliced the water like a warm knife through soft butter. The trade winds stayed steady even through the night and pushed us forward. We were fortunate to have a downwind rig; our aesthetically pleasing red, white and blue, butterfly-looking design, poled out on each side to form 180 degrees of massive propulsion. We could keep that rig up for days, until the wind surprised us and shifted from the rear quarter to the beam (side). On those rare occasions we would scramble to take down the massive sail coverage for a slightly slower point of sail. With our massive butterfly rig, *It's Enough* usually paced at seven to nine knots, and a couple of times we ticked off 200-mile days. On watch, I spent the time listening to books on tape, writing quick emails, drinking hot tea at the helm, and practicing an unsteady sort of yoga in the cockpit. I eased into the rhythm of the passage with, as Glen suggested, both my thoughts and my body.

Identifying the constellations of the Southern Hemisphere was a whole new game. The Crosby, Stills, and Nash song, *Southern Cross*, played in my head. "When you see the Southern Cross for the first time, then you'll understand just why we came this way…" Great song, nice lyrics, but in truth, the Southern Cross looks so, well... small—the entire constellation could fit snugly in Orion's Belt. But as I contemplated the endless patterns of stars, I realized the bigger-is-better approach to life did not apply to people who live on a sailboat. Living small made it easier to concentrate on things that matter most, like taking time to see the beauty and harmony around us.

Since departing the Americas, I noticed the waves and swells of the Pacific were bigger than the wind speed should have created when compared to what I had experienced in the Atlantic and Caribbean. During one of my night watches, it occurred to me that the extreme wave height was because of the vast expanse of the Pacific Ocean. The height of waves increases as they travel across the water, and the fetch—the distance traveled—is particularly long in the Pacific. Out of the blue (maybe where that expression originated), our boat would be thrown around by an exceptionally tall or rogue wave, forcing us to grab onto whatever was stationary and nearby. My appreciation for Otto, our trusty mechanical autopilot, grew as I learned its ability to steer a straight course was far superior to any human's—even through large, rough, and jerky seas.

Most days, the equatorial sun was so intense I wore long sleeves of light fabric, pants, and a brimmed hat for protection from the direct and reflected rays. At dusk the wind and waves calmed and the weather cooled off with the approach of night. Despite the need for constant lookout, when off-watch we found a comfy place and napped like cats as the need arose. Glen and I did not need to say much to each other during our off-duty time on those long passages, but we did converse during our meals together in the cockpit. As the designated galley cook, I tried to make our meager provisions appetizing, but our once-bulging hanging nets soon went from limp to empty. Just two weeks into the passage the only fresh food we had left was cabbage and a few onions, all of which grew softer by the day.

ESCAPE FROM THE ORDINARY

Chapter 23

After 21 days at sea we spotted a speck in the distance just as the sun was setting. The GPS and chart confirmed it as Fatu Hiva, one of a group of 15 French islands called the Marquesas. The chart showed no dangers, so we entered the bay and dropped anchor that night. Daylight revealed a splendor at which the light of the moon had only teased. While there is no such thing as an ugly bay in French Polynesia, I believe we had arrived in the most breathtakingly beautiful anchorage in the whole world. Formerly known as La Baie des Verges (The Bay of Penises), the anchorage was renamed La Baie des Vierges (The Bay of Virgins) by French Catholic missionaries. The penis version must have come from the looming, penis shaped rocks that lorded over the calm waters of the protected bay. There are many stunning islands, but sailors tout Fatu Hiva as the most magnificent in the world. When I first heard those superlative comments, I remember thinking, "How different can it be from all the other spectacular, mountainous islands we've seen?" But I soon learned—very different.

The beauty of Fatu Hiva defies comparison. Nearly vertical cliffs stood as sentries in the mist at both sides of the bay; lush, green valleys were dotted with small banana and coconut plantations; fruit trees and flowers thrived on the wild mountainous terrain; mountain goats could be heard bleating from crevices in the craggy rocks and hill tops, appearing as small, white dots to the naked eye. From the salty and slimy deck of our sailboat, I took in the entirety of the incomparable scene, and longed to reach shore where everything appeared to be vibrant and inviting—even the obsidian-black, volcanic-sand beaches.

Only one other sailboat occupied the harbor when we arrived, a French boat named Cigale—French for grasshopper, as in *The Ant and the Grasshopper* fable. The Cigale crew came to welcome us, and between our halting grasp of the French language and the couple's scanty English we managed enough common words to communicate. The French couple had been playing the grasshopper (having fun and enjoying the world) for a long time. They were on their fourth circumnavigation and had lived aboard sailboats for more than 20 years!

Jean Luc was an engineer who worked for months at a time on various French island territories around the world in order to fund their sailing life. He had worked in Fatu Hiva years ago and with his wife, Jeanne, offered to acts as guides to give us the grand tour of the island. They described a hike to a fantastic waterfall, and not given to missing opportunities, Glen and I arranged to meet with them that afternoon. Before leaving on the hike, S/V Skimmer, a boat we had known since the Pedro Miguel boatyard and the S/V Lazy Duck (the boat with the water-laden fuel tank in the Galápagos), cruised into the harbor within an hour of each other.

We greeted the two new arrivals, and after hugs, fits, starts, and dinghy launching, Jean Luc and Jeanne led our expanded troop of sailors on a hike to the 200-foot waterfall they had described. With the mist from the falls hovering above the lush, green trees, we stripped to our underwear to slowly sink into the chilly water. Jean Luc pointed to a ledge where locals would jump into the pool, but I was happy to let the spectacular beauty of the falls cascading into the pool welcome me to this new South Pacific phase of our sailing life.

After drying out in the sun, Jean Luc marshaled our group toward a village he knew. It was a small, tidy group of homes, with roofs woven out of palm leaves in the traditional Polynesian style. Next to the village houses, wooden platforms with tin roofs were used for drying coconut husks for the copra oil, the largest export from the island. Along the river and dirt road, pigs and cows were tethered to graze. Skinny cows, tangled amongst trees, were stuffing themselves with the thick green undergrowth, along with pigs with strange-looking long legs and narrow faces, reminding me more of wild boar than pigs. Jean Luc told us they were indeed wild pigs that the villagers, using dogs, hunted and captured.

The mixture of sights, sounds, smells, and language tugged forward a memory lost in the depths of my mind. The Pacific offered what Glen and I had talked and dreamed about. Despite the storms and dangers of the past few years, the sailing life tipped the scale heavily toward the right side of adventure. That scene was what we had longed for, and now we were living that very image.

For the next outing, Glen and I were on our own, hiking into the village where business hours were arbitrary and arrived happy to find an open store. After weeks of canned food, we both craved fresh fruit. Disappointingly, the store did not carry produce—families had more than enough growing on their own property. Inquiring where we could find fruit for sale, a woman in the store, who spoke some English, invited us to her house. Fruit trees filled her yard and she picked some lemons for us along with a dozen huge pamplemousse, a large type of grapefruit. When I asked if she knew where we could buy bananas, she took us to her sister's house where we chopped a stalk laden with the ripe yellow fruit. My mouth salivated at the sight.

Eating off the land appealed to me. I took a long look at a tethered pig—a roasted pork tenderloin would be a welcome change from fish. I gave the idea consideration: we could host an entire pig roast and invite our friends from the other three boats! The pig, however, remained tethered. I simply did not possess the language skills to figure out how to buy and butcher a pig on the hoof.

Struggling under the weight of our purchases, we waved down a lone truck on the island and were lucky enough to hitch a ride back to our boat. Fatu Hiva was a paradise unlike any we had seen, and without need for discussion, we both agreed to linger longer than planned in the Marquesas Islands.

Chapter 24

It was as if we had been adopted. The Marquesans tolerated our escape from land at night to sleep on our boat, but they filled our days from dawn to dusk (and sometimes well into the night) with trips across the island to visit relatives in a distant valley or village, some of whom spoke no French, much less English. One toothless and ever-smiling villager named Ruka prepared us a fish lunch, taught us how to eat poi (fermented breadfruit) with our fingers, and to sing along to the songs he played on a ukulele. We attended beach picnics with villagers and hiked to sacred sites as the generous Marquesans shared their food and told stories about the old days, which by any guess could have been 20 or 200 years ago.

The warm, friendly openness of the people was charming, especially given that in the past, seafaring visitors had brought nothing but trouble to their islands. Jean Luc, our friend from Cigale and somewhat of an historian of French Polynesia, told how groups of European missionaries had arrived in the late 1700s, intent on converting the islanders to Christianity. Disgusted by the natives' tattoos, uninhibited sex lives, nakedness, and lewd dancing, the missionaries forbade all of it, and convinced many islanders to accept the Christian way with the carrot of a free education and the stick of eternal damnation. Arriving uninvited at a foreign land and convincing the hosts that almost everything they believed was either wrong or evil was unimaginable. It surely required strong convictions and forceful personalities—the missionaries must have had both in abundance.

After the arrival of missionaries, it was whalers who taught the locals how to make alcohol from fermented coconut flowers. As with many other native tribes, this started an epidemic of alcoholism. Chilean slavers then came and captured islanders to work in guano mines, profiting from the worldwide demand for nitrogen-rich bird droppings fertilizer. Marquesans who managed to survive the atrocities at the hand of foreigners were then decimated by the strangers' smallpox, and much of the island's population was no more. It was a wonder the Marquesans let visitors in their harbor, let alone embracing them.

Native tattoo designs may be the most distinct aspect of Polynesian culture. According to Jean Luc, tattoos had been forbidden by the missionaries, and the traditional art form would have been lost forever were it not for a German doctor who visited the islands in the 1890s. During his trip, he completed sketches and recorded the details of the full-body tattoos of one of the island's last warriors. The striking designs, covering large amounts of flesh, could be imposing—likely the intended purpose. It could be daunting to approach a huge, scantily clad islander with his entire face and body covered with what were surely painful-to-receive ink etchings. A century later, the fierce images of some tattoo designs were entirely at odds with the personalities of those sweet, lovely people.

Timeo, an islander we befriended, literally wore his heart on his sleeve. His strong, thick arms extended from the cut-off sleeves of a frayed T-shirt. Etched onto his broad arms and muscular neck were traditional Polynesian tattoos depicting fish, turtles, and other marine life—all the things he loved—in the style of his ancestors. Giant Timeo could have squashed me like a breadfruit, yet he had a gentle, almost sweet demeanor as he apologized for the relentless, vicious, biting insects on the islands. "Squeeze some lemon juice on the bites and you will not feel it so hard," Timeo advised, his kind faced marked with concern.

Whatever I knew about flying, blood-sucking insects paled next to the over-subtly called *No-No flies*. There are three different kinds of No-Nos, all of them evil. Any mosquitoes you have ever encountered were amateurs compared to those micro-monsters. All species of mosquitoes insert a sharp, neat hypodermic into your skin to draw blood, but the No-No flies take a big bite out of your skin and then lap up the oozing blood. Lemon juice into an open wound did not sound enjoyable, but even if I got past the stinging burn, I doubted it could stop the pain or the itch. Not to insult Timeo with my doubt, we tried the remedy and were surprised to find it did help—a little. As though the No-No bites were not gruesome enough, Glen suffered the unfortunate experience of having one of the flies lay eggs deep under his skin and was only able to rid the resulting infection by squeezing the area with his fingers to expel the eggs. Yes, it was as gross as it sounds.

But the warmth and goodness of these islanders far outweighed the No-No flies desire to consume us alive and could be best described by an experience we shared one afternoon with other sailors anchored in the bay. Like our 4 p.m. beach parties in other parts of the world, sailors brought food and drinks to shore and used an old wooden cable spool on the pier as the table. A Polynesian family strolled by, and we invited them to join us. The family was embarrassed that island guests were reduced to eating at such a crude table and offered to bring a better one from their home. We tried to persuade the Marquesans our makeshift table was fine, but unconvinced, one of the native women removed her colorful pareu top and spread it over the spool as a makeshift tablecloth. Too stunned to protest, we averted looking directly at her when she unabashedly joined the party in her bra and pareu skirt. It was the defining generosity of our last few days in the Marquesas Islands.

Next stop: Tuamotu Island Group.

Chapter 25

A s a general rule, "What island is that?" isn't a question you want to hear coming from your captain. Following Glen's gaze, I spotted the unexpected island jutting up out of the water and dashed below deck to check our electronic charts and navigation program. Either that little island had recently formed from a volcanic upheaval, or our computer navigational chart was way off. Neither thought was comforting. Back when boats navigated by imprecise dead reckoning and celestial navigation, the Tuamotu Islands were known as the Dangerous Archipelago, a treacherous, threatening, and often deadly area for sailors. Atolls dotted that part of the ocean and were hard to spot until, at times, you and the boat were right upon them—sometimes, literally. They created a navigational slalom course that could be exhilarating in the daytime, but downright petrifying at night.

Choosing which atoll to visit was simplified because of the seventy-odd atolls in the Tuamotu chain, only about 40 had passes that allowed yachts to enter the central lagoon. Some of those 40 were designated as off-limits due to lingering radiation from years of French nuclear detonation and testing. We decided to visit Makemo, an atoll about 40 miles long, 1,000 feet wide and, most importantly, radiation-free.

When Charles Darwin spent time in the Pacific, he put idle time on the boat to good use. Besides working on evolution science, he pondered how atolls formed. Darwin correctly deduced they began as high volcanic islands such as the Marquesas, but after millions of years and movement of tectonic plates, the towering volcanic masses collapsed upon themselves, making a depression that eventually became a lagoon. Over the millennia, the volcano disappeared below sea level, and a coral rim formed a perimeter around the new atoll. After ages of settling, all that remained was a circular or horseshoe-shaped coral reef with a central lagoon. The eons and mighty forces it took to create it, one day at a time, were mind-boggling. The young, soaring volcanic islands of the Marquesas and the older, low Tuamotu atolls stood as illustration and geological record of earth's incredible power.

Understanding atoll formation was one thing but sailing into the slim pass of a circular ring of rock-hard atoll was something else. The pass we chose was slightly wider than a double-car garage and hazardous to traverse because of the strong tides pouring in or gushing out of the narrow opening. Having studied the tide chart on our way to Makemo atoll, we sailed under bare poles to reduce speed to time our arrival during slack tide as well as the best sun height to enter the lagoon. There were plenty of stories about yacht misadventures due to the presence of dangerous tidal flows entering lagoon passes, even during slack tide. We shored up our gumption and hoped we would not be recounted among the tales.

* * * * *

SAILMAIL: IT'S ENOUGH

TO: Jeanne

FROM: Julie

Hey Jeanne, we're doing okay considering we flubbed our first entry into Makemo, despite our best calculations. The inner lagoons are big, and the passes are narrow with strong, turbulent currents. If you arrive at slack water, everything should be fine. Reality is something else altogether.

Whitewater rifts in the pass were coming out of the lagoon, pushing against us and 20-kt winds blew us sideways. We were under bare poles—no sails—and motoring full power through the narrow slot but going backwards! After minutes of engine whining, Glen allowed the boat to slip back to the ocean in a marginally controlled zigzag motion, avoiding impact with the coral rock.

The lagoon at Makemo is so large and the coral so low on the windward side that at high tide, water pours into the lagoon and flows out at 10 or more knots through the narrow pass. We hove-to (hovered in place) for a few hours until the tide was more favorable. Glen wanted to launch the dinghy and fish along the reef, but I held sway: no fishing! Outboard trouble, hooking on to a big fish… A lot could go wrong to mess up our timing to enter the pass. A couple of hours later we made it through the pass and anchored near other sailboats across from the small village of Pouheva. Glen and I both collapsed in the cockpit, feeling like we had accomplished something worthy.

"Okay," I told Glen, "now you can go fishing."

Jeanne, visit us when we get to Tahiti. You will love it and can practice your French. I miss you!

Love, Julie

ESCAPE FROM THE ORDINARY

Chapter 26

I often reminded myself on those remote and beautiful Pacific islands that we were technically in France. One of the best remain-
ders of the French colonial empire was that French Catholic
missionaries, who had first come in the 1880s, also brought the gospel
of French baguettes and puffy pastries. All we had to do was fill our
pockets with money, take a short dinghy ride and with a slight command
of the French language, we could be savoring fresh baguettes piping hot
from an imported French oven. That's exactly what we did, and it was
well worth the effort of getting up early to enjoy them, still warm from
the oven, with double-cream French butter and strawberry preserves.
Fresh, delicious baguettes were ingrained in the island culture of French
Polynesia. Even the smallest of atolls had bakeries where every day (and
even a few hours on Sunday) one could buy baguettes, *pain au chocolat*,
and croissants. Forever emblazoned in my mind is the memory of a half-
naked, heavily tattooed, 300-pound islander in torn shorts and bare feet,
zooming by on a scooter while waving at us with his French baguette.

Pouheva, a village of about 600 people, was large enough to have a
path of white coral that functioned as what the islanders referred to as a
street. Our first mission ashore was to replenish our food stores at the
market. Thanks to French taxpayers, weekly cargo ships brought heavily

subsidized supplies, marked with red price labels, to all the inhabited islands of French Polynesia. The small markets were well-stocked with sugar, flour, canned corned beef, SPAM®, peanut butter (the French variety—runny and thin), beer, wine (a French staple), canned butter, canned veggies, and canned soups. Oddly, cans of Pringles® potato chips were found in six varieties. If we arrived within a day of the cargo ship, we were told we might also find various frozen meats, including leg of lamb, and a selection of French cheeses—an incredible range of goods for such tiny, secluded islands.

One day I went shopping immediately after the cargo ship departed and was able to purchase a bag of fresh lettuce and a few ripe, red tomatoes. The small bag of lettuce cost more than seven dollars, and the tomatoes were more than two dollars apiece. Glen and I ate slowly and savored every expensive, crunchy bite, but it was well worth it. I thought about that meal whenever I later opened a can of corn to mix with black beans and onions for a salad.

"Skip the middlemen," one sailor advised as he showed us a plastic bag of pearls he just purchased on a nearby pearl farm. French Polynesia is known for its pearls, and many sailors were buying them from cultivators at a fraction of the prices as sold in Tahiti. We visited a pearl farm by dinghy and were greeted by the owners. The wife spoke some English and explained that the black Tahitian pearls were cultivated on atolls like Makemo because the lagoon is a protected, warm, saltwater environment. She also demonstrated how the pearls were formed. Each day, a nucleus was grafted into 50 live oysters. In nature, the nucleus was often a parasite—not the grain of sand, as most people think. As a defense mechanism, the animal excretes a fluid to coat the irritant, layer upon layer. The nacre is deposited until a lustrous pearl is formed within shells, taking about 15 to 25 months. The couple harvested the pearls three times a year producing more than 50,000 genuine pearls. That was a small mom-and-pop operation, so it was hard to imagine the magnitude of pearl production at the other atolls where there were large, commercial farms owned by Asian firms, such as Hinano, which shipped their pearls directly to Tahiti.

I asked about the nuclei they implanted; was it artificial or from a different kind of oyster? The woman kept saying something like *meesipi*. When I cocked my head and looked puzzled, her husband came over and said the same thing. Eventually I understood their attempt at the English word. The nuclei used to inoculate the pearl oysters—bits of freshwater clamshell—came from Mississippi. I had never been one for jewelry and was happy to see other sailors taking up my buying slack, supporting the local islanders.

I craved some time out to read, write, and practice yoga on the beach. Glen, wanting to spearfish, felt the same. We headed for an uninhabited motu (a really small island within the lagoon of an atoll), located about an hour's sail away on the other side of the Makemo lagoon. Dropping anchor at the tiny, uninhabited motu, I told Glen, "Look at this view! This is the screensaver we used to have on our work computers!" Fifteen minutes would be all it took to walk the perimeter of our private motu, hosting not much more than white sand and four waving coconut palms. Our eyes took in the astounding beauty but, as we approached the far side of the small island, our noses were attacked.

A putrid smell grew stronger as we walked to the other side. There, we found a dead, decomposing sperm whale partially washed ashore. The high tide provided sharks enough water depth to tear at the flesh of the whale's underside as the large, lifeless body rocked in the waves reaching the shore. Gagging from the odor of death, we left, but returned at low tide when the sharks could not reach the whale. We wanted to try and figure out how the whale ended up on the beach. Other than the shark tears on the underside there were no visible marks of injury. It was puzzling... did the whale get beached accidentally?

The next morning, still anchored off the motu, we tuned into the morning radio cruiser net to hear if any boats we knew had arrived at Makemo. After check-in, we chatted with friends on another boat and mentioned the decaying corpse, not considering the local villagers would be listening in on our radio net. Word spread fast about the whale, and in less than an hour, we heard the villagers' outboard motors speeding toward the motu. Hurrying to the whale site, we discovered tattooed and bare-chested men extracting the whale's teeth with saws, hammers, and pliers. Carved whale's teeth, especially from a sperm whale, were highly prized and coveted in French Polynesia. The men were too focused to notice us and had tied cloths around their noses and mouths while working on the rotting animal amid the nauseating scene. The sight and smell of the operation made us gag, so we returned to our side of the motu and the haven of our boat.

For two days the island men worked at extracting the whale's teeth, but we did not return to watch. Weeks later we saw carved whale's teeth for sale in pricey tourist art galleries in Tahiti. The teeth were carved with traditional scrimshaw scenes of whaling days and old-style Polynesian designs, some selling for more than $1,000. I would like to think the teeth of our sperm whale would be carved, honored, and kept as family heirlooms by the natives on Makemo, as such pieces were part of their centuries-old traditions and culture.

We traveled out of Makemo through the familiar pass, this time on the correct side of the water flow. Our boat shot through the pass so fast on the outgoing swell, *It's Enough* felt like she was surfing. Glen and I looked at each other with the satisfaction of pros as we wordlessly watched the low atoll disappear in the waves behind us.

* * * * *

After three months exploring French Polynesia, it was time to move on. A few days before our visas expired, we officially checked out in Bora Bora. With little wind we could not go far from the long arm of the French gendarmes, so we motored 30 miles west to Maupiti Island. Though still part of French Polynesia, it was one of the more remote islands and a good place to wait until winds developed. The seas were calm with no hint of a breeze, but we were already preparing for the open sea, polishing stainless deck hardware and securely stowing things below decks.

Sitting in the cockpit, watching the sunset, Glen and I reviewed our time and the highlights of French Polynesia and afterward asked ourselves the questions all visitors to that part of the world must surely ask: Why did France continue to support its relationship with that beautiful yet far-flung place? From the Polynesians' point of view, the answer was clear. If you had a rich wife sending you baguette ovens and a billion Euros a year in support money and subsidies, would you want a divorce? Probably not. Visiting sailors appreciate the roads, infrastructure, internet cafés, and subsidized food and wine, but how did the average taxpayer back in France benefit? At one time, France needed the islands to test their nuclear weapons, but after that? Even French sailors didn't have the answers.

After a few days on Maupiti Island and with decent winds in the forecast, we set sail for the Cook Islands, a few hundred more miles to the west.

Au revoir! French Polynesia and *G'day* Cook Islands!

ESCAPE FROM THE ORDINARY

Chapter 27

T rade winds propelled us across vast stretches of the Pacific Ocean as bright, sparkling waves passed gently under *It's Enough*. After French Polynesia we stopped for fuel, food and snatches of adventure at the Cook Islands, among the dozen or so tropical territories of New Zealand.

On a sunny morning we were snorkeling on Aitutaki, one of the inhabited islands in the group, allowing our bodies to float with only an occasional flip of the fin. I stared into the puckered lips of a colorful parrotfish who eyed me with matching interest. Beneath the water, the Cook Islands were like other tropical havens we had visited, but ashore, posh hotels and restaurants lined the beach. The Cook Islands played host to no visible manufacturing or large-scale fishing operations, and with few international flights only the presence of a small number of wealthy tourists gave clue to its industry.

A sailor from another boat—a former tax attorney—was delighted to be the first to disclose the secret: The Cook Islands were an asset-protection haven for wealthy people. His arm swept across the view of the shore and its fancy hotels as he went on, "You don't really need to be that rich, just in an area of business that commonly gets sued. If a plaintiff wins a malpractice suit against his doctor who has a business back in the

U.S. or in Europe, the doctor could fly to these tiny islands in the South Pacific and plead his case again before a Cook's court, under Cook's law. This arrangement is mainly for professions such as real estate developers, doctors, corporate bigwigs and rich parents of teenage drivers."

The more I saw of the world, the more my eyes were opened to how many different ways people live their lives. With fresh perspective, I looked across what little I could see of the small Cook Islands in the middle of the Pacific. Lovely coral atolls, ideal for fishing and collecting pearls—and a global haven for offshore asset-protection trusts. Traveling to new shores, I learned to hold at bay my tendency to judge quickly, opening opportunities to ask questions and learn things. Using that new approach, I've learned far more about other people and places across this mostly blue planet.

There was one more atoll we wanted to visit in the Cook Islands, so with a clear weather window, Glen and I pulled anchor. Palmerston Island was far flung and required three days of sail passage, but we pointed *It's Enough* on course and allowed the winds to carry us away, leaving behind our opportunity to join the Cook Islands offshore tax haven.

* * * * *

"Palmerston Island, this is the sailing yacht *It's Enough*. We are five miles east and request permission to anchor for a few days," I said into the VHF radio. A man's voice answered with a curious blend of Polynesian and New Zealand accents, "Yacht approaching Palmerston, come in. We'll send a boat out to show you where to drop your anchor. Just circle around until we come out to you. Over."

Our navigational plotter led us to the leeward side of the island. We were uncomfortable with the thought of anchoring outside the protected lagoon, but there was no way for our sailboat to enter the shallow, coral-pocked inner waters. Our anchorage right on the reef would be dangerous if the winds reversed, and uncomfortable in heavy winds from any direction. Glen motored in a wide circle as we tried to decide if stopping at Palmerston Island was really a good idea. I looked down through the clear turquoise water and could visibly see the ocean floor that was littered with coral and only sparse sand to hold our anchor. If the anchor dragged while we were ashore, we would not find our boat before she sank on a reef. As we discussed our options, an aluminum skiff came racing out through a narrow passage in the coral reef, and two men pulled alongside our boat.

"I'm Edward," said one. "This is my brother Simon. Follow us and we'll show you where to go." We followed.

"Pull up here and drop your anchor!" Edward yelled. "You'll be okay." Glen and I looked at each other and shrugged as if to say, "It's only our lives and boat at stake here if the wind shifts." We did as instructed. Following our established habit, Glen dove on the anchor to set it more securely, and we figured—without certainty—we were probably alright if the weather held.

Palmerston Island soon took first place as both our favorite stop as well as the oddest island we had visited in the South Pacific. The social scene made it unique, with the added oddity that the 40-plus residents were all related; sometimes very closely and over many generations. Every resident could trace his or her lineage (or spouse's lineage) back to one person: William Marsters, a British ship's carpenter, who colonized the island in 1863 along with his three Polynesian wives (the second and third were cousins of the first). That interesting domestic arrangement eventually split the island's population between three family lines who continue to populate the island.

Marsters divided the island into sections, giving each wife her own space. He then spent years building houses using salvaged timber from shipwrecks. When Marsters died in 1899 at 78 years old, he had sired 23 children. Thousands of his descendants are now scattered around the Cook Islands and New Zealand, while a few dozen adults and children remained on Palmerston. Although all the families lived together on the same island, the community was still divided into three clans—the lines of descent from Marsters' three wives. The separate families seemed happy enough and made a concerted effort to avoid intermarriages. There was one school and one church, and each family shared the responsibilities of running the island by appointing an individual to a task (e.g., teacher, police officer, customs official, administrator). The New Zealand government paid the official employees, infusing the Marsters with outside income. Land disputes among the three Marsters families prevented an airstrip from ever being built, so supply deliveries were limited to one cargo ship, which visited every four to six months.

We decided to visit Palmerston a few months earlier while in Tahiti. There we met a sailor who told us about the intense and unusual family situation on Palmerston, including the minor feuds between the clans. We hadn't realized it at the time, but we were thrust into one of those feuds as soon as we approached the island. There had been two different voices on the radio trying to contact us as we approached. It wasn't until later we discovered the second voice was trying to intercept and win us. The dubious prize was the right to host us for the duration of our stay and consequently obtain any gifts such as books and DVDs we may have brought for the islanders. What happened behind the scenes was unclear, but the family clan of Edward and Simon, the interceptors, got us instead of whoever else was calling on the radio. We were prized.

Shortly after Glen secured our anchor, we invited Edward and Simon to join us for snacks and juice in the cockpit. Someone from the other clan, whose name was not offered, came out as the customs official for the island, looked over our passports, filled out paperwork, and collected the five New Zealand dollars per person check-in fee. During the customs formalities, Edward was quiet and stared at the horizon while Simon, who had a bad stutter, made small talk, though his stammering made for halting conversation. The customs agent—who was surely their cousin—wordlessly packed up his paperwork and returned our passports.

"Ready for lunch?" Edward asked. We were. The four of us piled into his skiff and he rocketed through the pass to the calm lagoon. Clear, blue water surrounded us, and we could easily see schools of grouper and parrotfish feasting on healthy, brown coral heads as we passed. Edward landed the skiff on the white beach bordering the island. We walked a sandy path toward the house, situated on a section of the island that belonged solely to his clan, who we met over lunch. The house, a three-room concrete block structure, was less than a quarter of a mile inland. Three young men prepared lunch as we watched, and the smell of fried fish wafted from the tiny, outdoor kitchen. Edward led us to an elderly woman who sat at the head of a long, wooden table, slouching comfortably in a plastic chair.

"This is my mother, Tuaini," he told us. "She raised 11 children." Tuaini flashed a toothless grin and deep wrinkles framed her face. "Yes," she lisped. "Five girls and six boys. Simon is my eldest and Edward is my youngest." Simon raised his shoulders, leaned back, and let out a hearty laugh. He looked at me, slowly blinked his eyes and smiled broadly; his perfect white teeth gleamed in the sunlight.

The table was set for a feast. Was this a typical lunch for them, or was it a meal to entertain prized guests? Bowls of white rice and coleslaw sat next to big trays of fried parrotfish and wahoo, a valued game fish. We sat on benches surrounded by the entire Marsters clan as they told us about life on the island, ancestors, hardships, cyclones, and the names of boats that had visited in the years before. Tuaini claimed to be an experienced midwife and self-taught healer. The friendly Marsters, whose lives were mostly free of television, movies, and contained few books, told us tales, and we were engrossed. The storytelling was a fine art of details that would carry their ancestors' stories faithfully to the next generations.

Our original plan was to bring canned goods and movie DVDs from the boat as hospitality gifts, but we were glad the canned items had been left behind. Food was certainly not in short supply on that island. They had two full walk-in freezers (including ice cream!) and a small metal warehouse of canned goods, soda, beer, and dry goods. Our cans of beans and Campbell soup would have been poor offerings, but the dozen movie videos presented were all ones they had never watched. It gave us pleasure when the kids jumped up and down with their gifts and headed straight for the generator to power up the television.

After the remarkable lunch, Edward and Simon took us on a tour of the island. Glen and I followed the brothers down a sandy trail edged by coconut trees and lights that were lit whenever the generator was running—even in the bright sunlight. We passed the two-classroom schoolhouse, sugarcane fields, and a few smaller, block homes. Ten minutes from their home, we arrived at what I called Main Street, a sandy lane stretching through the center of the island. Rather than being flanked by banks or stores, there stood only a modest Christian church, the original wood-plank home William Marsters had built, the family cemetery in which every gravestone bore the Marsters name, and a make-believe yacht club built to lure and entertain visiting sailors.

The islanders were not poor, nor did they seem to lack for anything. Each adult on the island who held an official, designated job received a salary from the New Zealand government. For added income the Marsters caught and sold parrotfish to Rarotonga twice a year at the market price and ate well from unlimited supplies of coconut, lobster, parrotfish, wahoo, dorado (mahi mahi), pig, chicken, and tropical bird. They had so much food, fields of pineapples went untouched because they were too difficult to harvest.

Glen asked about farming fresh vegetables, and Simon shook his head, explaining their only tractor had been broken for a long time. Glen, who can fix anything mechanical, asked to see the tractor, and Simon directed us to the sole vehicle on the island. The tractor was rusted and appeared forlorn when the tarp was pulled away. Simon recounted the good old days before the tractor broke down, when the family could gather mass quantities of coconuts to harvest the copra (dried coconut kernels that produce valuable coconut oil) and haul fuel barrels instead of wrestling them from the supply ship to their homes. For Glen, it was challenge accepted.

The next day, Glen rooted around our boat's spare-parts locker, and fabricated what he would need to fix several major problems with the tractor. After two full days of work, the tractor was up and running. Glen enjoyed a deep feeling of satisfaction as he stood among the entire smiling island population to watch the tractor chug by with a load of coconuts.

During our stay on the island, a few other much needed repairs cropped up that required Glen's magic multi-meter and engineering know-how. The most difficult task was the broken SSB/HAM radio, antenna, and wiring. Glen did not disappoint, and the Marsters family members in New Zealand were surprised and delighted to get a call from their relatives in Palmerston.

As Glen continued to work his electrical and mechanical miracles, we became favored visitors. The men took Glen spearfishing along the reef while the younger boys cast nets. At the end of the day, the men returned with the aluminum skiff filled with their daily catch. The extra fish they caught would be frozen and later traded for supplies brought by the infrequent trading ships. Eager to return the many favors they had received from Glen, with broad smiles they taught him the fast, Marsters' way to clean and filet fish.

I visited with Tuaini, the mother, and learned to weave palm fronds into mats and hats. She regaled me with sage advice about native medicinal concoctions made from ingredients such as sea urchins, local plants, and coconut milk. Tuaini, in her 70s, swam with me out into the ocean—she in her flowered dress—to show me exactly which sea urchin to use to treat dysentery. I donned swim goggles and snorkel and was surprised when she dove underwater without any equipment. She told me she had never used a mask before and the only ones on the island belonged to the men. I fit mine on to her face and once she got the hang of the snorkel, she swam all around the coral and came up giggling.

Glen, too, had taken note of the lack of good equipment. "They only have a few masks and a couple of cracked and broken fins for the entire island," Glen told me, "they strap on the fins with rope." We ransacked our lockers and came up with two extra diving masks and swim fins then presented them as gifts. The Marsters were truly grateful, and I knew our simple presents would make a difference in their lives.

On the fifth day, we announced we would depart the next morning. A special feast was prepared and every person in the family went to extra effort to show appreciation for all Glen's work. They rode their skiff out the next morning to say farewell as we once again took to the sea.

"Come back in a few years, on your next sail of the Pacific Ocean!" Edward called as he and Simon waved. The thought of another trip around the world jolted me, and laughing, I told Glen, "That's the beauty of naming the boat *It's Enough*. I don't think we'll need a second round."

It's Enough *flying her massive Amel papillon downwind sails. In trade winds we could log 200 miles a day.*

Glen designed this canvas awning and had it sewn in Trinidad. It took a while to assemble but made it possible to sleep below deck in the equatorial heat.

Inside the Pedro Miguel Boatyard. The nonstop action encouraged us to go traveling in Central and South America for a couple of months.

Julie at the top of Dead Woman's Pass on the Inca Trail.

Gathering with thousands of Incan descendants for unforgettable Inti Raymi, which invokes the return of the sun at the winter solstice.

Layered like an onion on the Inca Trail. Unmatched views during four days of hiking at brutal altitudes to arrive at Machu Picchu.

Galapagos encounter.

Native dancers in the Marquesas Islands are happy to have a reason to practice for Heiva, a Polynesian dance and sport competition held in Tahiti every July.

It's Enough at anchor in Fatu Hiva, Marquesas Islands, French Polynesia. Surely, one of the most beautiful bays in the world.

243

Hurricane season in the Pacific offered six months of exploring New Zealand. Making friends with one of the 60 million sheep in a country of 4 million people.

Dinner.

Glen fixing the only vehicle on Palmerston Island with spare parts from our boat. He also fixed their HAM radio so they could call relatives in New Zealand.

One of the tamer adventures in Niue.

Overlooking the Raiatea lagoon, Society Islands, French Polynesia.

Taking our bikes to shore, barge style.

Another moveable feast from freediver Glen.

Island Uber.

Waterfall hike to get some exercise after a 21-day passage from Galapagos to the Marquesas.

JULIE BRADLEY

Chapter 28

When we started the sailing circumnavigation, we figured it would take us roughly three years to get around the world and back to the Mediterranean Ocean and Europe, where we started. At the time, we thought getting back to Europe would be the final hoorah—the prize we earned after sailing around the world. But the beauty and people of the South Pacific made Europe a distant, abstract notion. I could not imagine a better place to explore from a boat than the South Pacific. The further we sailed, and the more islands we visited, the better it was. We had slowed our pace, realizing that finishing the circumnavigation in three years no longer seemed possible, or desirable.

What was important was getting out of the South Pacific islands for the six months of the tropical cyclone season, dictated by both common sense and the fine print of our boat insurance. Most sailors chose to spend the six months of tropical cyclone activity in Australia or New Zealand. If we spent the next six months in New Zealand, we could buy a car and explore by land. A half year in New Zealand sounded like a dream to both of us. With the decision made, we amended our cruising plans to include a small, special island that sailors had urged us to visit. As we departed the next morning with our new Five Year Sailing Plan, we set course for the island nation of Niue.

* * * * *

Niue was so small it would have to arm-wrestle the Vatican for claim to the title of World's Smallest Self-Governing State. At thirteen miles long and eight miles wide, it held a population numbering in the hundreds. Unlike the mostly flat islands in the Pacific, Niue was a wall of towering cliffs that looked like a cake floating on the distant ocean. It had no natural harbor and the only way boats could visit was by grabbing a mooring ball in an open anchorage on the lee side of the island, which was roiling even in settled weather. There were only 14 mooring balls and we were grateful one was available when we arrived after our six-day passage from Palmerston.

We arrived in late afternoon and were unsure if we would be able to clear customs that same day. By a radio call, we arranged for the customs officer to meet us at the dock an hour beyond normal business time, figuring we needed a good half hour just to get our dinghy to shore. Among sailors, the dinghy dock in Niue was famous—though not in a good way. There was no protected bay or harbor, so the town has developed a white-knuckle, nail-biting method for bringing dinghies ashore by crane. With dread about what we were about to face, Glen and I went to our mizzen deck to off-load our dinghy (stored upside down on deck during passages) and fitted it with the 15 HP outboard motor. Anywhere else, we would step into the dinghy and run to shore or a dock to check into the country, but Niue's crane process made getting to shore far more complicated. From rope, we devised a harness to which the crane at the dock could be attached and depending upon the weather was even more difficult a maneuver than it sounded. Everyone in the dinghy must be nimble and time their exiting climb out in concert with the motion of the waves. The person running the motor, now the only person remaining in the dinghy, would have to perform fast maneuvers to attach the dinghy to the crane hoist, turn off the motor and deftly clamber out of the boat to a ladder extending into the water.

When we reached the dock, I balanced in the rocking dinghy with hands outstretched like a cartoon zombie, then at just the right moment, grabbed the side rails, and scampered up the ladder. From the safety of my new perch, I lowered the crane hoist and watched as Glen, steering the outboard, made several attempts to attach the dinghy's harness to the crane hook. Adding unnecessary drama to an already tense situation, waves tossed Glen and the boat around in the exposed sea, foiling his best efforts to make the hook. Eventually, he was able to take advantage of a short lull in the frothy waves, attached the dinghy, and scurried up the ladder with a backpack full of papers and our valuable passports. When he reached the dock, I hoisted the dinghy with the motorized crane, swung it over with a rope, lowered it onto a trolley, rolled the trolley to an available space on the dock, and offloaded it so the trolley could be used by others. The perilous process ranged somewhere between edgy and death defying, and I was certain there were times when it would be too treacherous to land.

The convoluted landing process, however, was the perfect start for the overall adventure ashore in Niue. Having been briefed on the procedure over the radio by a fellow boater, Glen and I were successful in passing the dinghy proficiency test. The customs officer watched and gave us thumbs up as we conducted the dinghy maneuvering. Then, in what we would come to know as typical laidback and friendly Niue style, the officer told us a bit about life in Niue as we completed the compulsory paperwork.

Niue was self-governing but in free association with New Zealand. Niueans are New Zealand citizens, and Queen Elizabeth is the Head of State of Niue, as she is of New Zealand. New Zealand contributes money for infrastructure and tourism development; there are miles of developed trails and well-marked natural wonders to explore. Not many people beyond New Zealanders and a sprinkling of adventurous sailors even know of the glorious island.

Walking around the main town of Alofi, we regained our land legs. It usually took a couple of days to feel acclimated on land and the more I stayed off the boat, the quicker I adjusted. Besides, the dinghy landing was so complicated, we might as well stay awhile. Craving exercise, we rented mountain bikes and rode them to a supermarket well stocked with New Zealand products—a preview of what we would see on the shelves in New Zealand. Next, we hit an ATM for some New Zealand dollars, the official currency of Niue. With the sun slipping away, and the water calmer for the dinghy operation, we returned to *It's Enough*.

As we approached, we saw a group of fellow sailors in snorkel gear close to our boat; they were hovering near a mother humpback whale and her calf. Glen and I boarded *It's Enough*, then frantically tore off our clothes to get into swimsuits and snorkel gear, slid off the back of the boat, and entered the water hoping the mother and calf were still there. There was no need to rush. The two humpbacks had taken up temporary residence under a boat a few moorings away. The mother whale was down about 50 feet and the calf only 20 feet away. Mama whale kept a watchful eye and almost seemed to want us to appreciate her baby. After about 15 minutes of hovering over the pair, the mother turned to look us in the eye, and then slid away sideways so as not to hit us as she came slowly to the surface 20 feet away. She made eye contact again as she veered off further, surfaced, and fluked with her new calf following. We watched both above and below the surface as she dove again, surfaced, fluked, and dove again. She swam farther and gained speed, probably indicating she wanted some alone time and had enough of humans ogling her baby. The two whales checked in and out of our anchorage often, and we became accustomed to hearing whale song through the hull of our boat as we read at night. We made up themes for the different types of songs: a mother whale singing to her baby, a male whale crooning to a prospective mate, or a lonely whale searching for others in her tribe... The haunting whale songs drifted through the water and elevated our emotions to a new level of spirituality.

The morning after our whale encounter, we saw more marine life. I was ready to jump in the water to look for the whales when I spotted some pinkie-finger-sized snakes floating and swimming near our boat. A hasty reference to our marine wildlife book identified them as deadly poisonous krait, 20 times more potent than a cobra. The guidebook went on to assure us the snake's mouth was so tiny it could not open wide enough to bite a person, but those kraits seemed much too mellow even if they could. They were littered throughout the surrounding waters of Niue, and according to the records no one has ever been bitten. Eventually, we came to ignore them.

* * * * *

I had read the word chasm but was never quite sure what it meant until we were introduced to a quantity of them in Niue. The Anapala Chasm was a descent of more than 150 steps to a freshwater pool where we could swim. Ah, but no swimsuits! That didn't matter—we had it all to ourselves. We stripped down to our smalls, the New Zealand term for underwear, and swam in our private corner of a liquid heaven. We then visited Togo Chasm via an incredibly long ladder leading to a beach. The shoreline was isolated from the sea by a towering cliff but otherwise possessed all the properties of a beach that you might expect: sugary sand, palm trees, even seashells. Nature has a very good story there.

Another chasm formed a natural swimming pool with a mix of fresh and ocean water. When I first put my head underwater, I thought there must have been something wrong with my mask lens or my vision.

Where the seawater and freshwater came together it was like looking through a distorted kaleidoscope.

A few days later, we were with a group of sailors ashore for a happy hour gathering when a local Kiwi offered to lead sailors from several boats down into Vaikona Chasm the following day. When I asked for a rating of difficulty, he described it as "exciting but doable." That was our first encounter with Kiwi understatement.

We hiked two miles through bush to the opening, left our packs and food, then peeled down to bathing suits (this time we knew!) and t-shirts. We were told to leave our backpacks at the chasm entrance and, to keep our hands free, wore diving masks loosely around our necks. The moment we stepped into the opening we were looking down 50 feet at impressive and towering stalagmite and stalactite formations. Those formations were our handholds as we inched our way down the rock face, clinging to the occasional descending stalactite. We had never done any technical mountain climbing and I can't say this qualified because we had no special equipment or training. Our movements were slow, unsure and cautious. About 10 feet down, there appeared a thin, yellow rope attached to a stalactite to assist with our further descent. That so-called lifeline was a fraying, narrow, polypropylene twisted string that would not have been sufficient to even tie up our dinghy.

There were five of us sharing the adventure; another American sailing couple and a young Australian sailor whose wife had enough sense to stay back at their boat. As we crept down with careful steps, clinging to the thin, yellow, nylon rope—as though it could provide any aid whatsoever—we discovered the Australian was afraid of heights. His body shook like a quaking aspen, his comments unnerving me. I would have been shaking, too, had I ever looked down, but I was busy trying to focus on my next toehold. Glen, with his usual composure, went in front of me, offering occasional encouragement. Once we lowered ourselves down through the cave opening into the chasm itself, there was no turning back; the only way out was forward. Clinging with both hands and feet—and wishing for a prehensile tail—we climbed down the geologic formations to the chasm bottom among a cathedral of stalactites looming above us from an expansive ceiling. Rays of light penetrated small cracks and holes, becoming miniature spotlights for our three-ring circus.

At the bottom of the cavern was a pool of water so clear, Aquafina could bottle it. It was pure and bracing cold. We all jumped into the crystalline blue with our masks and snorkels to decompress from the stressful trek there. The sudden, biting cold took my breath away, then soothed me. But next I looked around, and it dawned on me: there was no other opening. Where could we go next?

Our guide told us to put on our masks and snorkels and motioned us to follow him as he ducked under water. He pointed to our exit. What I saw sent me into panic. We had to dive down four to five feet without a weight belt, enter an underwater tunnel, and swim its length for around five feet to where it would open up into a different cavern. If there was any way I could have turned around and escaped the way I came, I would have. We didn't have fins or weight belts and I was already exhausted. My feelings at that moment were indescribable. *Devastated* comes to mind but doesn't do justice to my despair. Glen and I looked at each other and shared a quiet understanding of how badly it could turn out. Our guide seemed surprised at our reactions and offered encouragement that we could all do this—we had already accomplished so much. We just had to see it through. His most convincing argument was, "Besides, there is no other way out."

Swimming through underwater tunnels seemed a bad way to die. Without the proper equipment, it would be difficult to swim downward to the tunnel opening. The pitch-black darkness ahead looked ominous; no more brilliant showers of sunshine trickling through the cavern to illuminate our path. The only source of light we had was the narrow beams from our underwater flashlights. Glen, a free diver who could hold his breath more than two minutes, went first. I could see he had arrived in the next cavern as he shone his lamp back through the tunnel. The dim light barely reached our side of the opening. Hopefully, the underwater stretch was truly not more than five feet. I was uncertain at even that distance. Taking a huge gulp of air, I dove down with all my might, groped the wall for the opening, then frantically pulled myself through, then up, and gasped for air as I surfaced. Finding and negotiating that tunnel was the worst minute of my life.

Our Kiwi guide chose that time to announce we had tunnels ahead as well. "Oh my God, Glen, I don't know if I can do another one." Glen held my hand, quietly pointed out we did not have any choice, and encouraged me with, "That was the longest and deepest tunnel and you made it." With that I set my mind, "Well, if they are shorter, maybe I can do it." I had to muster up some fortitude; we had two more underwater tunnels to negotiate. The second dive took us into another black cavern too dark to appreciate, had I cared. By that point I was too consumed by fear and focused on bracing myself for whatever lay ahead. Finishing the third dive completed what I called our water obstacle portion.

Just as I was rejoicing with a Snoopy dance next to a stand of stalagmites, I saw what was in store for us. The good news: we were past the water. The bad news: we had to creep along a ledge no more than two to five inches wide with tiny cracks for handholds and steps that were few and far between. Drowning, I imagined, would have been much more comfortable than crashing 50 feet down to land on a stalagmite.

The Aussie who was in front of me (and afraid of heights) kept muttering, "This is terrifying!" I begged him to only talk about toe and handholds as his fears were intensifying my own. I was on the razor's edge of panic myself. Very few visuals of that portion remain in my memory because if I'd looked down, I would have been a goner. Concentrating on finding my next handhold, I was glad for all the pushups and upper body strength from my Army career. Obsessively studying my hands and toes fitting into the narrow slots, never looking down, and imagining swimming with Glen and the whales under *It's Enough* were what kept me traversing the ledge.

Our Kiwi guide was leading the way, but we were on our own psychologically and physically. At one point, my rubber sandals slid on some slime, but Glen luckily caught me from falling more than a few feet. My arm was scratched up and some fingernails torn, but it could have been fatal if I had dropped the distance onto the solid stone ground.

Finally, after three hours in the bowels of the earth, we climbed into the sunlight like blinded moles—squinting and shielding our eyes. It was a brightness I thought we might never see again. All that remained was a mile or so of picking our way through sharp, pointy, coral potholes. I was too exhausted to high five Glen. Besides, there was no display of elation sufficient for having emerged from that ordeal in one piece.

We were above ground and alive. We retrieved packs and lunched. Still in shock, I wasn't hungry, but I knew my muscles needed the protein and downed my peanut butter and jelly sandwich. I sat contemplating what we had just done, quietly euphoric at having cheated death. The five of us sat in a circle quietly eating lunch, processing what we had been through. Exhausted and shell-shocked, we were survivors. Vaikona was my last chasm experience; on Niue or elsewhere on the planet.

I still shudder at what we got ourselves into that day. When I read about someone doing something stupidly death defying—Darwin award type stuff—I think of climbing through Vaikona Chasm. Later I saw a tourist brochure printed by the New Zealand government describing it as an extremely challenging climb.

Another Kiwi understatement.

"I'm adventured out," I told Glen. "Niue is great and all, but between chasming and getting our dinghy up that crane we may be using up our available luck. We still have half a world to sail through and explore." Glen rubbed the top of my head and said, "I can always generate more luck by rubbing strands of red hair together." He was good at summoning sailors' superstitions to fit his desires and I had to laugh, "It's going to turn grey if we stay here much longer."

Nature was in my corner as weather predictions indicated it was time to move on. Our exposed, rolling anchorage would soon become untenable with two-foot swells coming from an approaching low-pressure system. It was time to join the mass exodus of sailboats hurrying to open sea. When we checked out with the customs officer, a local U.S. Peace Corps volunteer named Mike approached and said he had been bumped from two consecutive once-weekly flights from Niue to Tonga. He asked if he could ride with us to Vava'u, the capital of Tonga, our next port and the site of a regional Peace Corps conference that was to start in five days. We would have some company on the next passage.

Next stop the Kingdom of Tonga.

Chapter 29

In the three days it took to sail to Tonga, Mike, our Peace Corps hitch-hiker, retched his guts out. He was just getting over his seasickness on the third morning about the time we spotted land. I called down and told him we were about an hour from making landfall in Nukualofa, the major town and site of the Peace Corps conference he planned to attend. That's all it took for his complete recovery. Mike got out of his bunk, showered, and dressed, just in time to be hailed as an adventurous hero by 20 or so of his fellow Peace Corps workers.

"I guess you really know how to sail now," said one of his friends. Mike played it cool and smiled. Glen and I introduced ourselves to the Peace Corps workers from throughout the South Pacific. From that time on, whenever Glen and I encountered Peace Corps workers on islands, we invited them aboard for a meal and to hear their stories. Their insights and company added an extra dimension to what we saw and experienced in our travels. Having delivered one of their own to the conference, we were universally welcomed by those attending. As an impromptu party formed in our cockpit, we quizzed the young volunteers about their experiences in Tonga. The Peace Corps workers agreed on one thing: Tongans generally kept to themselves.

"The way to get to know them is to attend church, which lasts a good part of every Sunday. Walk around the village on Saturday afternoon and you will be invited to church the next day. That could lead to further contact," we were told.

"A good start would be for Glen to wear a skirt," said another young man. "It will show his respect and interest in Tongan culture."

Glen pushed back on that idea, "You're not wearing one."

"Not for this Peace Corps conference," the volunteer told us, "but I do back in our home-base village."

The next day Glen tried on and ultimately purchased a *tupenu*; a skirt worn by men in Tonga. I bought one too because the extremely conservative and religious country had laws about modesty. Shorts of any kind were forbidden on Sundays. We weren't sure of the consequences if someone violated that local law, but generally it was our desire to be respectful.

We were surprised to learn Mormonism was the main religion in Tonga. Every island with a sizable village had a Mormon church doubling as a school. One reason for the success of the Mormon religion was free education and meals for the schoolchildren. By joining the church, Tongans had access to church-owned universities in Hawaii and Utah, giving them a chance at the American Dream. A Mormon missionary in Tonga told us more than 65 per cent of the Kingdom of Tonga population was Mormon. In other words, Tonga had the largest per capita population of Mormons in the world. The missionary also told us with that much influence in Tonga, the Mormon Church had a seat in the United Nations. I never considered the tiny Kingdom of Tonga with their 100,000 or so population holding much sway at the United Nations, but I guess it could be a start. In any case, there were large numbers of Tongan children receiving education and nutrition they otherwise might not receive from their government.

When I think of large-sized Pacific Islanders, I still think of Tonga. The sheer size of the people was stunning. They were very tall, and their girth was ample. To a Tongan, physical size was the measure of beauty. By local standards, that made for a lot of attractive Tongans.

It also made for many competitive athletes. The country was well represented with a sizeable number of participants at Pacific Rim rugby matches. The Mormons were also spreading the All-American sport of basketball. Since leaving North America I hadn't seen even one basketball court, but in Tonga I saw dozens.

* * * * *

For all the imposing looks, there was an interesting phenomenon in Tonga: the creation and high place in society of the *fakaleiti*. The fakaleiti caste was created when a family had too many boys and not enough girls to take care of the household chores. One of the young boys would be selected, dressed, and raised as a girl, then trained to perform the traditional female roles within the village. Often, the fakaleiti continued to dress and behave as women even into their adult lives. A percentage may have been gay, but not all of them. Some fakaleiti were married to women, while others related sexually only to other men. There was even a government sanctioned Tonga Leitis Association in the capital with sponsored events including a Miss Fakaleiti pageant. There was no shame and the villagers bestowed obvious respect upon their transgender population.

Life in Tonga seemed simple and from what I saw, was likely to stay that way. The ruling family and nobility ran the 170 or so islands without ever having to deal with pesky elected representatives. Tongans lived off basic subsistence farming of root vegetables, with limited income from kava, tourist shops and restaurants. But by far, the largest income for the country was in the form of remittances from other Tongans working overseas in New Zealand, Australia, and the USA.

Chapter 30

What made the passage between the Pacific Islands and New Zealand so dangerous was the severity and frequency of storms. To make it worse, there was no place along the more than 1,100-mile route for sailors to take shelter. True stories abound of sailboats and lives lost along the notorious route. Dangerous low-pressure systems periodically trudged their way up from the Antarctica in the Southern Ocean to the latitudes between New Zealand and the South Pacific. Whichever island group was the departure point—in our case Tonga—sailboats were certain to be hit by a storm along the way. The storm cycle was every five to seven days and the passage would take *It's Enough* eight or more days to complete. We readied ourselves and waited for the right weather window to depart.

On most mornings, sailors at anchor around us held radio sessions and talked about the latest weather fax and provided their opinion about passage timing. That may sound helpful, but weather in that area of the world was hard to predict, and even professional meteorologists often got it wrong. Sailors shared heated differences of opinion, one declaring such and such a day the perfect time to depart and another telling listeners they "would be sorry" if they followed such reckless advice. Some of the boat captains sounded knowledgeable while others sounded loud and scared. The arguments and educated guesses caused me anxiety and I began to obsess over the three daily weather fax downloads and Glen's analysis of the situation.

Stories of the storms and rough seas between the Pacific Islands and New Zealand deterred many sailors. They diverted and headed instead for the warmer climates of Cairns or Brisbane, Australia. However, we would be better positioned to explore Fiji, Vanuatu, and New Caledonia the following year if we based out of New Zealand. Even though sailing to New Zealand and staying for six months was tantalizing, it was clear that getting there would be difficult.

Considering what was at stake, sailors from one of the larger boats paid a meteorological service out of California to pick a weather window, giving the rest of us updates from the experts. The Californians finally reported that a good weather window was approaching, and in two days there would be an opportunity for a New Zealand departure. Suddenly there was a flurry of preparations in port. Sailors were double-checking equipment, sails, engine, electronics, fueling, preparing meals in advance... Almost a dozen boats waiting in our harbor decided to leave with the big, lead boat that was following the meteorological service's advice. But we would not be among them.

After the four-day Force 10 storm we had sailed through in the North Atlantic, Glen had developed a keen interest in forecasting the weather and devoted much time to it. For the past month in Tonga, he downloaded weather fax charts three times a day, comparing them to the weather we then encountered. He did not agree with the meteorological service analysis of the weather conditions and was concerned about the possibility of a nearby low-pressure system deepening. I argued for leaving, but not too much. After our big weather fiasco in France, Glen and I knew that impatience in a boat could be dangerous. Sitting tight and waiting for optimal conditions was more likely to get us to the desired destination—not always when we would like—but at least safely.

The day the fleet departed for New Zealand we rode out in our dinghy to bid farewell to friends, handing out Oreos for scurvy, and promising to reconnect soon in Opua, the northern port of entry in New Zealand. We took some good ribbing from sailors we had come to know well on various Pacific islands, who threatened to take the prime marina dockage before we arrived. Writing down the departing group's radio net schedule to monitor the travel conditions, we promised to keep in touch. *It's Enough* would follow in a couple of days, if all turned out as favorably as their *expert* forecasted.

Waving goodbye to our friends in the overcast sky felt odd. "Knowing that no matter when we leave, we are bound to get hit with something, makes this even more difficult," I told Glen.

We would see how things unfolded from our now nearly deserted anchorage in Tonga. From safe anchorage, we listened in that night on the fleet's radio net conversations but did not participate. There were plenty of check-ins, and we plotted the general positions of the fleet of boats on a paper chart to follow their progress. The lead boat captain was in twice daily contact with the met service over his satellite phone. Two days after the mass departure, the lead captain reported that the California weather gurus had sent him a message, "Turn back to Tonga!"

I heard those words, stopped cooking dinner, and called Glen to come listen as well. The boat captains in the fleet discussed the possibility of returning to Tonga, but after much back and forth, the entire group decided to tough it out. The return trip to Tonga would be upwind and the consensus was it would be quite uncomfortable against the wind and waves, with the possibility of getting smacked by the storm anyway. Every boat in the group chose to hold tight through what was described by the met service as a "deepening low" with winds in the 40 to 45 MPH range, gusting to 60. Those were wind speeds we had all been through, and they were neither comfortable nor desirable—but as long as no equipment broke or sails tore, highly doable.

Twelve hours later, we heard an unfamiliar meteorological term—weather bomb. The California weather experts urgently warned the boats that a weather bomb would reach them within 24 hours and explained the term as explosive cyclogenesis—which sounded even scarier. A storm *bombs* when a low-pressure area deepens more than 24 millibars of pressure within a 24-hour period. The effect of that kind of fast drop in pressure within a low-pressure system creates explosive winds, rain, and waves. It is called a bomb because the wind revolves so fast it creates a cyclonic mix of steep waves and rain so torrential a human would not even be able to stay standing.

The updated forecast predicted, "Winds in excess of 60 miles an hour, gusting higher." The question was, "How much higher than 60?" The possibilities were ominous. Waves were forecast at 25-35 feet high, breaking into flying foam. Memories of our North Atlantic storm three years before flashed through my mind and tears welled in my eyes. The danger for our friends enroute to New Zealand had escalated exponentially since the last forecast.

Sailors unlucky enough to get caught out in a weather bomb have two survival strategies: reduce the sails to handkerchief size and heave to or run under bare poles (no sails) with knotted ropes or a series drogue towing behind to break speed and avoid pitch poling in the massive seas. Though immensely relieved at having remained at port, Glen and I were very afraid for our friends. During the last radio communications before the big storm, the voices of the captains were breaking as they reported the building lightning, torrential rain, mounting winds, and fuming seas.

The sailors out there agreed there would be no further radio nets until after the storm. All hands were needed to prepare their boats and crew. (In most cases, as on our own relatively small craft, the crew was the captain's wife.) We plotted the boats' last-reported positions on our charts. As bad as the wind and seas were reported to be, the worst of the storm was still 12 hours away. The boat crews would have to use that time for everyone to get some sleep and food while they could. We heard weariness and fear in their quaking voices and hoped fervently that the convoy of boats would have the stamina required for the coming conditions. Though not religious people, there are forces at work beyond our understanding, and we prayed the crews would survive.

Safe at port in Tonga—400 miles away—Glen and I weathered the distant edge of the storm with winds of 45 gusting to 55. We were in a well-protected harbor but started anchor watch—24-hour monitoring of our GPS coordinates to make sure we did not drag to shore or hit a reef. Throughout the night and the next day, we covered two radio frequencies: the mayday frequency and the group's radio net frequency. To our great relief, there were no distress calls.

Once the storm passed, we finally heard a few boats come up on the net. Within another day, all the boats reported in. Everyone, however, sounded exhausted, beaten, and in low spirits. Some reported breakage or loss, mostly equipment or sails lashed on their masts or decks. Fortunately, there was no dismasting, pitch poling (when the boat is flipped over from end to end), or knockdowns/rollovers (when the boat rolls sideways and the mast goes under the water)—a major miracle given what they had been through. A few injuries were reported: broken ribs, an injured back, cuts, serious bruises, total exhaustion, dehydration from seasickness... but nothing that would require medical evacuation at sea.

How bad had it been out there? The dozen or so boats talked about that for a while and in the end could never agree. They said whatever wave height they reported would be wrong—they had to look too far up the mast to accurately assess. As for wind speed, their instruments were nailed at 60 knots, the top of the gauge, but the highest winds during the storm went well beyond that measure with explosive turbulence.

After the surprise weather bomb, most boats at anchor in Tonga no longer wanted to sail to New Zealand and departed for Australia instead. Overwrought that we too would be blasted on our way to New Zealand, I was ready and willing to abandon our plan of a six-month visit to New Zealand.

"Let's sail to Australia, leave the boat in a marina and just fly to New Zealand from there," I proposed to Glen. "Please?" I pleaded with tears in my eyes. "It's too dangerous." I still experienced occasional panic attacks triggered by big storms or even the prospect of heavy weather. My nervous system took a beating following the progress of the weather bombed boats. I could not sleep from worry. My hairbrush was packed with an unbelievable amount of hair, falling out from the stress. I had been in their place before and knew how it felt to expect that each mountainous, crashing wave would be the one to destroy your boat. I was ready to skip New Zealand, the country I had most looked forward to on our circumnavigation.

As the storm weakened, Glen continued to analyze the weather data and came up with a departure plan. We would leave that afternoon!

He convinced me by showing how the extreme low-pressure system had been very large and that if we left right then, in its aftermath, we would increase our odds of being in New Zealand before the next one formed. Even though we would depart in less-than-ideal stormy conditions, we would have two things going for us: we knew the winds would only decrease in strength as we sailed out of the low-pressure system, and if we moved with as much sail out as we could handle, achieving 200-

plus miles a day, we could potentially arrive in New Zealand before conditions worsened... but we had to leave immediately.

"Immediately" seemed to be the watchword of our entire circumnavigation. My agreement to leave for New Zealand in 30- to 35-knot winds and heavy rain was the strongest testimonial of my trust in Glen's judgment. After all, he got us alive to where we were thus far.

We stowed the dinghy on the mizzen deck and outboard in the large aft locker. I did my part preparing and stowing things securely down below. I turned on our reverse-osmosis water maker to top off our fresh water tanks for the passage, and pulled out the peanut butter, the only thing I could keep down in rough seas. Pulling anchor from Tonga, I called our storm-surviving companions on the radio, and with a lump in my throat, told them, "See you in New Zealand!"

* * * * *

It was counter-intuitive to leave a safe and protected harbor in high winds and rain, but we did. Little did we know at the time but leaving at the tail end of a bad storm would become our strategy for cruising between the Pacific Islands and New Zealand. Glen's approach proved sound. We toughed out a couple days of 35-knot winds and huge, leftover waves, but we reached our goal of 200-plus-mile days. By day three, we had sunshine and 18- to 25-knot winds that carried us on the fast track toward Opua, New Zealand, the northernmost and closest port of entry. As dawn broke on the seventh day, I saw glimpses of land in the distance and woke Glen with a hearty cry of, "Land Ho!"

Soon we responded to a radio call from a patrolling New Zealand Coast Guard Orion aircraft requesting our information and destination port. The pilot asked if we knew gale force winds and rain were expected that afternoon. We assured him we did and that we had as much sail up as we could handle. All we could do at that point was lean forward and cross our fingers we would beat the storm. Entering the Bay of Islands, the light rain grew heavier and the winds picked up. They increased to gale force and pelting rain as we breathlessly pulled up to the quarantine dock seven-and-a-half days after departing Tonga. Safely and without incident, we had arrived in Kiwiland.

Totally spent, but with *It's Enough* secured to the quarantine dock, Glen and I slept and held each other for 12 hours that night and woke up to a new chapter of our sailing life. We had worked and played hard to get from France to New Zealand in two-and-a-half years and traveled more than 12,000 nautical miles. For the next six months we planned to take it easy and live aboard *It's Enough* in a New Zealand marina. We might even splurge to buy a used car to explore both large islands. Mentally and emotionally, I felt as solid and stable as I had in a long while. The boat, Glen, and I had been through a lot. The choices we made in and about our boat had more than proven themselves while the rigors and joys of the cruising life were well and truly in our blood. At last we would have six months in a first-world country full of marinas, keen sailors, and daily access to a laundromat—simple but wonderful little pleasures!

Awakened the next morning by a crisp knock on the side of the boat, two customs and one immigration inspector greeted us, and one handed me a sheet of paper to fill out. "Our goal is to be the friendliest and most helpful customs and immigration in the Pacific," the customs form declared in prominent typing at the top. Really?

"What a charming way to greet visitors to your country. People from the United States must think it's a trick," I told the inspector, recalling surly border officials in the States.

"We hear that a lot," answered one of the three inspectors who removed their shoes before boarding. The inspectors were friendly but also very serious about their inspection. They required us to open our safe (the first and only country to do so), they checked below the floorboards, in the freezer, the fridge, and all the little nooks and crannies only sailors are supposed to know about.

The unexpected thoroughness was worrisome. We did not carry drugs or much of value on our boat, but we did possess one tiny little thing we had never admitted to having: a 9mm sidearm with a box of ammunition. In our years of voyaging, we had never even pulled it out of its almost inaccessible hiding place. It was onboard for security, and thankfully, we had never been threatened or boarded by bad guys. If the New Zealand customs officials found it, they would fine us heavily, take the gun, and possibly bar us entry to the country—or all three.

The New Zealand customs inspectors did not find our handgun, but they came close. During the check-in to dozens of countries, very few—not even the U.S.—had come aboard to inspect our boat. The others were mostly happy for us to bring our paperwork and passports to their office, collect their check-in fee, and rubber-stamp our papers. The New Zealanders were on the business end of what was mainly an agricultural inspection. Prior to arriving, we had been told that eggs, meats, cheese, milk, butter, honey, nuts, dried fruit, grains, fresh produce, and more were all restricted from entry into New Zealand. While cruising the western Pacific we ate through our provisions fairly well, and the limited selection in Tonga made it easy to finish off our existing storage. It was understandable for customs to purge so much of our food stores as much of New Zealand's economy is based on dairy and agriculture. Who knew what bugs could be lurking in a package of flour bought on a remote island? We did!

Inspection complete, we were legally and officially landed, and felt like celebrating. We walked to the Opua Sailing Club that night to celebrate with a proper meal and reunited there with dozens of other sailors we knew from the previous seven months of our Pacific crossing.

Everyone was talking about a major news headlines, "Littleton Marina Boats Destroyed in Storm." The storm that swept in as we entered the dock the day before had hit Christchurch in South Island with 110 mile-per-hour winds. The waves pounded over the breakwater and swept away the entire marina.

I read aloud the article about the destruction of boats and docks in Littleton Marina. In the rest of the world, a 110 MPH storm warrants a name. Usually it's a title that begins with typhoon or hurricane. In New Zealand it was just a storm. By Kiwi standards, it was big enough to make headlines, but did not qualify for the record books.

There's a reason why New Zealand grows strong sailors. It's surrounded by water with the Southern Ocean calling all the shots. Sub-Antarctic winds and storms blow across the small nation with not much in the way of landmass to weaken or slow them down.

"We need to be careful selecting the marina where we dock," said Glen. "We don't need to lose our boat and lives while we're asleep!" That thought changed our criteria for choosing our base of operations for the next six months. The day before, we had wanted to live on South Island within walking distance of shops and a quaint main street to better appreciate a small-town culture. Instead, we would find a marina on the North Island, which is further from the Southern Ocean, in a marina with a natural harbor, sheltered from prevailing winds and a tall breakwater protecting the entrance. In Christchurch, the Littleton Marina entrance had been open to prevailing winds, and the man-made breakwater was not constructed for the caliber of weather the Antarctic can muster.

Our research began in earnest. Talking with salty sailors native to New Zealand waters we settled on a new stormproof marina called Gulf Harbor, about 45 miles north of Auckland. On the upside it provided excellent protection for our sailboat. On the downside, the marina was part of a new housing development that lacked charm, and the nearest grocery was a distant 15 miles away.

As it turned out, Kiwis love visiting sailors, and we were warmly welcomed at Gulf Harbor in a way that might not have happened in downtown Auckland, the boating capital of the country. During that time, visitors appeared to outnumber the Kiwis in the city of Auckland. Several months earlier, Team New Zealand had successfully defended the America's Cup, and the city was still teeming with foreign sailors and tourists. Glen and I likely would have had fewer chances to forge real friendships in Auckland amid all the America's Cup visitors.

On the other hand, we had arrived in Auckland too late to watch the America's Cup sailing competition. New Zealand had retained the Cup and would have to defend it in two years with the venue once again in Auckland. Most of the sailing syndicates, with hundreds of support personnel, decided to stay and practice in Auckland until the next Cup series. The City of Auckland was like a smaller version of an Olympic sailing village: fun to visit for a while, but not the real New Zealand. In contrast, normal sailors like Glen and me blended comfortably into everyday Kiwi life and were welcomed by local sailors on the docks in Gulf Harbor, 45 miles north of Auckland.

Chapter 31

I hope driving on the left side of the road works for us. For that matter, we haven't driven in three years, so maybe the entire act of driving will be strange," I said excitedly as I scanned the Auckland newspaper classified section looking for the perfect car for our six-month stay. The used-car ads were chock full of late-model cars with low miles and low prices. The cheap price tags seemed at odds with the country's relatively high housing, food, and fuel prices. The contrast left us perplexed.

Glen and I decided to go to a dealership near us to look at a used Nissan Pathfinder listed for what we figured had to be a misprint. We caught a ride to the car lot and were welcomed by the owner as if he knew us. He had done a lot of business with visiting sailors over the years and came up with a win-win arrangement for both parties. The unbeatable price was available to us on the condition we would let him sell the car when we departed New Zealand in six months. We could not imagine a better situation and swiftly tried to put a deposit on the car using our credit card. However, they did not do things that way in New Zealand.

Whenever we could get to the bank, a check would be fine. Until then, the dealership's insurance would cover us if we wanted to go ahead and drive the vehicle off the lot. Glen asked if we could take it to a mechanic for an inspection and the owner told Glen he would give us a warranty for any major repairs for the next six months. Was there a hidden camera somewhere? We were flabbergasted by the easy transaction that truly seemed to be mostly to our advantage. "If the whole country is this nice, we may never leave," I thought to myself as Glen drove off the car lot.

Later, a Kiwi friend told us the reason why cars in New Zealand were so affordable: there was no import duty on used vehicles in New Zealand and the previously owned cars were mainly imported from Japan and Singapore. Those left-drive countries are geographically small, which kept mileage accumulation low, and nearby which reduced shipping costs. Japan and Singapore both stimulate their economies with a tax on vehicles more than four years old. Instead of registration costs going down as vehicles age—like in the U.S.—those Asian countries raise those costs, prompting residents there to get rid of their moderately used cars. Lucky New Zealand. Lucky us.

New Zealanders have cracked the code on travel within their country. Kiwis, as they liked to be called, stay at holiday parks. Space could be rented for one's own caravan (the Kiwi term for an RV) or stay in one of their parked caravans or cabins equipped with kitchens and cookware. The holiday parks had a communal kitchen and fire ring area for campers to gather, where we met other traveling New Zealanders. The only people we found in B&Bs were other foreigners.

In the states, "motel" can in some places have a negative connotation. In New Zealand, motels are always good and at times excellent. Each room was more like a small apartment with a complete kitchen stocked with fresh foods such as milk, bread, eggs, butter, coffee, and occasionally yogurt. The New Zealanders we met who had visited the United States complained about American motels that in their opinion "short change the traveler" due to lack of a kitchen. On the other hand, they had nothing but praise for our inexpensive and large restaurant serv-ings, which they declared big enough for two people.

* * * * *

Buying a serviceable and late-model used car was easier than driving on the opposite side of the road. It soon became obvious we weren't the only ones making big mistakes in that department. New Zealand welcomed as many as two-three million visitors a year, quite a lot for a country with a population of four million. That would amount to one to two tourists for every local Kiwi!

Many of those visitors were Americans and Europeans accustomed to driving on the right side and, like us, had a hard time staying on the opposite side of the road. It's not a habit to be corrected overnight. Even after driving on the left side became second nature for us, it was not uncommon to encounter a rental car or caravan driven by tourists com-ing head on. We could never drop our guard and my sentiment was, "How ironic it would be to survive ocean crossings and mighty storms at sea only to bite the dust driving the roads of New Zealand!"

* * * * *

"Is it possible for us to purchase a summer membership for your Manly Veterans Tennis Club?" I asked. "We are both Veterans of the United States Army; here's an ID card to prove it." Glen and I had tennis rac-quets in one hand and military ID cards in the other.

The tennis club looked like a scene out of Wimbledon: tennis whites, five well-maintained courts, a leader board sign-up for doubles play, and a fine-looking clubhouse where I imagined social events if they allowed us to join. Best yet, we would be playing folks our own age instead of trying to return the super hard serves of college-aged players. The lady I asked introduced herself as Wendy. She was a fellow redhead (or, as the Kiwis pronounced it, *reedhead*). I felt a little uncomfortable because it looked like she was trying not to laugh, and I couldn't figure out why.

Wendy answered, "I will talk to the Club Board, but I believe we can create a type of temporary membership for you. Come back tomorrow morning at 9:00 with your racquets, and you should be able to play with us." The next morning, Glen and I arrived sporting our tennis whites (okay maybe off-white from too many washings in a bucket at sea). At the club, play stopped, and a few dozen Kiwi tennis players— middle aged and older—greeted us with good-natured salutes, kidding about a military invasion by the Americans.

Finally, one woman I spoke with told me, "Never mind them. In New Zealand we use the term veteran for anyone over the age of 45—it has nothing to do with military service. You don't need your military IDs here and you are most welcome."

Glen and I joined the Veterans Tennis Club and most mornings played tennis with a group of friendly and sportsmanlike Kiwis in the village of Manly. Joining their potlucks, playing in their tournaments, we ended up good friends with more than a few. Their advice and guidance gave us insider tips on their favorite towns, hikes, and places to experience in New Zealand.

One man from the southern part of North Island asked us if we liked rivers as much as oceans and recommended a canoe trip close to his family farm. He invited us to stay at his home, then directed us to join what he claimed would be a memorable time on the water—even for blue-water sailors.

Chapter 32

Minutes earlier, the river had been a sun-filled, cheerful place. Canyon walls framed the cloudless, blue sky tented above us, and white water from occasional boulders added interest to our remote surroundings. But during the second hour of day one, things on the Rangitikei River took a serious turn.

"Get ready to paddle hard!" Glen called out as we approached the churning water of a large eddy. He was steering and paddling in the back and I was like a machine up front, beating at the water from side to side like a mad woman. My arms and shoulders were burning with the effort, but all it took to convince me to paddle harder was a glance downstream at Cadillac-sized boulders forcing the water into fast, massive waves of white water. Setting my jaw, I was determined to stay upright through the rapids. We stretched our arms, planted the paddles deep, and pulled hard to make it past a dreaded eddy… but an invisible hand reached out, grabbed the boat, and shoved us straight toward a wall of rock. I threw the paddle inside the boat, braced myself, and THUD! We crashed head-on into the side of the gorge wall. It stopped us cold. The 17-foot-long Dagger canoe recoiled and shuddered with the impact, but miraculously stayed upright. Water splashed around my knees and the canoe reeled crazily. There was a hole in the bow. Water surged in and covered our legs. It was like trying to steer a bathtub. The canoe went belly-up and we were destined to navigate at least some of the rapids on our unprotected butts.

The icy cold of the snowmelt river water shocked my muscles and lungs. Gasping for air and pedaling my legs I tried to find ground, but the water was too deep. Despite the roar of the river, I could hear our guide yelling out advice, "Feet down river!" I commanded my limbs into action and flogged freezing arms and legs, attempting to gain steerage while avoiding gigantic, jutting rocks. Expedition mates, still in their canoes, paddled past screaming out unhelpful survival tips as I tried to gain my bearings and frantically searched for Glen. Time stood still, and everything seemed to move in slow motion.

Shivering, with feet rigidly pointed down river, I struggled to assess my predicament. The canoe had been sidelined with a gaping hole and there was no other way into or out of the steep rock canyons but down the wild river. Something short of panic gripped me. Glen suddenly appeared in the water ahead of me, and I forced myself to gain control. My frozen extremities barely responded to make an all-out effort to swim toward and follow him. As I neared, we found shallower water, clawing and dragging our uncooperative bodies toward the pebbly bank. My feet were so cold I could barely feel them, and I stumbled several times before reaching solid land. Unable to stand, I shivered on all fours and wondered if—hoped—this spelled the end of our four-day whitewater canoe adventure. Gaining control of basic functions, I looked around, but the dry land revealed no clues as to how we could get out of the remote Rangitikei River without our canoe, clothes, and gear. Assessing the fantastic possibility of a helicopter rescue, I saw Royce, our Kiwi guide, had intercepted our half-submerged canoe and waterproof-bag of dry clothes and sleeping gear.

So much for a quick helicopter exit; the trip would go on.

The Rangitikei River was not for beginners, as we most decidedly were. Glen and I had never set foot in a canoe until that morning, but the company brochure promised "two hours of instruction," that turned out to consist of 15 minutes of introductions and a life-vest fitting.

"You two are world sailors," Royce had assured us. "If you can cross oceans, our little Rangitikei River shouldn't be so hard for you. Just follow behind me and try to avoid the eddies. You'll be 'right." Typical Kiwi understatement (of which I had heard plenty). In New Zealand, the country that invented bungee jumping, flying fox box, and *gorp* balls, there was no such thing as baby steps or ramping up. Just get out there and hang on tight.

Once I could feel my feet, I stood up on the bank and put my arms around Glen. "I tried to point out that eddy," worried the spill had been my fault.

Perhaps Glen thought so too, "I still haven't seen it," he replied wryly. "Maybe we need to work on hand signals." Glen and I stood trembling while our fellow canoers banked their boats and laughed at our sorry, dripping selves.

"We never thought world sailors would be the first in," said a pharmacist from Christchurch who stepped out of a perfectly intact canoe. In Kiwi speak, comments like that are designed to *take the piss out of someone* with a bit too much arrogance.

"Maybe we shouldn't have mentioned we sailed to New Zealand," I answered, which brought a laugh and seemed to humble us sufficiently. As we ducked behind a tree to change into dry clothes, the guide pulled out shortbread cookies and put on the *billie* to boil water for tea. Slowly our canoe drained of river water and Royce, a strapping twenty-something native Kiwi, pulled out duct tape for an on-the-spot field repair. The canoe would be our transport out of the challenging river gorge after all.

There's no better way to get to know complete strangers than spend four days with them in the wilderness. To that point, our friendships with Kiwis had been forged on the dock at our Auckland area marina. Our New Zealand acquaintances so far were affable, hardcore local sailors who wanted to talk sailing and sailboats. On the river, we had opportunities to listen to the life stories of Kiwis from different backgrounds and parts of the country: the pharmacist, a dairy farmer, an avocado farmer, a politician, a couple of university students, and two river guides.

All in the group had our little quirks, but even with our disparate backgrounds everything meshed. The dairy farmer was the first one up in the morning to make a fire and put on the tea. Meal preparation was a team effort to which Glen and I contributed American flapjacks to the *brekkie*. Lunch was quick, simple sandwiches, so by supper we had worked up healthy appetites. The dinner menu reflected a normal Kiwi fare of meat, roasted veggies, and dessert bars they call slices. We begged off telling our voyaging tales, so we could hear everyone else's stories. After long talks and getting to know each other around the campfire, we fell asleep not to the usual slapping of waves against the hull of our sailboat but to the quiet roar of the Rangitikei rushing past.

The last night we told our own story and offered invitations to our bonded group to come for a visit and possible sail. We scribbled down everyone's contact information and during the next few months reconnected with the dairy and avocado farmers. They graciously gave us tours of their farms and we met their wives, who had already heard about the world sailors who couldn't handle the Rangitikei River.

* * * * *

"Tramping is just walking," a Kiwi friend assured me as Glen and I studied the New Zealand Tramping Guide to the Great Walks. That figured. New Zealanders were so understated they called five-day hikes tramping. For a country the size of Colorado, New Zealand seemed to get bigger the more we saw of it. We had explored the area around Auckland but were getting antsy to strike out and see the entire country top to bottom. A Great Walk looked appealing, the most famous being the Milford Track, rated the "Finest Walk in the World" by those who had experienced it. One of our Kiwi friends surprised me with different advice.

"None of them!" he said. "Why waste five days on a walk that requires reservations for lodges along the way and costs thousands of dollars? Milford Track is just another beautiful walk in New Zealand except it's filled with tourists and it rains a heck of a lot in that region. Explore New Zealand like a Kiwi. Every town from top to bottom has trails and paths built by the locals, and it's a great way to see the country. Drive for a couple hours and when you feel like stretching your legs, stop at the next town or village tourist information office and ask about the best hike for the time you want to spend. Travel like a Kiwi—laid back!"

At the risk of stereotyping four million people, we had noticed that most Kiwis really were laid back. Their endlessly optimistic attitude was best evidenced by their *fun comes first* work ethic and what seemed to be their favorite saying, "She'll be 'right." We noticed when a Kiwi said, "She'll be 'right," it was often an extremely challenging if not downright hopeless situation. Strangely enough, everything usually did turn out all right. One of my goals for our six months in New Zealand was to develop a "She'll be 'right" attitude. My life as an Army Major was completely upended in the land *down under*.

One other thing that surprised us on a regular basis was how Kiwis were always undervaluing themselves to outsiders. New Zealand was founded by farmers and sheepherders whose lineage was self-effacing and humble to the extreme. The more successful the individual, the more modest he or she was. Whenever we complimented them or their country, they would find some way to fend off the kudos.

A Kiwi friend acknowledged that the extreme humility was grounded in New Zealand history. He explained that for a long time the small nation of immigrant farmers and sheep ranchers were all equal in their standard of living and existed as one big social class. When different social classes emerged, or someone got ahead, there was a tendency to cut down those who stood out. "Tall poppies get cut," was an expression left over from those early days. It was quite an interesting outlook for me, coming from the U.S., the land of many tall poppies.

Before arrival in New Zealand from Tonga, I wondered if we would get island fever being land-based for six months. But traveling *like a Kiwi*, New Zealand felt a lot bigger than it looked on the map; it could take a lifetime to fully explore its many wonders. On the volcanic North Island in Rotorua, we soaked in hot springs and hiked along bubbling mud and sulfur pits. On less populated South Island, we saw places that reminded us of Maine, Scotland, and Colorado, not to mention the breathtaking fiords of which we had never seen the likes. Finally, our six months in the land filled with picturesque beauty and high adventure were coming to an end. I expressed my desire to stay longer, but Glen reminded me of our larger quest to sail around the world.

The goodness and sincerity of the Kiwis stole our hearts. Saying farewell to our good friends in New Zealand was very tough, but as the weather turned cold and rainy it became easier to depart. It would be a tight schedule with only six months available in the South Pacific islands before the tropical cyclone season forced us to Australia. We would be hard pressed to fit in three major island groups in that time. Fiji alone has more than 300 islands, and that was where we headed.

Chapter 33

Glen stuck his face up into the cockpit and asked, "What's up?" So much for stealth. Minutes before I had taken in about half the sails as quietly as possible, but the giveaway flapping sound and the winch creaking under a change in the load woke Glen from a sound sleep.

I don't know why, but I always felt like I had done something sneaky when I reduced sail on my night watch. Glen usually thought I was wimping out on the opportunity to rack up some fast miles on a passage. Sometimes, I suppose, I really was overly cautious. If the boat was heeling at too much of an angle, it didn't give me any wiggle room for strong gusts, but my real fear (one of so many in cruising life), was that if we experienced a rogue wave while already at a steep angle of heel it could put the mast in the water. Called a knockdown, it happened to two couples we knew, and more than the day was ruined for them. As to the conversation at hand, I had other motives.

"I reduced sails because we were going to arrive at dark," I called back to Glen. "I'm slowing us down. Airbrakes. I'll wake you up when we get close enough to see the lights of Suva. Go back to bed for another couple of hours."

Suva, the capital and main port of Fiji, was a busy place. Island freighters, tankers, and yes, a few sailboats all converged at a narrow opening. In reef-strewn waters with poor navigational markers, such as around the islands of Fiji, landfall to a new place was wisely accomplished during daylight hours.

We didn't plan to spend much time in Suva. The tensions between the native Fijian and East Indian population had resulted in a small but violent coup earlier, and we wanted to stay clear of the unrest that caused it. The day we arrived we learned something about the friction between the two groups.

Having successfully entered the port and checked in with the authorities, we hailed a taxi to get to a grocery store. The rickety cab reeked of sandalwood incense. Hindi music blared from the radio, and a red elephant Ganesh Hindu god stood guard, suctioned to the dashboard and bobbing its head at passengers. The driver was dressed in traditional Hindu clothes and spoke with a strong Indian accent. That experience on a Fiji taxi ride was unexpected, so I could not resist the urge to ask the driver where he was from.

"Gujarat in western part of India," the driver, whose name was Raj, replied with some head wobbling, "but I was born here in Suva."

"How did you come to speak Hindi?" I asked, referring to the Hindi radio station, "When was the last time you visited India?" Raj shook his head. "I have never been to India. My great grandparents were brought to Fiji in 1890 by the British to work the sugarcane fields. We have our own Indian schools here, and we speak Hindi at home." As we drove through industrial downtown Suva, we passed Indian shops and restaurants housed in well-kept buildings. Raj told us that 40 percent of the population of Fiji was of East Indian origins. It was evident they had clung to their ancestral culture and language. He told us the farmland on the two big islands was all owned by native Fijians; by law only Fijians could possess land. East Indians leased the land to farm sugar cane, but many Fijians were refusing to renew the leases to the farmers. "Fiji for the Fijians!" was the new strong slogan in the country and was splashed across signs along the roadsides. To make a living, Indians turned to shop keeping, starting restaurants, and driving taxis in the larger towns.

"You will never see a Fijian driving a taxi," Raj continued. I kept an eye out the whole time we were in Suva; he was right. Later we found out the Fijians wanted the Indians to stay on the two larger, mainland type islands to keep the out islands reserved for native Fijians. It was a perfect storm for discontent and unrest.

* * * * *

The racial tensions that oppressed in Suva dissolved behind us as we headed toward the outer islands where life was simpler. Despite their attitude toward East Indians, Fijians were friendly to visitors, providing we understood and observed their cultural practices. In Fiji one must be invited as a guest of the village to drop anchor in front of an island. Fijians don't consider their village and property to stop at the high-water mark. To them, the ocean surrounding their island and the fish on their reefs were also their property. Anchoring in front of their village designated the sailors on board as houseguests. It could be a sticky situation in some cultures, but Fijians had an ancestral custom that allowed visitors, even other Fijian travelers, to approach and gracefully ask permission to stay. It was a ceremony called *sevu* and included a ritualized gift giving of the native kava root from the visitors to the chief and elders of the village.

Kava is a brown root both cultivated and grown wild in much of the South Pacific. It is ground into a fine powder, mixed with water, and consumed in large quantities by native men in kava-drinking groups. Kava drinking is a social and manly part of village life that starts most afternoons with the pounding of the roots and the consumption of the saturated kava-root water after dinner. Called grog, it is a tranquilizing, non-alcoholic drink that numbs the tongues, lips, and even faces of novices such as Glen and me. The village men were so accustomed to it, they could drink entire bowls of grog, and afterwards it was hard to see any difference. Visitors could buy half a kilo of kava root at the markets wrapped in festive strings and paper, ready for sevu presentation. Kava was a cash crop in Fiji and a main source of income since being identified by western cultures as a tonic for stress.

Our first opportunity to present sevu was on the remote island of Dravuni, one of eight or so islands enclosed within the lagoon formed by Astrolabe Reef. In Suva we purchased a dozen bundles of kava, each wrapped in the brightly colored gift paper. Readying for the formal ceremony, Glen and I dressed conservatively, covering as many body parts as possible. For myself, that meant a long skirt and a shirt with sleeves. Glen found the longest pair of shorts he owned, which he paired with a long-sleeved shirt. In proper attire, we gathered our little bundle of kava, beached our dinghy, and asked the first person we saw to take us to the turanga-ni-koro, or village chief.

After a trek through the village we were greeted by the chief who invited us to sit on the ground outside his bure (house with thatched roof). Glen placed the sevu gift of kava on the ground in front of the chief and said, "We seek your permission to anchor on the islands within the lagoon and fish their waters from time to time for food." Speaking slowly and using hand signals he bridged the language gap, and broad smiles flashed. The chief picked up our offering, signaling his acceptance, then performed a hand-clapping welcome blessing our home country and family. With the ritual concluded, we relaxed, and the chief waved other villagers over to meet us.

One young man spoke excellent English and told us, "The chief asks you to not visit one of our islands. Our village is receiving money from an American television company to keep a group of people on the island without any food to see if they can survive. It's strange to us, but if anyone goes there, we will lose our money." Glen and I looked at each other in surprise. A Survivor show on a nearby island! The villagers would earn a great deal of money for hosting the shoot. We made a mental note to one day look up that episode and enjoy a flashback to the beauty of those islands.

The ceremony initiated us as part of the village, and we were invited to join in most activities including the kava group in the evenings. Before we tried kava, I wondered why its recreational popularity had not spread to the West since it was legal all over the world. My first taste of kava gave me the answer—it tasted like dishwater. Not to be outdone by the alcohol-based drinks popular the world over, with repeated consumption, kava reportedly ruins a person's liver. I believe this to be true. Many older Fijian men had yellow eyes—an indicator of liver damage—and they moved at a consistently slow pace. Maybe the laidback Fijian attitude imprinted from drinking thousands of gallons of kava!

Big island, little island, it didn't matter. In Fiji, no matter where we were, at 4:00 p.m. we could hear the beat of heavy metal or wood rods pounding out the powder for that evening's kava gathering. Only men were allowed to sit around the large kava bowl, but women did their own drinking of kava in a more private setting. Because we were guests we were invited to attend, but never stayed long. Yellow eyes were not in my future. The first time, I filled the kava cup with only a sip and still it numbed my lips. The second time around, it froze my whole face and made me so relaxed I could barely keep my eyes open.

The best part of the sevu ceremony was the sense of belonging to the island and the freedom to come and go along its beaches and hills. It was such a joy to get off the boat and get some land time, walking and climbing over the rolling terrain. The permission granted by the chief gave us the liberty to explore the islands without worrying about intruding on a village or interrupting the residents' daily life. In fact, once we were part of the island, the friendly natives truly wanted to mingle and do things with us. During one of our walks ashore, Glen was invited to go spearfishing with two young men. Since the reef was a kilometer away, we decided to take the two men aboard, sail to the spot, and use *It's Enough* as the mother ship while the spear fishermen threw their bloody catch in the smaller dinghy. Our sailboat was anchored directly off the reef, and it was my job to stay on board in case the wind tried to shift us onto the coral. The entire time I was nervous as a treed cat, peering off the bow to make sure the anchor was not dragging or damaging the precious coral reef. It also gave me a front-row seat to the men's activities.

Get two or more guys together and whatever they are doing turns into a competition. Glen and the two village men were out for hours, moving up and down the reef, spearing grouper and snapper, then throwing the gory fish into the dinghy. What does blood in the water attract? Sharks! When several of the blood-craving creatures appeared, the men climbed into the dinghy and moved up the reef. That happened over and over. Not wanting to let the spearfishing competition die, the men continued to reposition their fishing spot. At one point, I saw them as a speck in the distance and was left to worry not only about the sailboat getting blown on the reef, but the likelihood of a shark finding a tasty Glen in the bloody waters.

When the three men finally returned to *It's Enough* with a couple dozen nice-sized fish for the village, one of them casually mentioned that the prior year he had been attacked by a great white shark around that very spot. "I'm glad I didn't hear that story earlier!" I admitted.

"Oh no worries," the villager explained, "Sharks only attack when you've been bad so that's why we were okay this time. Last year, the day before I went fishing, I had bad words with my father's brother. He told me to watch out because something bad always happens to people who show disrespect. He was right because the next day the shark got a bite of my leg." I did not notice before but, sure enough, the man had a huge chunk of skin gouged out of his discolored calf. "If we are guilty of having done something bad, we must go to the village chief with an offering of *yaqona* (kava), tell what we did bad and be forgiven," he continued. "Then we can spearfish."

That was the first (but not the last) person I knew to be bitten by a shark. It was clever how the Fijian beliefs encouraged harmonious village life. Not only that, the belief system fostered a lack of fear while spearing food for the village.

I told Glen, "I'm taking more kava to the chief to protect you from sharks while you're spearfishing!"

"No need," he said. "I'm good all the time."

* * * * *

Normally we would go out of our way to avoid mangrove swamps. The murky brown water from the swamp made it hard to see coral heads or marine life, and at low tide, it was smelly. That said, there we were, heading straight for the mangrove trees amongst an armada of dinghies filled with other sailors anchored on the island of Makongai in Fiji.

Bright and early that morning, Wonga, a Fijian man we met a few days earlier, paddled to our boat asking if we wanted to go see the turtles. Although not sure what that might entail, Glen hopped into the dinghy and skittered around to the other sailboats at anchor to see if they wanted to join the expedition. Early morning projects could be a bit iffy with laidback cruising sailors and we weren't sure how much participation to expect. But the sheer mystery about the outing added to the interest. Ten of us from five sailboats piled into three dinghies as Wonga directed us to the other side of the island.

Wonga urged Glen to max the throttle, saying time was running short. His familiarity with the area told him that right then the large, green turtles were in the mangroves. Slack tide was minutes away and it was necessary to get to the mangroves before then. Once the tide started ebbing or receding the turtles departed in droves, leaving their leafy green meals until the next high-tide cycle. To consume as much as possible, the turtles would leave at the last minute, creating a fast and furious exodus as the tide went out. With five-foot tides found in that area of Fiji, the turtles didn't want to get stranded in the swamp.

Anchoring the dinghies where instructed, we lined ourselves in thigh-high water, using the natural reef to help channel the turtles past us. Truthfully, none of us expected to see too many turtles as they can be rare and difficult to spot. But what a treat for us doubters. Once the water started creeping lower and lower on our legs, the mass turtle exodus began. Dozens of sea turtles, some several feet long, glided and maneuvered to get out of the mangrove swamps to the wide ocean waters. They shot right past us with their little turtle feet paddling impossibly fast—like the wind-up tub toys for kids. Crowded in the same funnel as the escaping turtles, we could see the detail and designs of their shells as well as their pointy little heads as they zipped past us—not to be delayed by pesky humans. As they swam for deeper water, we could see several different turtle species. Clever and fast, the turtles avoided colliding with each other, the reef, or us.

Once the exodus was over, we figured it was the end of the show, but Wonga had other plans. He pulled out a dozen empty burlap flour bags and told us it was time to hunt for crabs. With lots of family in Louisiana, I was pretty sure there should be more equipment needed to hunt crabs than a burlap sack. Wonga showed us otherwise. He took us into the bush behind the mangrove trees and told us to check the crab traps.

The Fijians had built permanent crab traps close to the mangroves, seeded them, then checked for bounty periodically. The bait to lure them was made by piling rocks one deep in a circle and filling the shallow pit with cracked coconuts. They then covered the coconut meat and shells with palm fronds, creating a protected nest for the crabs. As the coconut meat aged and started stinking, the foul odor attracted crabs from all over the marsh. Crabs love to munch on rotting coconut meat, and Wonga said it made them taste sweet. Searching at first for the traps that had not been checked in a week, our noses led us right to the spot.

We came upon the first trap too noisily with ten of us talking, laughing, and behaving in a generally non-stealthy manner. About the time the smell hit our nostrils we saw the frightened crabs scurrying away. Surely, we had blown the chance of harvesting crabs from that trap, but Wonga flung away the palm fronds to reveal a teeming mass of what looked like coconut shells but were actually coconut crabs. As our eyes adjusted, we saw dozens of them trying to burrow beneath the husks of empty coconut shells, while others tried to make a break for the perimeter. The quantity and size of the crabs were startling. With large, red pincers they snapped everywhere at once and I wasn't sure of the right technique to safely grab one. When it came to collecting the crabs, we sailors proved worthless. But not Wonga! He moved with purpose and expertly grabbed the big ones while avoiding the hazardous pincers. When things calmed down, Wonga taught us where and how to grab the crabs, so we could be more helpful with the other traps.

By the time we got to the next crab trap we were psyched and raring to go. That time, not a crab knew we were there. Glen flung the next set of palm fronds aside, then joined the rest of us in a madcap snatch of the teeming crabs as we shrieked and laughed at the chaos. More than a few got away, but still our burlap sacks were a writhing, snapping mass of coconut crabs. If anyone ever wanted to devise a carnival event that was an adrenaline rush and extreme fun, snaring snapping crabs could be the answer. A competition for size was waged and after the fourth trap, we ran out of burlap sacks. Two additional unchecked traps would have to wait for another day. We seeded the traps we had already sprung with more cracked coconuts and palm fronds. By the time we finished, the smell of rotten coconut no longer bothered us—it was the fragrance of bounty.

Wonga took all the crabs back to the village and invited our group of ten to his house that afternoon for kava followed by crabmeat cooked in coconut milk. As it turned out, there is more claw and shell than meat on coconut crabs. Crabmeat was sparse despite the number we had caught. As we sat around picking crab shells out of our meal (their shells are very thin and difficult to crack whole), we congratulated ourselves on our hunting and gathering skills, then drank kava with Wonga and our tribe of cruising sailors.

* * * * *

Confronted with 330 Fijian islands to explore within only a few months, we relied on word of mouth advice from other sailors. I compared my notepad of recommendations with our navigation chart and saw we were close to an uninhabited resort island owned by the wealthy Forbes family of magazine and political fame. Malcolm Forbes bought the island in 1972, turned it into a coconut plantation, and later into a resort. The resort closed following the political coup in Fiji, but there were still dozens of rows of coconut trees planted all the way down to the water. That island felt eerie.

There we stood on a deserted island, surrounded by posh buildings, careful landscaping and well… no one else. As if we were the only survivors in some post-apocalyptic world; castaways with a sailboat. It reminded us that we were quite self-sufficient on our own boat. Glen speared all the fish we could eat, at times taking orders: grouper, flounder, snapper, the occasional lobster… Then there was the gathering category of food, which included papayas, mangos, breadfruit, and coconuts.

One night, Glen and I ate a true castaway meal on the beach of our deserted island that would have catapulted us to the finalist section of the Survivor Fiji episode. Dinner consisted of a speared grouper grilled on the fire, rice cooked in coconut cream, breadfruit wrapped in foil on the coals, and coconut cake I had baked in the pressure cooker for dessert. It was about as perfect a meal as I could imagine, sourced from local bounty.

Much of our meal had come from the coconut palms towering around us. No wonder it was rare for Pacific Islanders to possess a Western Type A work ethic; there was so much abundance to be had for very little effort. Even coconut trees were hard to beat for sheer output and versatility. Each tree produces about 50 coconuts a year, all year, for 60 years. Try that with a tomato plant!

On other islands we had been offered an alcoholic brew made from the top flowering parts of the coconut palm tree. Called *arrack*, the brew was extremely potent, and to keep peace, arrack was outlawed on most Fijian islands by village elders. Besides food and drink the coconut tree supplied anything needed for a simple island life. We saw palm fronds woven into roofs, baskets, floor mats, and general shelter. Coconut shells were used as cups and made excellent firewood. Rope, brushes, and *coir* (heavy matting) were woven from the hairy fiber of the coconut husks, and the trunks of the trees provided timber for building.

It was easy to tell which islands had cultivated coconut plantations as opposed to the random growth on most islands. Palms planted during the British colonial era stand in rows as straight as a military formation from the hills right down to the water line. Astonishingly, Southern plantation-style homes with sweeping verandas still dotted some remote Pacific islands, transporting me back to antebellum plantations I had toured in the Southern states. Like Forbes Island, some of those Fijian island plantations had been converted into tourist resorts, complete with warning signs for guests, "Beware of Falling Coconuts!" Even paradise has its hazards.

Chapter 34

After a couple days of nonstop rain, we sailed fast and hard to arrive at everyone's favorite part of Fiji, the sunlit Yasawa Islands. The white-sand beaches on the west side of Fiji were a striking contrast with the east side's tall, green, rain-soaked volcanic islands where deep water from the volcanic slope made anchoring difficult and reefs for fishing scarce. Within hours of our arrival on what we called the "sunny side" of Fiji, Glen and I were in the warm, clear water.

"Can't you float through with me?" I asked Glen. "They're so huge—the two of us floating together would be a bigger mass for them to avoid." Our rubber dinghy was anchored in the middle of what sailing friends had been calling Manta Ray Pass, a narrow strip of water between two islands, where manta rays feed in large numbers.

Glen shook his head, his dive mask adding emphasis. "The current is too strong here. There's no way either one of us will be able to swim back to the dinghy. I'll drop you off here at the head of the current then pick you up downstream after you drift through the mantas. After that, you drop me off, I'll float through, and we can do that routine as long as we want."

I slid into the water to go first. A very strong current tugged my body through the pass, threatening to make me lose my white-knuckle grip on the dinghy. I struggled to hang on tightly and secure my dive mask at the same time. Through my mask, I watched the mantas swirling gracefully and effortlessly against the current. A half dozen skimmed through the water with barely a flick of bat-like wings that must have measured 12 feet from fin tip to fin tip.

Mask in place, I lifted my face from the water, "I don't know—their mouths are wide open and they have hundreds of teeth! Are you sure this is safe?" I was afraid of Glen abandoning me to the huge, toothy beasts. With the tiniest smile, he answered with a confidence I did not share. "You'll be fine! See you down the pass in five minutes." Letting go of the dinghy I called back to him, "Okay, but if they eat me, promise you'll finish the voyage in a 20-foot rowboat—by yourself!"

The current was so powerful, I felt like an astronaut stepping from a space station in zero gravity, but without the security a tether would have provided. Flying through the water, I panicked when the first manta ray swam directly into my path with its mouth open, a set of pointed teeth in full display. I kicked my fins to dodge the oncoming mouth, but the huge manta easily avoided me, passing within inches of my body. As it glided past, I was caught in its swirling wake. Untouched and unhurt, my pounding heart began to regain its normal rhythm. I gained courage as one after another the rays glided by without the slightest contact. The giant, open-mouthed manta rays displayed their hundreds of teeth as they sailed by my body to feed on tiny plankton critters at the low end of the ecosystem's totem pole. Surely at one time, the animal's distant ancestors used those teeth to consume a food source larger than the miniscule plankton they were now downing around me. Despite their straight from sci-fi appearance, they were gentle giants with no interest in humans who inserted themselves in their feeding ritual. Unlike their much smaller stingray cousins, they have no barbs on their tails, so at least I was saved from an inadvertent, but deadly, swing of a tail.

Glen and I swam with the rays and drifted through the pass for more than two hours. Exhausted, we finally helped each other back into the dinghy and shared the near-spiritual feeling that gliding with the mantas had stirred.

Chapter 35

We were at anchor off one of the hundreds of remote islands in Fiji. Off the bow of the boat were a white sandy beach, palm trees, and the occasional coconut crab scurrying around. I was in my own sweet place in the cockpit looking out upon the harmony of nature that lifted my spirit. That was my world... early morning quiet time. I went above and wiped the dew off the cushions so I could sit down with my cup of tea and enjoy the sunrise. Glen, never an early riser, was down below decks, still in bed. The sun was rising fast, the water was calm, and in the soft sunlight I could see colorful fish swimming against the sandy bottom—a perfectly assembled aquarium for my personal enjoyment.

Someone called to me from a sailboat anchored not far from us. "Julie... Julie... over here!" A Canadian sailor I barely knew stood on the deck of his boat, wildly waving his arms calling out my name and yelling something. I moved to the stern of *It's Enough* so I could hear him better. "BBC... go listen. BBC!" the Canadian shouted, but I couldn't hear the rest. He raised his voice and I thought I heard him say, "America is under attack." *What?* "Julie, turn on BBC radio. Bad news. Radio. BBC. Now!"

Shaken, I rushed to the single sideband radio. The authoritative British voice was garbled but as I prodded the tuner, the news announcer's words became clear. The normally calm British voice was breaking with emotion and talking fast in frantic sentences, "Two planes attacked the World Trade Center in New York, possibly killing as many as 100,000 people. Reports coming in say another commercial airplane has hit the Pentagon, killing untold numbers, with reports of yet another heading for the White House or Capitol building. As yet there are no reports of attacks elsewhere in America."

Dumbfounded, I tried to absorb the information. In disbelief, I rose on legs of jelly, stumbled to our stateroom, and sunk to the bed—no longer able to stand. Between sobs, I woke Glen and told him of the un-believable devastation.

Glen kept shaking his head and told me, "Julie there must be some mistake. That can't be right," as he got out of bed and rushed to the radio at the navigation station. The British voice still wavered as he reported the horrific scene: smoke, flames, and people leaping from the windows and roofs of the skyscrapers. Stricken with what we were hearing and unable to imagine it getting worse, the first tower then collapsed, trap-ping emergency responders and those left in the building. Unable to do anything, we listened with aching hearts to what should have been im-plausible news. So many people dead...

As a child, I heard Pearl Harbor spoken of by my parents and grand-parents, always with reverence in their words and grief and sorrow on their faces. Sitting at the radio that morning, I already knew the term 9/11 would join the atrocities of Pearl Harbor as an incomprehensible world event. Tears rolled down my cheeks and a lump formed in my throat as the BBC newsreader updated listeners with the shocking news. It was some time before I could process what I was hearing, and as I did, the news grew worse. Another plane flew into the second tower and it collapsed a short while later as well. BBC continued to paint a visual image of what was happening at the World Trade Center for those of us who could only hear the news on the radio.

Glen and I were sitting in front of the radio, stunned. We barely registered the sound of sailors from two other boats rapping on the side of *It's Enough*. New Zealand and Canadian sailors had driven their dinghies over to join and comfort us. I was numb, body and soul, but went through the motions of making coffee and setting out a pack of shortbread cookies that would have to do for breakfast. The six of us sat wordlessly listening to the radio, unable to endure what we were hearing, yet unwilling to turn it off.

Glen and I needed to get somewhere with a phone and television. My family was in Seattle and Glen's was in Arizona—surely, they were safe. Then my thoughts hung on our friends and former colleagues working in the Pentagon.

From that remote island in Fiji it was impossible to imagine the impact the attack was having on the lives of everyone in America—for that matter, around the world. We needed to get the full story and check on the safety of our families.

I feared most that 9/11 would be like Pearl Harbor: a shocking singularity leading to war. In those early hours no one knew who was behind the attack. *What country could, or would, have attacked the superpower of America?*

Would I be recalled to active duty? It had been three years since I retired from the Army as a military intelligence officer. My last assignment had been conducting nuclear weapons inspections in Russia. I did not believe Russia could be behind the attacks—after all, they were newly open to capitalism and world trade. But if they were the attackers, I knew I would be recalled to active duty immediately. My specialization in Russia, nuclear proliferation, and weapons of mass destruction would be required.

We needed to get to an island where we could get more information and contact our families. Glen pulled out a navigation chart, pointed to a speck in the ocean and said, "Malolo Island looks good; it has a small airstrip and a resort called Musket Cove, which likely has satellite television and possibly a landline telephone where we can place a call to the States." Musket Cove was only a day sail away and our New Zealand and Canadian friends at anchor nearby told us they would follow. They too felt the need to contact family and be among others. They understood this tragic event was shared by the entire world.

Pulling anchor, we sailed through the day arriving at Musket Cove as the sun set. Word had gone out on the sailors' radio net about our makeshift meeting place and soon other sailboats from other Fiji out-islands joined the growing fleet. Glen and I drove our dinghy ashore and parked it on the beach next to a dozen others. The iridescent blue water and white sand beach were invisible to us—all we could think about was the attack. Ashore we found Musket Cove to be a small, family-run resort with a large television where guests and sailors were already gathered. There was a single landline pay telephone which would become our connection to family and friends back home.

I stood in a long queue for the phone to check in with my family. My aviation family worked for Boeing and all traveled for their jobs. Though the odds were small they had been on those airplanes, I had to make sure they were safe. I was relieved to hear their voices and learn they were all at their homes in Seattle. My brother told me, "All airplanes in the country are grounded—people from work are stranded all over the world. Don't even think of coming home right now. No one is even sure exactly who was behind this attack, but it does not look like Russia was involved." We called Glen's son and daughter in Arizona, and they too were safe. Glen's son Scott, a flight instructor, was grounded for the foreseeable future along with every other airplane in the country.

Gathering our news from the radio had been shocking enough, but I could not have predicted the gut-wrenching impact of seeing graphic footage of the attack and aftermath on television. My imagination had formed the scene while listening to BBC radio, but the unthinkable and unspeakable events replayed on film were now forever seared in my brain on September 11, 2001.

Being among sailing friends who had gathered on the island brought solace. Even so far from the disaster, we shared a collective trauma. To be a New Yorker, watching helplessly from the streets of Manhattan, must have been unbearable. The announcers came up with vague theories as they tried to describe the loss but found themselves without adequate words to express the horror of what had happened. Deep down we all knew that, like Pearl Harbor, the horrifying attack signaled the end of an era and would shape the course of the world forever.

Within days, the anchorage at Musket Cove filled with sailboats from Germany, Australia, New Zealand, France, Canada… The international sailing community on Malolo Island was like a floating and grieving version of the United Nations. The normally carefree group was somber, reflective, and any one of us could burst into tears or choke up watching or hearing news updates. Sailors and Fijians alike cried and averted their eyes as the news replayed the horror of people leaping from burning skyscrapers to their death.

Among the American sailors was a stockbroker who, until his retirement two years before, had worked on the upper floors of the World Trade Center. He lost his former colleagues and office workers that day.

Glen had worked in the Pentagon, but details about that attack were far less detailed for security reasons, so we had no idea if friends had died. The hearts of all nations went out to America. Nearly every sailboat, no matter what its nationality, flew the American flag as a show of support for what the United States had suffered. Still in shock for days after, I believe everybody, no matter where they were from, got the sense their homeland too could be vulnerable. One German sailing couple motored over in their dinghy with homemade coffeecake, and as we sat in the cockpit together, he said, "If this can happen to the great and powerful country of America, which of us is next?"

Flags are an important part of what sailors carry onboard, as it is customary to fly a small courtesy flag of the country being visited as well as a larger flag of your own country. In an embrace of solidarity and support for the United States, every single sailboat in the anchorage flew the American flag. It brought tears to my eyes to see such collective kindness and sympathy for all that was lost. When we were among other Americans, one comment surfaced often, "I didn't know any country or people hated America so much." In post 9/11, would such a simple act as flying an American flag inflame the hatred we witnessed during that attack?

It was days before we learned it was a rogue act of Islamic terrorists. Those in the military understand and accept that life can change or end in a flash. But to imagine sitting on the ninety-ninth floor of the World Trade Center on a beautiful, early fall morning, sipping coffee at your computer while men who believe 72 virgins are waiting for them in heaven, fly an airliner through your window... well, that creates uncertainty on a far larger scale.

For many of us, the question now was: how can we finish sailing around the world without risking our lives? Dictated by geography and landmass, most sailors are channeled toward areas where it now seemed Americans—and westerners in general—were unwelcome, or worse. It would make no difference to a pirate or terrorist whether a boat hailed from Annapolis, Maryland, or Hamburg, Germany. Ocean sailing on small boats is perceived as a Western pursuit. Anyone who wanted to return to Europe or the United States from the Pacific Ocean would have to put themselves at life-threatening risk well beyond that of storms and hurricanes.

Although Glen and I had studied world-sailing routes for decades, we pulled out our charts as though the geography of the world had somehow changed, along with everything else. It had not. There were still only two approaches to sailing around the world: south along the tips of Africa and South America or through the Panama and Suez Canals. It is the rare sailor who seeks out the extreme weather and dangers of Cape Horn and Cape of Good Hope, churned up by the fierce Southern Ocean. On the other hand, the dangers of Cape Horn could be predicted. Sailing through the Gulf of Aden and the Red Sea presented entirely different threats. Piracy off countries such as Somalia and Yemen had always been economically driven. It was rare for pirates to kill sailors; instead they took money, electronics, and anything of value on board. Now, things were unpredictable and potentially dangerous toward Americans in that part of the world.

In the weeks that followed I became more worried I would be recalled to active duty and started having dreams where I was wearing my Army uniform but had forgotten where to put the insignia. I also wondered how the Army would reach me, considering we were still anchored in the Pacific Ocean. Since our voyage, I had changed so much as a person and doubted it was even possible to revert from the life of a sailing vagabond to the Army way of thinking. However, I did feel guilty, perched upon turquoise waters surrounded by white sand beaches while there were such terrible things happening in our country. For most of our adult life, Glen and I had been closely involved with our national security—suddenly we were distant and irrelevant.

My mother, who collected, sorted, and forwarded our important mail, sent an email telling me I had a letter from the Department of the Army. I called her and asked her to read it aloud over the phone. The letter from the Army said I was "invited" to return to active duty. I had Mom read the sentence with "invited" twice. That one word made all the difference. If it had said, "ordered", I would have been arranging the first available flight back to the States. I had been in a category of commissioned officers called regular, which meant I could be recalled to active duty at the discretion of the Army. Recall was presently optional for anyone in certain fields who desired to leave retirement and return to active duty. I contacted the Military Intelligence officer assignment branch and informed them I chose to stay retired. Guilt pangs troubled me at first, but that inner conflict dissolved when it was determined the attack was one of terror from the Mideast—not my area of experience or knowledge.

The financial news worsened daily. Many sailors, including us, had what was left of our life savings in the stock market. As news emerged of a global financial collapse, friends who relied on IRA and 401k stock investments announced they would to have to unretire, quit their sailing voyage, and go back to work. Our savings too were heavily depleted by the world financial collapse, but we knew we could live on our boat at a fraction of the cost as on land. Every day we heard from friends among us or by email of dire changes to their future.

A Seattle sailing couple we knew stopped by to ask us to pass around a For Sale flyer for their boat. Over a period of days, they cobbled together a new life plan. Closely watching the weather, they planned to depart at the first clear passage window for Australia where they would sell their sailboat and fly back to the States. They had already been in contact with their former employers about going back to work. In a strange turnabout of the way things usually happen, they would live with their grown children until they once again had steady income.

Every sailor in that harbor—and surely people all over the world—stepped back and reevaluated their life's plan, unsure how the financial collapse would affect them. Originally, we planned for our sailing voyage to last three years, but the events of 9/11 forced a conversation about the larger picture of our life. The attack on US soil directed toward Americans made us think twice about rushing to finish. We had no home to return to, could no longer afford to buy one, and had no idea where we would choose to live. There was no reason to lurch forward for an arbitrary number of years to complete our circumnavigation. After a few days of discussion, Plan B started to form.

Instead of sailing west and hurrying toward Australia, we decided to return south to New Zealand. There, the American dollar was still strong, and we could live simply and affordably on our boat for the next six months of the tropical cyclone season. Surely, things in the world would settle down and we would sail onward to complete our circumnavigation. If we needed new charts for the Cape of Good Hope, around the tip of Africa, we could acquire them in New Zealand. With so much uncertainty in the world, at least we still had each other and *It's Enough*, our floating home and only possession of value we had left in the world.

Glen and I stayed in Fiji for several weeks. It occurred to us that Plan B would have us living in New Zealand during the upcoming America's Cup competition and that appealed to us. It was a glimmer of something positive to chase away the terror of 9/11. Possibly we could participate in the America's Cup as volunteers. It was worth exploring when we returned to Auckland.

Deep in the back of our minds, we knew that the detour back to New Zealand was delaying our passage through dangerous oceans and outlaw territory, but after that short break, there would be little choice. Without benefit of foreseeing the future, how could we have known what waited on the far side of the world?

A Sneak Peek

An excerpt from the continuing adventures in the
sequel: *Crossing Pirate Waters*

A ttention all ships! Attention all ships! Piracy attempt on a southbound cargo vessel Latitude 03 15, Longitude 100 23. All ships enforce anti-piracy measures transiting the Malacca Straits," boomed over the distress channel of our marine radio.

"Glen did you hear that?" as I plotted our present coordinates. "That's only two miles from our present position!" My voice raised an octave. "What should we do?" I rummaged in a drawer for our pepper spray. Glen raised his eyebrows at my anti-piracy measure: a six-inch can that was rusty from salt air. Who knew if it would even work…

The Strait of Malacca was a natural haven for seafaring bandits. Just a slim highway of water, the eastern shoreline of the Straits belongs to Malaysia, the other to Indonesia. Their coastlines offered a maze of dense, jungle inlets and coves that favored pirates' small, maneuverable vessels over slow, hulking ships. The narrow route ran 550 miles, roughly the distance between San Francisco and Las Vegas. Envision a bottleneck carrying one-half of the globe's shipping trade with over 50,000 ships per year transporting everything from computers to much of the world's oil supply. Piracy in the Straits of Malacca was an age-old tradition. Eighteenth and nineteenth century European spice traders lived in terror of Malacca Strait pirates who killed all aboard for the valuable cargo and ship, all staged from the same shores we were passing.

Just like in the bodice ripping pirate movies, stealing cargo and ships was a quick route to riches. The risk to the pirates was minimal, and piracy was even culturally admired in the ports that harbored them. The pirate friendly terrain in the strait wreaked havoc on my ability to sleep as we made our way from Singapore to Thailand.

In Singapore Glen and I had attended an anti-piracy briefing designed for people like me who dreaded the thought of meeting face to face with real-life pirates. The slide show turned it into a numbers game with data on ships taken and valuation of cargos heisted so far that year—statistics that made me wonder why the Indonesian and Malaysian militaries were not on top of the situation. Notably, the briefing lacked advice on how to fend off the bandits or avoid abduction. The expert's parting words were, "Personnel are rarely recovered. Remember that the objective is a big payday. Crews are not important." In other words, the pirates may not attack us for just being Americans—they really wanted our boat, electronics and valuables such as night-vision goggles and cash. My mind shifted to the small 9mm handgun we had hidden under the floorboards in the galley. If that was our ace-in-the hole against pirates, we were in trouble.

Acknowledgments

It is to my husband, Glen, that I owe my deepest gratitude. He has loved me beyond measure and worked hard to help bring our dreams to life. This book is, of course, yours as much as mine. Force 10 storms aside, we would never have made it without your ready sense of humor, ability to find the silver lining in everything, and willingness to figure out how to solve any problem—both mechanical and in our relationship. Beyond this book, I want to thank you for making my life full of possibility, wonder, and love. Our life together is, and always will be, an adventure.

I owe much to the Army for my twenty-year career. I went in a troubled, broken teenager and came out a disciplined person with stamina to face tough situations. I took for granted the mighty team watching my back all those years and there were times in the Gulf of Aden and Indian Ocean I yearned to have all that force again. Through luck and pluck we made it through on our own.

For their encouragement and steady support, I'd like to thank my women's writers' group. Without a doubt I extracted more than I gave. Barb Davis, Vicki Sandler, Cyndie Shaffstall, Carol Sletten, Amy Hanridge, Marilyn Binion, Michelle May, and our organizer, Diane Wise— all authors and friends who were there for me along the way. Cyndie

Shaffstall gets special thanks as my mentor and advisor on all aspects of publishing and digital marketing; great to have you in my corner. Vicki Sandler, raising my consciousness did wonders for my writing and relationships. I'm also deeply indebted to Carol Lacy-Salazar for her eye to detail. Carol, you are the only person who understands when the occasional Russian word slips into my Spanish. Super-special bonus thanks to my friend and neighbor, Sue Sitko, with whom I have walked hundreds of miles in the forest talking through ideas while immersed in nature. Your grounding and humor are appreciated.

To my niece, Chiara, and nephews, Troy, Tyler and Gabriel, in hopes that you dream big, too. If only you had been able to share the best of this adventure.

To Glen's grandchildren, Brittany, Bria, Brandon, Preston, Connor, and Hannah. This book explains all those photographs of your parents visiting Grandpa Glen and Nona all over the world. I hope this book inspires you to choose extraordinary paths.

I am deeply indebted to friends who joined us on ocean passages. Sometimes there was more adventure than any of us wanted, but you hung in there with positive vibes and support. A big thank you to great friends Lee and Ines Oppenheim, Bob and Cyn Starr, Allan Gainok, Ron McInnes, Don Albright, and Jerry Durbin for sharing both challenging and great times together on passages.

A deep bow to the beautiful friends and sailors who shared our adventures along the way. First and foremost, Ann Harsh and Ralph Nehrig on S/V Harmony, who inspired us to go for broke with our great Amel sailboat and helped immensely in our planning. Your tales of rounding the Capes served as an object lesson that the canals were our routes of choice. So many more... Charlotte and Heyward on S/V Skimmer, Paul and Terry on S/V Catofun, Rob and Dee on S/V Ventana, Miles and Lisa on S/V Ladybug, Tom and Bonnie on S/V Toujours... it would take pages.

To my sister, Jeanne, and brother, Johnny; you both took a far different path in the life we once shared and ended up with beautiful families and super successful careers. You both found a way to get paid for traveling all over the world... okay, so you do have to work when you get there.

I'm deeply grateful to my mother, Judy Redshaw Guess, who made me strong enough to handle everything that has come my way so far. She also made me wise enough to know when I found my perfect life mate. Thank you also for my red hair. Who knew it would cause children on remote islands to break out in tears?

Mom, I value every minute we now get to spend together. Extra special thanks to Mom's kind, charming, and wonderful husband, Stan Guess, who came on to the scene too late to join us on our voyage. You are a true friend, a fine pilot, sailor, and know how to keep your cool. It would have been fun.

To my father, John, to whom I owe my adventure and travel genes. Growing up on his stories of pet monkeys in the jungles of Burma and his time among Gurkha soldiers nurtured my desire to travel. I miss my Dad's love, sense of humor, and encouragement. I wish I could have had more time with him and that he had lived long enough to know how well my life turned out.

I'm deeply grateful to the friends who have nurtured and loved me. There are too many to name. I can only say you know who you are and I'm so fortunate to have you in my life. I am humbled by your friendship and kindness.

Lastly, I am forever indebted to Diane Wise, my lovely and tactful editor who corrected countless mistakes and cut the slow bits to keep things moving. Looking back at my first draft, I see how she deftly guided my writing style from intelligence report to telling my story. The strengths of this book are a result of Diane's recommendations and guidance, while any faults are all mine. I appreciate the unwavering support even though editing my book took her away from writing her own. Also, despite her best efforts, I have to apologize for still not knowing how to correctly use a semicolon.

Made in the USA
Coppell, TX
24 January 2020